you & **your**

Jaguar
XK/XKR

Also from Veloce Publishing –

Essential Buyer's Guide Series
Jaguar E-Type 3.8 & 4.2 litre (Crespin)
Jaguar E-type V12 5.3 litre (Crespin)
Jaguar Mark 1 & 2 (All models including Daimler 2.5-litre V8) 1955 to 1969 (Thorley)
Jaguar New XK 2005-2014 (Thorley)
Jaguar S-Type – 1999 to 2007 (Thorley)
Jaguar X-Type – 2001 to 2009 (Thorley)
Jaguar XJ-S (Crespin)
Jaguar XJ6, XJ8 & XJR (Thorley)
Jaguar XK 120, 140 & 150 (Thorley)
Jaguar XK8 & XKR (1996-2005) (Thorley)
Jaguar/Daimler XJ 1994-2003 (Crespin)
Jaguar/Daimler XJ40 (Crespin)
Jaguar/Daimler XJ6, XJ12 & Sovereign (Crespin)

Great Cars
Austin-Healey – A celebration of the fabulous 'Big' Healey (Piggott)
Jaguar E-type (Thorley)
Jaguar Mark 1 & 2 (Thorley)
Jaguar XK A Celebration of Jaguar's 1950s Classic (Thorley)
Triumph TR – TR2 to 6: The last of the traditional sports cars (Piggott)
Volkswagen Beetle – A Celebration of the World's Most Popular Car (Copping)

General
1½-litre GP Racing 1961-1965 (Whitelock)
AC Two-litre Saloons & Buckland Sportscars (Archibald)
Alfa Romeo 155/156/147 Competition Touring Cars (Collins)
Alfa Romeo Giulia Coupé GT & GTA (Tipler)
Alfa Romeo Montreal – The dream car that came true (Taylor)
Alfa Romeo Montreal – The Essential Companion (Classic Reprint of 500 copies) (Taylor)
Alfa Tipo 33 (McDonough & Collins)
Alpine & Renault – The Development of the Revolutionary Turbo F1 Car 1968 to 1979 (Smith)
Alpine & Renault – The Sports Prototypes 1963 to 1969 (Smith)
Alpine & Renault – The Sports Prototypes 1973 to 1978 (Smith)
An Austin Anthology (Stringer)
An Incredible Journey (Falls & Reisch)
Anatomy of the Classic Mini (Huthert & Ely)
Anatomy of the Works Minis (Moylan)
Armstrong-Siddeley (Smith)
Art Deco and British Car Design (Down)
Austin Cars 1948 to 1990 – a pictorial history (Rowe)
Autodrome (Collins & Ireland)
Automotive A-Z, Lane's Dictionary of Automotive Terms (Lane)
Automotive Mascots (Kay & Springate)
Bahamas Speed Weeks, The (O'Neil)
Bentley Continental, Corniche and Azure (Bennett)
Bentley MkVI, Rolls-Royce Silver Wraith, Dawn & Cloud/Bentley R & S-Series (Nutland)
Bluebird CN7 (Stevens)
BMW 5-Series (Cranswick)
BMW Z-Cars (Taylor)
BMW Classic 5 Series 1972 to 2003 (Cranswick)
BMW – The Power of M (Vivian)
British at Indianapolis, The (Wagstaff)
British Cars, The Complete Catalogue of, 1895-1975 (Culshaw & Horrobin)
Bugatti – The 8-cylinder Touring Cars 1920-34 (Price & Arbey)
Bugatti Type 40 (Price)
Bugatti 46/50 Updated Edition (Price & Arbey)
Bugatti T44 & T49 (Price & Arbey)
Bugatti 57 2nd Edition (Price)
Bugatti Type 57 Grand Prix – A Celebration (Tomlinson)
Carrera Panamericana, La (Tipler)
Car-tastrophes – 80 automotive atrocities from the past 20 years (Honest John, Fowler)
Chrysler 300 – America's Most Powerful Car 2nd Edition (Ackerson)
Chrysler PT Cruiser (Ackerson)
Citroën DS (Bobbitt)
Classic British Car Electrical Systems (Astley)
Cobra – The Real Thing! (Legate)
Competition Car Aerodynamics 3rd Edition (McBeath)
Competition Car Composites A Practical Handbook (Revised 2nd Edition) (McBeath)
Concept Cars, How to illustrate and design – New 2nd Edition (Dewey)
Cortina – Ford's Bestseller (Robson)
Cosworth – The Search for Power (6th edition) (Robson)
Coventry Climax Racing Engines (Hammill)
Daily Mirror 1970 World Cup Rally 40, The (Robson)
Daimler SP250 New Edition (Long)
Datsun Fairlady Roadster to 280ZX – The Z-Car Story (Long)
Dino – The V6 Ferrari (Long)
Dodge Challenger & Plymouth Barracuda (Grist)
Dodge Charger – Enduring Thunder (Ackerson)
Dodge Dynamite! (Grist)
Dorset from the Sea – The Jurassic Coast from Lyme Regis to Old Harry Rocks photographed from its best viewpoint (also Souvenir Edition) (Belasco)
Draw & Paint Cars – How to (Gardiner)
Drive on the Wild Side, A – 20 Extreme Driving Adventures From Around the World (Weaver)
Dune Buggy Files (Hale)
Dune Buggy Handbook (Hale)
East German Motor Vehicles in Pictures (Suhr/Weinreich)
Essential Guide to Driving in Europe, The (Parish)
Fast Ladies – Female Racing Drivers 1888 to 1970 (Bouzanquet)
Fate of the Sleeping Beauties, The (op de Weegh/Hottendorff/op de Weegh)
Ferrari 288 GTO, The Book of the (Sackey)
Ferrari 333 SP (O'Neil)
Fiat & Abarth 124 Spider & Coupé (Tipler)
Fiat & Abarth 500 & 600 – 2nd Edition (Bobbitt)
Fiats, Great Small (Ward)
Fine Art of the Motorcycle Engine, The (Peirce)
Ford Cleveland 335-Series V8 engine 1970 to 1982 – The Essential Source Book (Hammill)
Ford F100/F150 Pick-up 1948-1996 (Ackerson)
Ford F150 Pick-up 1997-2005 (Ackerson)
Ford Focus WRC (Robson)
Ford GT – Then, and Now (Streather)
Ford GT40 (Legate)
Ford Midsize Muscle – Fairlane, Torino & Ranchero (Cranswick)
Ford Model Y (Roberts)
Ford Small Block V8 Racing Engines 1962-1970 – The Essential Source Book (Hammill)
Ford Thunderbird From 1954, The Book of the (Long)
Formula One – The Real Score? (Harvey)
Formula 5000 Motor Racing, Back then ... and back now (Lawson)
Forza Minardi! (Vigar)
France: the essential guide for car enthusiasts – 200 things for the car enthusiast to see and do (Parish)
The Good, the Mad and the Ugly ... not to mention Jeremy Clarkson (Dron)
Grand Prix Ferrari – The Years of Enzo Ferrari's Power, 1948-1980 (Pritchard)
Grand Prix Ford – DFV-powered Formula 1 Cars (Robson)
GT – The World's Best GT Cars 1953-73 (Dawson)
Hillclimbing & Sprinting – The Essential Manual (Short & Wilkinson)
Honda NSX (Long)
Immortal Austin Seven (Morgan)
India – The Shimmering Dream (Reisch/Falls (translator))
Inside the Rolls-Royce & Bentley Styling Department – 1971 to 2001 (Hull)
Intermeccanica – The Story of the Prancing Bull (McCredie & Reisner)
Jaguar from the shop floor (Martin)
Jaguar E-type Factory and Private Competition Cars (Griffiths)
Jaguar, The Rise of (Price)
Jaguar XJ 220 – The Inside Story (Moreton)
Jaguar XJ-S, The Book of the (Long)
Japanese Custom Motorcycles – The Nippon Chop – Chopper, Cruiser, Bobber, Trikes and Quads (Cloesen)
Jeep CJ (Ackerson)
Jeep Wrangler (Ackerson)
The Jowett Jupiter – The car that leaped to fame (Nankivell)
Karmann-Ghia Coupé & Convertible (Bobbitt)
Kris Meeke – Intercontinental Rally Challenge Champion (McBride)
Lamborghini Miura Bible, The (Sackey)
Lamborghini Murciélago, The book of the (Pathmanathan)
Lamborghini Urraco, The Book of the (Landsem)
Lancia 037 (Collins)
Lancia Delta HF Integrale (Blaettel & Wagner)
Lancia Delta Integrale (Collins)
Land Rover Design - 70 years of success (Hull)
Land Rover Emergency Vehicles (Taylor & Fletcher)
Land Rover Series III Reborn (Porter)
Land Rover, The Half-ton Military (Cook)
Land Rovers in British Military Service – coil sprung models 1970 to 2007 (Taylor)
Lea-Francis Story, The (Price)
Le Mans Panoramic (Ireland)
Lexus Story, The (Long)
Little book of microcars, the (Quellin)
Little book of smart, the – New Edition (Jackson)
Lola – The Illustrated History (1957-1977) (Starkey)
Lola – All the Sports Racing & Single-seater Racing Cars 1978-1997 (Starkey)
Lola T70 – The Racing History & Individual Chassis Record – 4th Edition (Starkey)
Lotus 18 Colin Chapman's U-turn (Whitelock)
Lotus 49 (Oliver)
Making a Morgan (Hensing)
Marketingmobiles, The Wonderful Wacky World of (Hale)
Maserati 250F In Focus (Pritchard)
Mazda MX-5/Miata 1.6 Enthusiast's Workshop Manual (Grainger & Shoemark)
Mazda MX-5/Miata 1.8 Enthusiast's Workshop Manual (Grainger & Shoemark)
Mazda MX-5 Miata, The book of the – The 'Mk1' NA-series 1988 to 1997 (Long)
Mazda MX-5 Miata, The book of the – The 'Mk2' NB-series 1997 to 2004 (Long)
Mazda MX-5 Miata Roadster (Long)
Mazda Rotary-engined Cars (Cranswick)
Maximum Mini (Booij)
Meet the English (Bowie)
Mercedes-Benz SL – R230 series 2001 to 2011 (Long)
Mercedes-Benz SL – W113-series 1963-1971 (Long)
Mercedes-Benz SL & SLC – 107-series 1971-1989 (Long)
Mercedes-Benz SLK – R170 series 1996-2004 (Long)
Mercedes-Benz SLK – R171 series 2004-2011 (Long)
Mercedes-Benz W123-series – All models 1976 to 1986 (Long)
Mercedes G-Wagen (Long)
MG, Made in Abingdon (Frampton)
MGA (Price Williams)
MGB & MGB GT– Expert Guide (Auto-doc Series) (Williams)
MGB Electrical Systems Updated & Revised Edition (Astley)
MGB – The Illustrated History, Updated Fourth Edition (Wood & Burrell)
Microcars at Large! (Quellin)
Mini Cooper – The Real Thing! (Tipler)
Mini Minor to Asia Minor (West)
Mitsubishi Lancer Evo, The Road Car & WRC Story (Long)
Montlhéry, The Story of the Paris Autodrome (Boddy)
MOPAR Muscle – Barracuda, Dart & Valiant 1960-1980 (Cranswick)
Morgan Maverick (Lawrence)
Morgan 3 Wheeler – back to the future!, The (Dron)
Morris Minor, 70 Years on the Road (Newell)
Motor Movies – The Posters! (Veysey)
Motor Racing – Reflections of a Lost Era (Carter)
Motor Racing – The Pursuit of Victory 1930-1962 (Carter)
Motor Racing – The Pursuit of Victory 1963-1972 (Wyatt/Sears)
Motor Racing Heroes – The Stories of 100 Greats (Newman)
Motorsport In colour, 1950s (Wainwright)
N.A.R.T. – A concise history of the North American Racing Team 1957 to 1983 (O'Neil)
Nissan 300ZX & 350Z – The Z-Car Story (Long)
Nissan GT-R Supercar: Born to race (Gorodji)
Northeast American Sports Car Races 1950-1959 (O'Neil)
Norton Commando Bible – All models 1968 to 1978 (Henshaw)
Nothing Runs – Misadventures in the Classic, Collectable & Exotic Car Biz (Slutsky)
Pass the Theory and Practical Driving Tests (Gibson & Hoole)
Pontiac Firebird – New 3rd Edition (Cranswick)
Porsche 356 (2nd Edition) (Long)
Porsche 908 (Födisch, Neßhöver, Roßbach, Schwarz & Roßbach)
Porsche 911 Carrera – The Last of the Evolution (Corlett)
Porsche 911R, RS & RSR, 4th Edition (Starkey)
Porsche 911, The Book of the (Long)
Porsche 911 – The Definitive History 2004-2012 (Long)
Porsche – The Racing 914s (Smith)
Porsche 911SC 'Super Carrera' – The Essential Companion (Streather)
Porsche 914 & 914-6: The Definitive History of the Road & Competition Cars (Long)
Porsche 924 (Long)
The Porsche 924 Carreras – evolution to excellence (Smith)
Porsche 928 (Long)
Porsche 930 to 935: The Turbo Porsches (Starkey)
Porsche 944 (Long)
Porsche 964, 993 & 996 Data Plate Code Breaker (Streather)
Porsche 993 'King Of Porsche' – The Essential Companion (Streather)
Porsche 996 'Supreme Porsche' – The Essential Companion (Streather)
Porsche 997 2004-2012 – Porsche Excellence (Streather)
Porsche Boxster – The 986 series 1996-2004 (Long)
Porsche Boxster & Cayman – The 987 series (2004-2013) (Long)
Porsche Racing Cars – 1953 to 1975 (Long)
Porsche Racing Cars – 1976 to 2005 (Long)
Porsche – The Rally Story (Meredith)
Porsche: Three Generations of Genius (Meredith)
Powered by Porsche (Smith)
Preston Tucker & Others (Linde)
RAC Rally Action! (Gardiner)
Racing Colours – Motor Racing Compositions 1908-2009 (Newman)
Rallye Sport Fords: The Inside Story (Moreton)
The Red Baron's Ultimate Ducati Desmo Manual (Cabrera Choclán)
Roads with a View – England's greatest views and how to find them by road (Corfield)
Rolls-Royce Silver Shadow/Bentley T Series Corniche & Camargue – Revised & Enlarged Edition (Bobbitt)
Rolls-Royce Silver Spirit, Silver Spur & Bentley Mulsanne 2nd Edition (Bobbitt)
Rootes Cars of the 50s, 60s & 70s – Hillman, Humber, Singer, Sunbeam & Talbot, A Pictorial History (Rowe)
Rover Cars 1945 to 2005, A Pictorial History
Rover P4 (Bobbitt)
Runways & Racers (O'Neil)
Russian Motor Vehicles – Soviet Limousines 1930-2003 (Kelly)
Russian Motor Vehicles – The Czarist Period 1784 to 1917 (Kelly)
RX-7 – Mazda's Rotary Engine Sportscar (Updated & Revised New Edition) (Long)
Schlumpf – The intrigue behind the most beautiful car collection in the world (Op de Weegh & Op de Weegh)
Singer Story: Cars, Commercial Vehicles, Bicycles & Motorcycle (Atkinson)
Sleeping Beauties USA – abandoned classic cars & trucks (Marek)
SM – Citroën's Maserati-engined Supercar (Long & Claverol)
Speedway – Auto racing's ghost tracks (Collins & Ireland)
Standard Motor Company, The Book of the (Robson)
Steve Hole's Kit Car Cornucopia – Cars, Companies, Stories, Facts & Figures: the UK's kit car scene since 1949 (Hole)
Subaru Impreza: The Road Car And WRC Story (Long)
Supercar, How to Build your own (Thompson)
Tales from the Toolbox (Oliver)
Tatra – The Legacy of Hans Ledwinka, Updated & Enlarged Collector's Edition of 1500 copies (Margolius & Henry)
Taxi! The Story of the 'London' Taxicab (Bobbitt)
This Day in Automotive History (Corey)
To Boldly Go – twenty six vehicle designs that dared to be different (Hull)
Toleman Story, The (Hilton)
Toyota Celica & Supra, The Book of Toyota's Sports Coupés (Long)
Toyota MR2 Coupés & Spyders (Long)
Triumph & Standard Cars 1945 to 1984 (Warrington)
Triumph Cars – The Complete Story (new 3rd edition) (Robson)
Triumph TR6 (Kimberley)
Two Summers – The Mercedes-Benz W196R Racing Car (Ackerson)
TWR Story, The – Group A (Hughes & Scott)
Unraced (Collins)
Volkswagen Bus Book, The (Bobbitt)
Volkswagen Bus or Van to Camper, How to Convert (Porter)
Volkswagens of the World (Glen)
VW Beetle Cabriolet – The full story of the convertible Beetle (Bobbitt)
VW Beetle – The Car of the 20th Century (Copping)
VW Bus – 40 Years of Splitties, Bays & Wedges (Copping)
VW Bus Book, The (Bobbitt)
VW Golf: Five Generations of Fun (Copping & Cservenka)
VW – The Air-cooled Era (Copping)
VW T5 Camper Conversion Manual (Porter)
VW Campers (Copping)
Volkswagen Type 3, The book of the – Concept, Design, International Production Models & Development (Glen)
Volvo Estate, The (Hollebone)
You & Your Jaguar XK8/XKR – Buying, Enjoying, Maintaining, Modifying – New Edition (Thorley)
Which Oil? – Choosing the right oils & greases for your antique, vintage, veteran, classic or collector car (Michell)
Wolseley Cars 1948 to 1975 (Rowe)
Works Minis, The Last (Purves & Brenchley)
Works Rally Mechanic (Moylan)

www.veloce.co.uk

This edition first published in August 2015, reprinted October 2018 by Veloce Publishing Limited, Veloce House, Parkway Farm Business Park, Middle Farm Way, Poundbury, Dorchester DT1 3AR, England. Tel 01305 2600668. Fax 01305 268864 / e-mail info@veloce.co.uk / web www.veloce.co.uk or www.velocebooks.com. ISBN 978-1-787113-92-3 / UPC 6-36847-01392-9.
© 2015 & 2018 Nigel Thorley and Veloce Publishing Ltd. All rights reserved. With the exception of quoting brief passages for the purpose of review, no part of this publication may be recorded, reproduced or transmitted by any means, including photocopying, without the written permission of Veloce Publishing Ltd. Throughout this book logos, model names and designations, etc, have been used for the purposes of identification, illustration and decoration. Such names are the property of the trademark holder as this is not an official publication. Readers with ideas for automotive books, or books on other transport or related hobby subjects, are invited to write to the editorial director of Veloce Publishing at the above address. British Library Cataloguing in Publication Data – A catalogue record for this book is available from the British Library. Typesetting, design and page make-up all by Veloce Publishing Ltd on Apple Mac. Printed in India by Replika Press.

you & your

Jaguar XK/XKR

Nigel Thorley

Buying, enjoying, maintaining, modifying

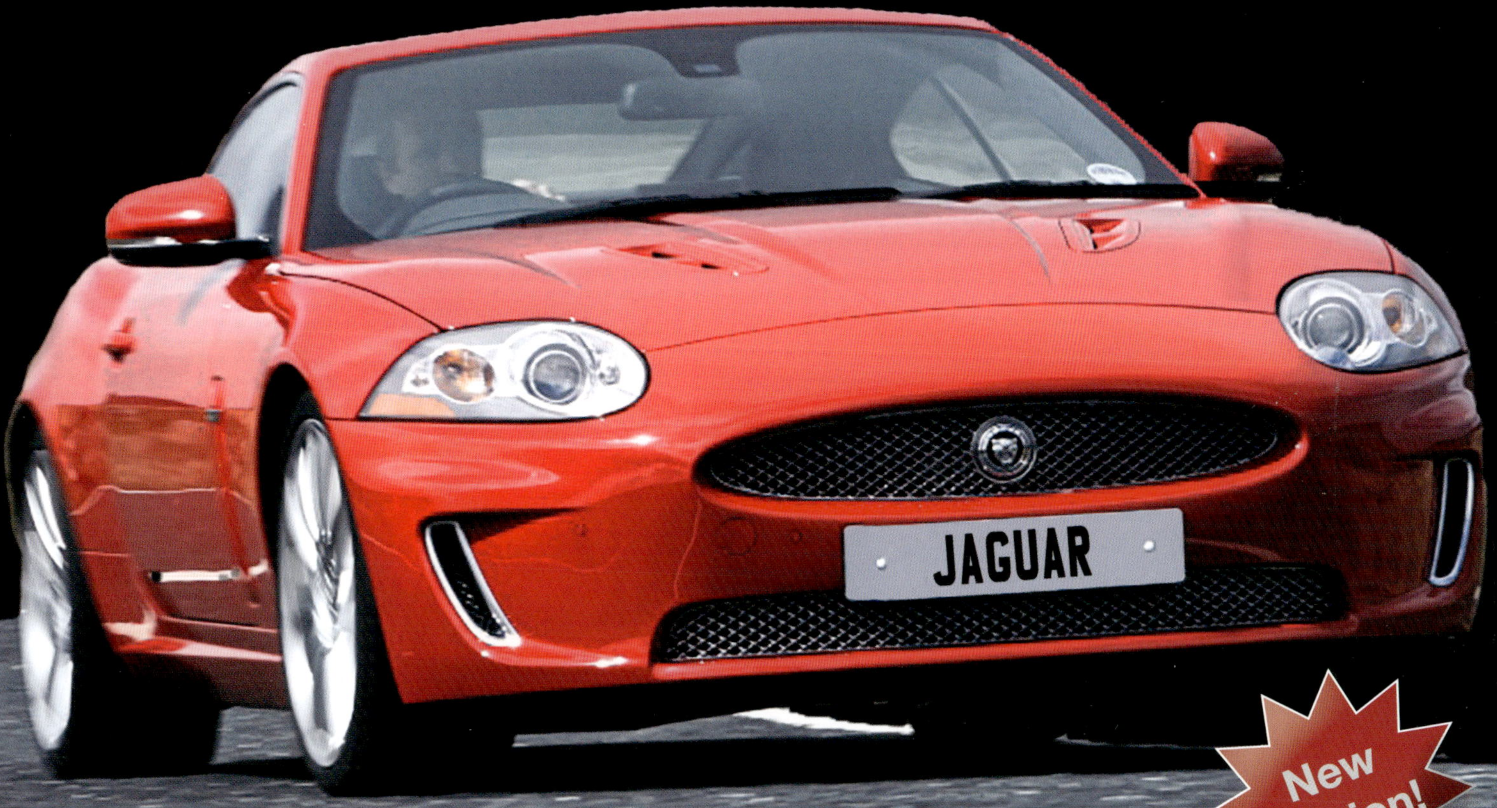

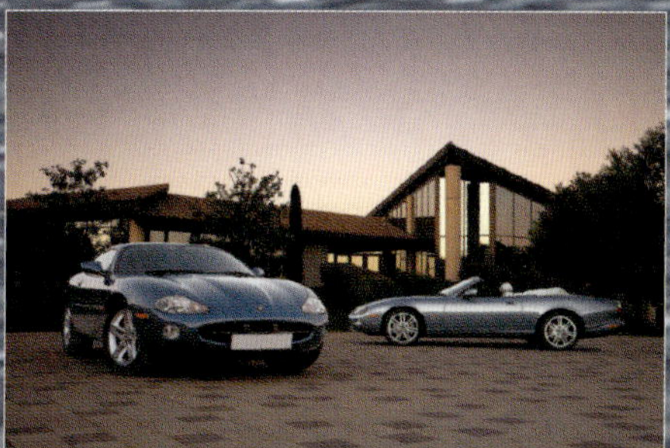

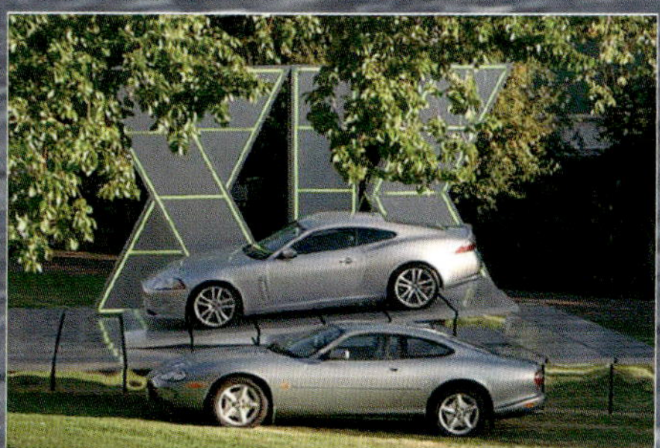

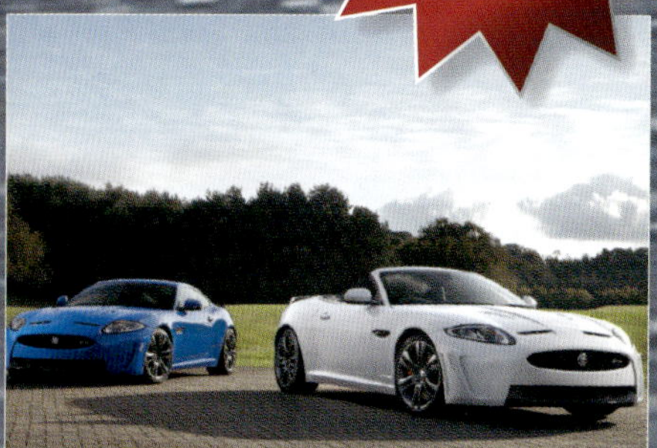

Contents

Acknowledgements **6**

Introduction **7**

X-100 to XK8 in under five years 9
Background to change 9
Development of a new sports car 11
1992: work begins. 12
External styling 14
Enter Clay A 17
Interior design 18
1993: moving forward 22
A new car, a new engine and new transmission. .. 23
Financial support and final approval 25
1994: X-100 is a goer. 26
1995: a hectic year of testing 28
1996: the final goal in sight.. 29
Summary 30

The new car in detail 32
AJ-V8 contemporary comparisons with the
opposition. 33
Transferring the power 34
At the wheels 35
Security and safety aspects 36
Interior features 37
External attributes 39
What price success?.. 39

The cat is back 40
Shaping up to the competition. 44
What the press and the people said. 44

R-rated 50
First-hand report 50
Boom time 51
A Police XK8? 53
Into 1998 53
Enter the R 54
More press comments 58

Ongoing development and excitement.. 61
Special Vehicle Operations 62
The ultimate driving experience 64
1999 model year changes. 65
XK6? 67
Key personnel changes 68
R-Performance.. 68
1999 Press reviews 70

The millennium and beyond . .. .71

2000 model year changes 71
Competition in 2000. 72
The F-type unveiled.. 72
Silverstone special edition 74
2001 and more updates 75
Centenary car 78
Flying the flag 78
Production figures 78
Press comparisons 79
XKR-R 80

The new generation XK. 82
Falling sales.. 82
Six-speeder 83
2002 changes 83
Engine comparisons. 84
The competition 86
Another special edition 87
The last chance Coupé and Convertible 88
Interior alterations 89
Special option packs 91
Introducing carbon fibre.. 91
2005 V for Victory and S for Superb. 91
Closing comments 95

Buying an XK8 97
Decide on your budget 97
The choice of car 98
SPECIFICS – 1996 to 2005 models 100
Body and trim 100
Interior trim.. 102
Electrics 103
Mechanicals.. 103
In conclusion 104

Owning, running and caring for your
1996-2005 XK8/XKR 105
An overview.. 105
Engines . .. .106
Nikasil engine linings 107
Timing chain tensioners 108
The fuel system. 110
Cooling system . .. .110
Gearboxes. 111
Front suspension.. 112
Rear suspension 113
Brakes 114
Regular servicing.. 115
Variable valve timing 123
Throttle bodies . .. .123

Emissions . .. .123
Electrics 124
Air-conditioning 125
Trim 125
Hood problems. 126
Rear bumper mountings 127
Window trim strip corrosion 128
Spare wheels. 129
Parts availability 129
Keeping your XK clean and presentable 130

The shape of things to come. 131
Exterior design features 131
Interior designing. 132
Engineering 133
And where from here? 133

The XK8 is dead, long live the XK. 134
What car to build? 135
Computer Aided Design 138
Power train 138
In-built safety 139
Building the new car 140
First off the line 141

The new XK in detail. 142
The powertrain. 142
Suspension, steering & brakes 144
Exterior styling. 145
Interior design 147
Safety features 149
Wheels & tyres 150
So, what's in a name? 150
Enter the Convertible 150
Public launch 154

XKR returns 155
The supercharged 4.2-litre engine and powertrain. .155
Chassis, suspension and brakes 157
Exterior and Interior trim changes 157

New XK ongoing developments. 161
XK 3.5s? 161
New XK styling pack. 161
XKR Portfolio 163
XKR-S 164
XK60 Special Edition 165

Enter the 5.0-litre. 166
Enter the 5.0-litre . .. .166
The new 5.0-litre AJ-V8 Gen III engines 166
Upgraded transmission 169
Active Differential Control and Dynamic
Stability Control 169
Suspension 170
Exterior design . .. .171
Interior design 171
User-friendly technology and driving aids 172
Equipment levels 173

**More changes, new models and the return of a
name 174**
XKR 75/175 174
Arden 75 176
Startech XK 176
2011 model changes . .. .177
Interior changes 177
XKR-S returns 180
XKR-S Special Carbon Fibre Pack 183
XKR-S Convertible 183
Fast and Black 184
The XKR Speed Pack 184
The XKR Black Pack . .. .185
XKR Dynamic Pack 185
Artisan SE 186
Indian Special Edition XKR 187

The grand finale 188
XKR-S GT 188
Yet more special editions . .. .191
XK66 191
XK Signature & Dynamic R 192
The Final Fifty 193
End of the line 193

Buying a New XK 195
The choice of car 195
4.2 or 5.0-litre 196
Body and trim 197
Interior trim 198
Electrics and lighting 199
Mechanicals 199
Road test 199

Owning, running and caring for your New XK 200
An overview 200
General servicing 200
Other maintenance 201
Additional maintenance and care issues. 203

Modifications and miscellanea. 205
Factory accessories 205
Alloy wheels 206
R-Performance (X-100) models 207
Outsiders 207
How to improve the looks of your XK 208
How to improve safety and comfort 209
How to improve performance 210

Appendices 216
International clubs 225
Monthly magazines with regular XK content 227
Brochures, handbooks, press releases and other
paperwork. 227
Sales, servicing, other maintenance and
enhancements 227

Index 232

Acknowledgements

The earlier title *You and Your Jaguar XK8* proved very popular, as not only was it one of the few publications to cover the Jaguar sports models from 1996 to 2005, but it was also the most comprehensive in its detail. This type of book is an ideal 'vehicle' (pardon the pun) to explore these particular cars, both for the general enthusiast, and for car owners who want to learn more about the marque. Now, therefore, seems the ideal time to consider a revised publication to include the New XK range of models from 2006 to 2014.

It would not have been possible for me to write this book without a great deal of help from many people, and my apologies for any that I miss in this brief acknowledgement.

Firstly, of course, Jaguar Land Rover who designed, built and sold the cars in the first place. The XK models were in production for a total of 18 years, and the changes, modifications, model revisions, etc, have been numerous. Fortunately, they provided access to their records for me to use freely. Allied to this were the services of the Jaguar Heritage Trust, the charitable organisation set up by Jaguar to secure and maintain their archive for future posterity. Their resource is immense, and extremely useful to authors like myself.

Many thanks also to the Jaguar independent specialists, David Marks (David Marks Garages of Nottingham), and Ian Kelsall/Gavin Jones (XJK Ltd, Stoke on Trent) whose wealth of knowledge on modern Jaguars is unsurpassed; technical experts for the Jaguar Enthusiasts' Club, they provided a great deal of assistance in the preparation of the Purchase and Maintenance chapters in this book.

The Jaguar Enthusiasts' Club has also played an important part. The largest Jaguar club in the world, the Club offers immense support to owners and enthusiasts of the XK models, and has formed a special XK Model Forum through which members can communicate on all matters relating to the cars. This has also proved a good source of material for this work and many thanks to Mike Horlor, XK enthusiast and co-ordinator for that club forum.

Thanks also to my publisher, Rod Grainger at Veloce, for his commitment to continue and expand this publication. He spurred me on to update this important book to provide a detailed insight into the development, purchase and running of these fine Jaguar sports cars.

Last, but not least, I, as usual, have to thank my wife Pauline for putting up with my consistent and obsessive involvement with the Jaguar marque; the fortunate aspect being that she loves our own XK!

Nigel Thorley
Doncaster, South Yorkshire

Introduction

The background and history of the Jaguar marque has been adequately documented many times before in other more detailed publications than this. Suffice to say at this point that the original business (the Swallow Sidecar Company) commenced operation in the town of Blackpool in England in 1922, as a partnership between William Walmsley and William Lyons.

The business eventually moved on to produce stylish bodies on existing motor car chassis, primarily for Austin, later for Morris, Standard and many others,

which resulted in the company relocating to Coventry in Warwickshire, the heart of the British motor industry.

In 1932 it produced the SS1 two-door Coupé. Not only was this the first use of the 'SS' brand name – later to be changed to Jaguar, after the Second World

The five generations of Jaguar production sports cars – from the rear forwards, 1930s SS100; 1948–61, XK120 (including XK140 and XK150); 1961–74, E-type Series 1 (also Series 2 and 3); 1975–96, XJS and XK8 (including XKR), 1996–2005. (Nigel Thorley)

War – but it was also the company's first in-house designed car. Interestingly, it set the scene for the future development of other two-door models which eventually led to the XK8, the subject of this publication.

By the late 1930s, the company's emphasis had switched to saloons (now carrying the title 'SS Jaguar'), plus a small-production-run rakish sports car, the SS100 and, after the War, the XK120. This latter, highly successful, two-seater was updated in the 1950s to become the XK140 and 150, before ending production in 1961, to make way for the next generation of Jaguar sports car, the legendary E-type. The E-type remained in production for a total of 13 years, and, during that time, a 2+2 version appeared, a reflection of the need then, as now, for extra seating in a sports car.

When the E-type finally met its demise, Jaguar, like many other manufacturers, turned its attention to 'grand touring' cars, still sporting in nature but with extra seating within a two-door arrangement, and providing supreme comfort within a quality and performance package. From the then superb XJ saloon, the XJ-S was born in 1975.

Unloved at first, mainly due to its avant-garde styling, the XJ-S grew in both stature and quality over an enforced production run amounting to 21 years, during which time Jaguar went through its troubled British Leyland era, leading almost to oblivion, then privatisation and revitalisation, and, finally, to Ford ownership in 1989. Ford spent £1.6 billion, buying Jaguar, paying off its debts, dealing with redundancies, and putting the product quality right.

Prior to all this, in 1980, the Italian coachbuilder Pininfarina had shown its concept Jaguar Spyder, achieving a contemporary interpretation of the 1960s E-type. This sparked Jaguar's own development project, leading up to the Ford takeover, of what it thought would be the eventual XJS replacement model, coded XJ41, to become known as the 'F-type' – which Ford duly assigned to the scrapheap.

Eventually, with Ford money and advances in technology, the car code-named X-100 was launched, in 1996 – the XK8. A great achievement for Jaguar then, and a car that stood the test of time against stiff competition from other manufacturers.

That XK range was replaced, in 2005, by the New XK (as Jaguar Cars called it). Although retaining much of the mechanical aspects of its predecessor, it was an entirely new design – built in aluminium, at a time a relatively new process for Jaguar, first seen in the X-350 (XJ saloon) in 2003. The New XK, and all its derivatives, lasted until 2014, when Jaguar finally closed down production of the model.

At the time of writing, there isn't a direct replacement for the XK, the position of Jaguar sports cars being taken over by the F-Type two-seater – so ended 18 years of continuous XK production.

This book tells the story of all the XK models from 1996 to 2014, their development, their pros and cons, and it will hide nothing from the enthusiast owning, contemplating the purchase or just interested in these models.

Chapter **One**

X-100 to XK8 in under five years

Background to change

Jaguar was well known for the longevity of its models and designs – take the XK120, for instance, launched in 1948, which in its last (XK150) form was still around in 1961. But even by Jaguar standards the XJ-S was getting a bit long in the tooth by the end of the 1980s.

The constant upgrading and modification of an existing product can sometimes cost as much as, if not more than, starting with a clean sheet of paper, so for some considerable time Jaguar engineers had been working on an entirely new sports car project to eventually replace the XJ-S. This was codenamed XJ41, later to be known as the F-type.

Loosely based on the XJ6 (coded XJ40) – the saloon car range already under development and finally introduced in 1986 – the XJ41 used that vehicle's floorpan, AJ6 engine and transmission. Later developments included a turbocharged engine, four-wheel drive, and a convertible version (coded XJ42). But ideas constantly changed, money was short, development was stunted by the redirection of resources to the saloon cars, and there appeared to be little co-ordination between the people involved in the project. Eventually it became a standalone project distinct from the XJ40, which made it even more expensive. By this time it was overweight and would have under-performed, and it just didn't gel as a viable successor to Jaguar's sporting car line.

Various examples of XJ41 (the stillborn Jaguar F-type sports car project) that never made it to production. (JDHT)

The Convertible XJ41 in its final form, displaying elements of US rear styling. (JDHT)

By the time XJ41 was a drivable vehicle ready for evaluation it had become clear that it had out-stayed its welcome: it was cramped and uncompetitive in the market place that had developed by that time. Then, after the Ford takeover of Jaguar in 1989, the project was scrapped (writing off about £15 million of work), although elements of the styling eventually found their way back in the form of the Aston Martin DB7.

The final interior layout of the XJ41 showed a lack of finesse to the styling and certainly less legroom and headroom than in an XJS. (JDHT)

John Egan (at the helm of Jaguar prior to the Ford takeover) had done a remarkable job bringing the company back from the brink after the British Leyland era. Overall quality had improved, money exchange rates had helped profitability, privatisation had boosted morale, and the XJ40 resulted in world record Jaguar sales in 1988 and 1989 that wouldn't be exceeded again until 1998.

Jaguar's first new Ford boss, Bill Hayden, re-emphasised the goals set previously by John Egan. Even better build quality would be vital if Jaguar was to stay in existence. After the despatch of an XJ40 saloon to the States for Ford to review, strip and evaluate, it was clear that although Jaguar had made great strides since the early 1980s, there was still a great deal of

The XJ41 Coupé shows design elements of the XJ220 and XK8 at the front. (JDHT)

work to do. Fortunately, this led to improvements in the design and reputation of cars like the XJ-S, at that time still Jaguar's only sporting model and destined for an elongated lifespan beyond its sell-by date.

Ford's first priority as far as new cars was concerned, however, was the saloon car range, because that was where the volume sales, and therefore the profits, were to be found. Although the XJ40 was still in essence a good car, it had to be brought up to date if Jaguar was not to suffer a set-back against ever stiffer competition. Hence the X-300 project was born, Ford's input helping Jaguar build a substantially better car, with a return to more curvaceous styling. The 'heritage' card also came into play, as the new saloon not only looked like previous XJs but was carefully marketed as such.

The X-300 was a tribute to what Ford had brought to the Jaguar table, and to the Jaguar design team that had been able to make so many improvements in so short a time, as it went into production in 1994, less than four years after its inception. It showed the world, and the company's Ford bosses, that Jaguar was still a viable company producing great cars.

Development of a new sports car

With work on the X-300 saloon coming along nicely by 1991, thoughts turned to what would be the next new project. Would it be an upgrade to the existing XJ-S, at this time still selling well; a completely new replacement; or another, perhaps smaller, saloon? As we now know, the first stage was to commit £50 million to a facelift of the XJ-S (thereafter known as the XJS),

which appeared that year. This gave Jaguar time to consider its future plans.

Bob Dover, a relatively late arrival at Jaguar from Land Rover, was appointed head of the Sports Car Team. It was very late in 1991 that a decision was taken to look to an XJS replacement, even though finance would continue to be a major problem, and there was no commitment from Ford to approve such a project – a situation that would continue for some considerable time.

The X-300 (XJ6, seen here in XJR supercharged form) was a tremendous step forward, and brought a lot to the table in terms of the XK8 sports car. (Nigel Thorley)

BOB DOVER

Bob Dover started his career in mechanical engineering, becoming an apprentice at Farnborough in 1962, and in 1968 he joined British Leyland as a project engineer. By 1978 he was working for tractor manufacturers Massey-Fergusson, and then in 1988 he moved to Land Rover as Director of Manufacturing. He joined Jaguar in 1990 as Director of Manufacturing, New Products, and in 1992 became head of the X-100 team as Chief Programme Engineer, Sports Cars. He later moved over to Aston Martin.

GEOFF LAWSON

Born in Leicester, the brilliant stylist Geoff Lawson studied design and took a Masters degree in furniture design at the Royal College of Art. He joined Vauxhall Motors in 1969 as a designer and worked on car and truck programmes in Europe and the US for General Motors, progressing to Chief Designer level. He was appointed Jaguar's Director of Styling in 1984. His work with Jaguar included the facelifted XJS, the X-300 saloon, the XJ220 supercar, the New Series XJ saloons, and the XK8. Geoff died suddenly in June 1999 at the age of 54.

Feeling that a fresh outlook was needed (as the XJS was very much a grand touring car rather than an out-and-out sports car like its predecessor, the E-type), the marketing strategy for the proposed 'new' model would change, because the 'S' had never been as popular in the valued US market as the E-type had been in its day.

1992: work begins

Bob Dover's Sports Car Team was made up of a mere 24 people, including Jaguar's Chief Stylist Geoff Lawson. They had to work to a very strict brief to produce an entirely new Jaguar sports car to a relatively minor (and at the time somewhat theoretical) budget of £300 million, which had to accommodate an existing floorpan and a new AJ26 engine, yet to be built.

A further facelift to the XJS was considered, which would have been economical and would have provided a quick-fix, even to the point of grafting on an X-300 look-alike front, but it was inevitable that styling cues

Interesting styling alternatives for the XJS considered as a stopgap until an entirely new sports car could be produced. (JDHT)

TIMELESS	✓	BEAUTIFUL	✓
FASHIONLESS	✓	HONEST	✓
ELEGANT	✓	WANTABLE	✓
ENGLISH	✓	JAGUARNESS	✓

from the E-type or even the XJ220 supercar would have to be considered. Although the concept of reviving the XJS didn't go away for quite some time, Jaguar finally committed to the preparation of designs and the building of four clay models to evaluate the possibilities for an entirely new car, coded X-100.

External styling

Geoff Lawson assigned Fergus Pollock as X-100 Project Leader, and they commissioned four clay models to be created for evaluation. This coincided with Bill Hayden's retirement from the company. He was replaced at the helm of Jaguar by Nick Scheele, another ex-Ford man who had run its Mexican operation. He arrived at a crucial time in the early days of the X-100 project, with great enthusiasm for both the car and the company.

As well as two in-house designs from Jaguar's Whitley Engineering facility, Geoff enlisted the help of Ford's own styling department in the US, as well as its Italian coachbuilding subsidiary, Ghia. The results were ready in March of 1992 and were based on four specific themes, entitled 'Evocative, Radical, Progressive and Evolutionary'. At this point only the Coupé was being

Clay No. 2 emphasising just how radical this design was for Jaguar then, as it would still be now. (JDHT)

worked on, Geoff Lawson considering that this was the most vital design to get right and that the Convertible would more easily follow from it.

Clay No. 1: Evolutionary design

This was a design created externally for Jaguar by Moray Callum, a Ghia designer, the brother of Ian Callum of Aston Martin and now Jaguar fame. Based on the concept of a traditional luxury GT design to appeal to existing XJS type customers, the 'evolutionary' aspects of the design would, hopefully, also appeal to new customers enticed away from Jaguar's competition.

A relatively pretty design, although somewhat slab-sided, it bore some resemblance to a Porsche 911 yet retained a touch of Jaguar traditionalism with an oval grille, not too dissimilar to earlier Jaguar models and, in hindsight, remarkably close to the S-type saloon grille from 1999. With a very large rear screen, and an enormous and severely tapered rear end, this clay got through the initial assessment in March but was abandoned next time around in June.

Clay No. 2: Radical design

This was an in-house design created by Jaguar's team at its relatively new Whitley Engineering Division in Coventry. One of several designs worked on by Keith

Helfet (one of the few engineers and designers at Jaguar who had worked under Sir William Lyons, the founder of the company) and his boss Geoff Lawson, this was to be an avant-garde, almost adventurous design, to get a feel for how far Jaguar could go within contemporary design.

With a pronounced windscreen, Porsche-style doors, no rear side windows, a roofline somewhat reminiscent of a TVR Cerbera, and a severe rear overhang and taper, this was moving right away from anything Jaguar had done before. Nevertheless, the front end sported a grille somewhat resembling that of the racing C-types of the 1950s.

This Radical concept was also carried over to the next review in June.

Clay No. 3: Progressive design

The second non-Jaguar design, created for it by Ford in the US, was derived from the XJS. It again used the oval style of radiator grille but with frontal lighting not too distant from what would eventually be the XK8 design. From the side this concept was decidedly XJS in the lower section, and even the door aperture owed much to the old car. At the rear was a very large tailgate and a rear window with an unusual lighting technique. An interesting detail was the use of bumper bar blades, a

Another styling exercise that enjoyed a short stay of execution. (JDHT)

feature to appear later on cars like the S-type and many competitors' vehicles.

This concept was out of favour at the first viewing in March 1992.

Revised Clay No. 2 design was, however, also later abandoned. (JDHT)

Clay No. 3 was heavily derived from the XJS, though from this angle it has a distinct Porsche 911 look to the side rear. This clay was ruled out very early on. (JDHT)

Clay No. 4: Evocative design

The second of the Jaguar Whitley concepts, this was designed to create a style echoing previous Jaguar sporting car successes like the XK120 and E-type. Meant to appeal to a younger audience but not to be so contemporary as to put off existing XJS or other Jaguar owners, it also used a traditional radiator grille but of smaller dimensions and with a prominent centre rib (à

Clay No. 4, an in-house design that it was felt had the greatest promise from which to generate another clay. (JDHT)

la Mark 2 of the 1960s). With concealed headlights, the bonnet line and auxiliary lighting features would later be seen in the 'real' XK8. The side view also showed touches of the final car, and they retained the rear quarter-windows with a nicely sloping roof section. At the rear there was still a lot of work to do, obviously. Note the return of the centrally mounted exhaust pipes (à la E-type).

Along with the other Whitley design, this concept carried over to the next stage in June, by which time the designs had gone through the various stages of their viability studies.

After another review mid year it was Clay No. 4 (the Whitley Evocative concept) that was chosen for further development, although it was decided that

another clay model should be produced to move the theme forward. This became known, confusingly, as Clay A (for 'Alternative').

Enter Clay A

Much better proportioned than Clay 4, this design was shorter. It featured sculptured sill and rear valance areas not unlike the XJ220 supercar and even had a nose not too distinct from the old E-type and the newer XJ220. Geoff Lawson, Jaguar's own stylist, had a strong

This was Clay No. 4 at a later stage in development, by this time renamed Clay M. Clear signs of XJ220 and the eventual XK8 are coming through at the front, but although not noticeable in this view it still had a very pronounced rear overhang. (JDHT)

Clay A, and the XK8 as we know it takes shape. With its shortened rear overhang and tidy up of the frontal view, this is now very close to the final design, though the front wing curvature still has to be altered, as does the door style and form. (JDHT)

Another angle of Clay A, showing its very close relationship to the final car from the rear. The idea of a differently coloured rear bumper continued for a while. Also note the addition of a badge on the boot lid, which did not appear in production form until the original XKR model. (JDHT)

belief in what Jaguar was all about, and felt that the heritage of Sir William's style should not be ignored, and this was apparent in this concept. Although there was still lots of work to do, the XK8 was now beginning to take shape.

Interior Design A was too traditional for the new Jaguar sports car. (JDHT)

Interior design

Work on the interior design and layout of the new car went on alongside the external styling. Care had to be taken not to upset existing buyers who loved Jaguar's well known traditional touches of leather and wood, nor to be too outrageous and get sucked into the world of gadgetry. Five possible choices were arrived at for consideration, half-sized models of which were produced.

Design A: Traditional

This was indeed quite traditional, and was to be saloon car-derived in order to provide good parts interchangeability – indeed, some of these styling

features found their way into the later X-308 (XJ8 saloons) launched in 1997. It was a good 'safe' design but was not sporty enough for the X-100 strategy, so was abandoned.

Design B: Progressive

This design had an enlarged sweeping centre console design. The passenger side was devoid of any detail while the instrument pack ahead of the driver was obviously derived from a Ford Scorpio. At the time this design was considered a good base to work from, but more design choice was requested. Although abandoned, areas like the centre console seem to have later found favour in the Aston Martin DB7.

Interior Design B was what Jaguar termed 'Progressive'. It was ultimately deemed unsuitable – and just look at those door trims! (JDHT)

Design C: Evolutionary

Trying to achieve a halfway compromise between the traditional and the new, this design incorporated loads of woodwork and a somewhat squat centre console area. It was ruled out in the first review in March 1992.

Interior Design C was still traditional in the dashboard layout, acres of wood on the door trims and unusual shaping to the centre console area. (JDHT)

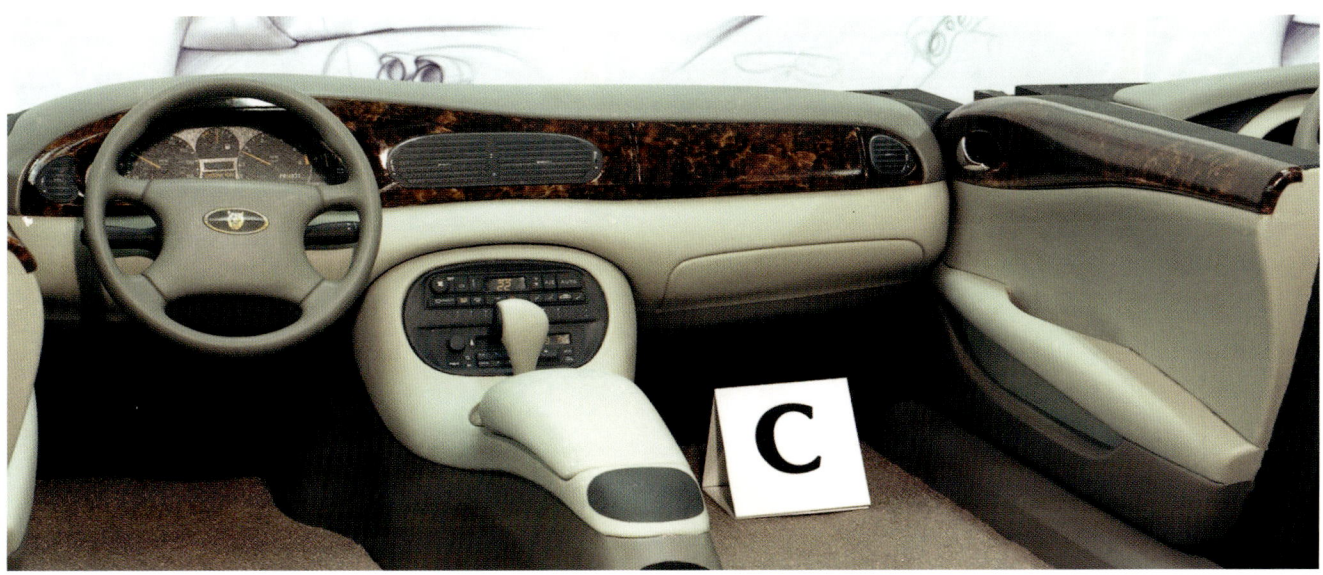

Interior Design D, which seemed – even to the layman's eye – to have nothing favourable about it. (JDHT)

Design D: Avant-garde

This was like nothing Jaguar had ever tried before. With no wood and somewhat featureless details, it received the thumbs down right from the start and was instantly rejected.

Design E: Radical

This was to be Jaguar's radical alternative with sweeping curves everywhere, no pronounced centre

The 'Radical' Design E interior concept, which was just that! (JDHT)

console area at all, and a definitely American influence to many features.

Not convinced that these concepts were the way forward, in June 1992 more choices were provided in the form of sketches, and one particular example found favour. With a full-width veneered dashboard with curved top, this became known as the 'Spitfire wing' design. Although it was indeed very traditional – particularly so in the original drawing, which seems to have taken some cues from much earlier cars, like the 1950s Bristols – a later derivation in October was more subtle and was adopted for further development.

From this point it didn't take long for the final style to emerge, with the main instruments in front of the

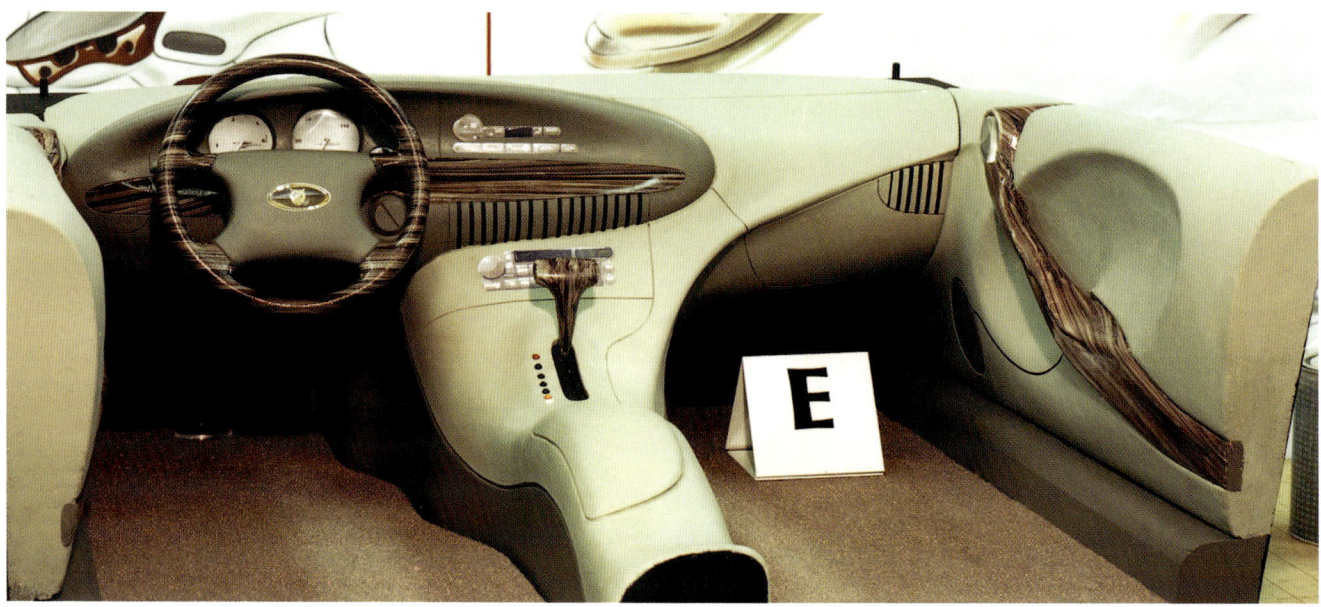

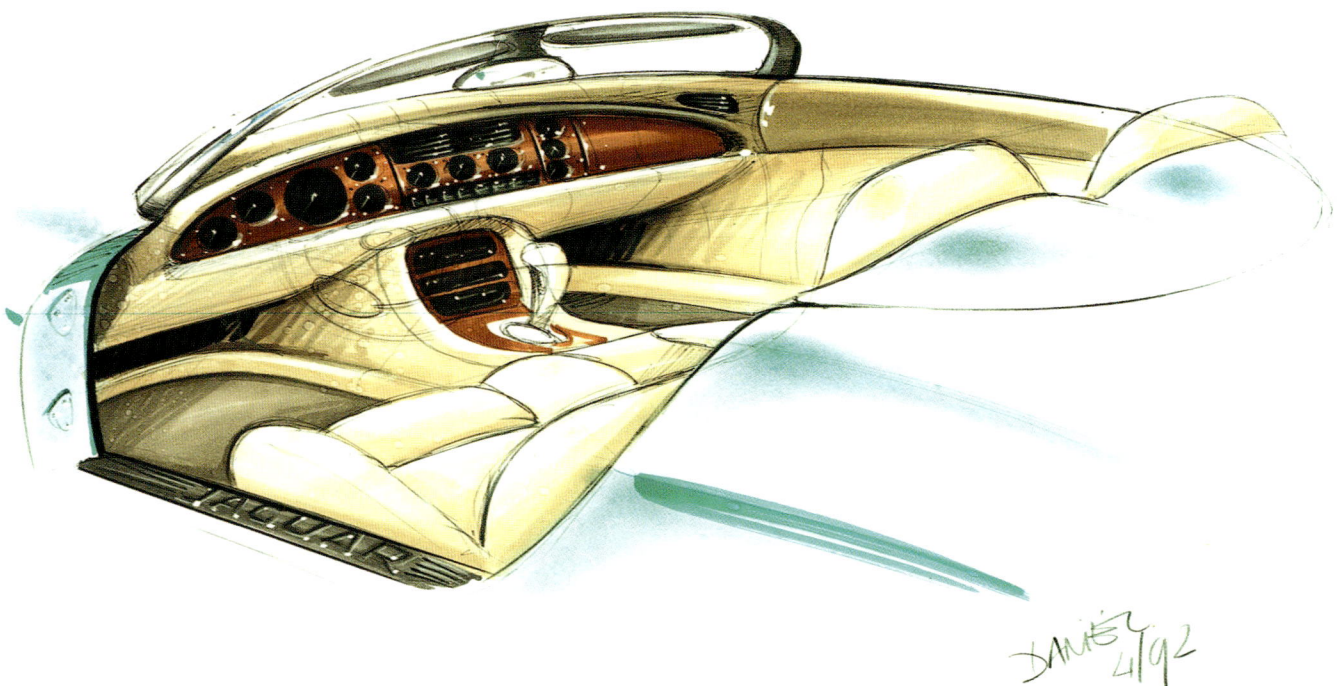

driver and ancillary gauges in the centre section above an X-300-derived centre console area. The choice of dashboard 'finish' came up for review and no fewer than nine types were focus tested across the world – everything from traditional walnut veneer, through grey stained wood, brushed aluminium, carbon fibre and even Chinese lacquer.

At the time it was only the walnut and grey staining that proved popular, and these finishes were finally agreed for the early cars.

During 1992 Jaguar carried out some major market research by organising focus groups. The one held

in the US was shown pictures of the various designs, while a later one held at the National Exhibition Centre in Birmingham was shown the modified Clay 4 (now confusingly renamed Clay M), displayed alongside Clay A, the existing XJS, and the competition from other manufacturers like Mercedes. On the latter occasion a specially chosen audience of 300 potential customers for such cars was selected for a detailed evaluation of the vehicles.

Perhaps not surprisingly both the new Jaguar proposals were rated equally highly, although Clay A (more akin to the eventual final design) rated better in Convertible form than Coupé.

The first mock-up of what would eventually be the XK8 dash layout. (JDHT)

Six days after this focus group – by which time all the results had been evaluated – Jaguar finally sanctioned Clay A, although it must be emphasised that even at this point Ford had not given approval for the project to go into final development and production. With the final external design agreed, outside consultants could now digitise the styling model to create a fibreglass representation for final detailing. Two such cars were built for various show purposes, but neither were runners at this stage.

The Jaguar team were now fired up over the X-100 project under the ultimate leadership of Nick Scheele and other key personnel, the only major problem being that Ford had still not given its global approval to finance it. However, Ford itself was at

November 1992, and *Autocar* were on the trail of the new Jaguar. (Reprinted from *Autocar* magazine)

the same time developing its own new Mustang, so the interchange of ideas helped both projects but predominantly gave Jaguar some credence in the Ford camp.

In November 1992 Jaguar set about the sourcing of parts to build the X-100 and found tremendous support from suppliers, despite the fact that there was no money on the table at this stage or, indeed, an agreement to produce the car. The very same month *Autocar* magazine published an 'exclusive' on the new Jaguar V8 sports car. Splashed across its front cover was a very credible artist's impression of the car, although the inside pictures owed more to the stillborn F-type than the X-100. In its editorial, headed 'The F-type lives', it demonstrated first-hand knowledge of what had happened that year, even down to Jaguar's thoughts about using a modified version of the existing XJ-S suspension. However, the impression was given that Ford had now backed the project officially. Its closing statement said a lot: 'For the lovers of Jaguar sports cars, the next three and a half years (until the launch of X-100) are going to seem interminable'!

To summarise, once the design strategy had been conceived and the concepts prepared, the sequence of events that accompanied the hectic birth of the X-100 project in 1992 was as follows:

- March – Theme selection
- March/April – Feasibility review
- June – Market research
- June/July – Post-research design changes
- June/July – Review and agreement on one design
- July – Review clinic in the USA
- August – Post-US review design changes
- September – Feasibility review
- September – Overall review

1993: moving forward

And so into 1993, only the second year of the X-100 design programme, with Jaguar working – unofficially – towards a launch date of 1996. The first move came in February, when a fibreglass representation of the car was shown to the US dealer network, where it was met with great acclaim, although the network wanted changes like more chrome and good old-fashioned wire wheels. This provided positive feedback for the Jaguar team and must have sown the seed of Ford eventually giving the project its final approval – but not yet! Ford still considered that 80 per cent of the Jaguar business depended on saloons, so it was difficult to justify major expenditure on a new Jaguar sports car.

In March 1993 the options were still open-ended and varied. Jaguar could carry out yet another upgrade to the existing XJS design (which, of course, happened anyway); it could fit its forthcoming new engine (the AJ-26) into the XJS bodyshell with or without further design upgrades; or it could continue with development of the X-100, but only as a convertible (to save money) though making it available with a fitted hardtop.

Back in the UK, Jaguar remained convinced of the potential of the X-100, and work had to get under way quickly on the many aspects of the car. Firstly, and right from the outset, the X-100 would have to use the existing XJS floorpan (which dated right back to 1968 and the first XJ6). This requirement was set in stone, as the floorpan is arguably the most expensive item to engineer; there wasn't the money or time to develop a new base for the car, so the good old XJS would be recycled for this purpose.

With this firmly in mind, the next consideration was the existing suspension layout. A famous bit of Jaguar engineering – the independent rear suspension, that dated back to 1961 and the E-type, and had served the company admirably – was considered, to save money. The same also applied to the front suspension, as both would easily fit onto the existing floorpan. The rear package was not considered a viable option, however. Suspension technology had moved on, and at this time the XJS still had inboard rear disc brakes (more costly to service), although this was soon to change. The next choice was to adapt the floorpan to accept the newer, more practical and economical alternative, the X-300 saloon rear suspension, itself based on the XJ40.

The front suspension also caused problems, since the XJS fitment couldn't be achieved given that the X-100 would be powered by the new AJ26 V8 engine, which was smaller, lighter, and would sit further forward in the car. The main oil sump was also situated at the front of the new engine (not at the rear as with the Jaguar V12 and AJ6 engines), so it would foul the existing XJS subframe. Height restrictions under the sloping bonnet of the X-100 also affected engine mounting, and here too the technology had moved on, which would mean unreasonable changes to the existing set-up. Lastly, the existing XJS subframe was not known for its longevity and this too had to be addressed in the new car.

Jaguar's thoughts therefore turned to using the subframe developed for the X-300, but again space was

a problem so initially a steel subframe was designed before worries about fatigue ruled this out. Eventually new technology came into play, with an intriguing light and stiff alloy design being adopted which would be unique to the X-100.

As for the bodywork, Jaguar had learnt a lot from Ford with its new Mustang design, and the 'no adjust' body-build principle was adopted, so that instead of car bodies being designed and built with adjustable hinges and tolerances to allow for manual adjustment on the assembly line, tighter tolerances and better build quality enabled each panel or door to fit first time. This eliminated the need for the hand-fitting of panels during assembly, and the expensive and time-consuming use of lead loading, shimming, etc, all of which made the car easier and cheaper to build.

Conceived back in the 1960s, the XJS floorpan – indeed, the car – was always a heavy structure, so it was necessary to lighten everything where possible. For example, a lot of the old style strengthening was removed in favour of panel upgrades with smaller, higher stressed reinforcements. There would also be a 60 per cent reduction in the welding required on the car's bodyshell, as the number of panels required to build an X-100 were 30 per cent fewer than in an XJS.

All the tooling work for the X-100 body was given to the Japanese Ogihara company, well known for its expertise and quality and already working on the Ford Mustang project. It also worked closely with Jaguar to set up the body-in-white assembly facility at the Castle Bromwich factory in Birmingham.

A new car, a new engine and new transmission

As already mentioned, it was always intended that the new car would take the latest AJ26 Jaguar V8 engine, under development at the time. The AJ26 was only the fourth completely new engine totally designed and built by Jaguar. The first, the well-known XK six-cylinder engine, had powered all Jaguar models from 1948 until 1971 and remained in use in a substantial number of cars even thereafter; then had come the legendary V12 unit used from 1971 through to 1997; and most recently there had been the AJ-6 (later AJ-16) multi-valve straight six, built from 1983 to 1997, which replaced the XK unit. Jaguar's problem was that a new engine was vital to reduce the overall weight of the car, to improve efficiency and to retain refinement. Jaguar's V12 engine was costly to build and wouldn't pass updated US emissions controls in place since 1995, and the six-cylinder engine was not refined or efficient enough and was too heavy.

The new V8 represented a major step forward in technology and performance terms, for which Jaguar had started with a clean sheet of paper in the late 1980s. Surveying the needs and perceptions of the Jaguar market, it was decided that the most vital requirements were good performance with refinement, a high standard of durability and quality, and reasonable cost of ownership and maintenance. As well as these idyllic objectives Jaguar also had to consider ever more stringent legislation worldwide on emissions, fuel consumption, CO_2 and even noise pollution. Safety issues were also a factor, since a neat compact engine provided the designers with the optimum amount of space to protect occupants from front-end collisions.

The tradition of utilising six cylinders was soon abandoned for reasons of refinement and possible problems with hydrocarbon emissions. Ten cylinders would have created inherent imbalance problems for

such a refined car, and 12 cylinders were immediately vetoed on a cost basis. Nevertheless, it was recognised that a V formation would make for a compact unit, and would be very acceptable in the valued US market. The solution, therefore, was to use eight cylinders, which offered a good weight saving and, ultimately, excellent engine refinement.

The concept of a V8 engine had been mooted by Jaguar earlier, even before the Ford take-over, but this time round it was a serious contender from the outset. It was considered vital that the refinement of the finished product should be at least as good as the then current Jaguar V12 power unit, and, indeed, competition was particularly stiff from the likes of Lexus, who in 1990 had launched its own superbly designed, refined and economical V8 engine for its top-of-the-range LS400 saloon. It was considered equally vital that a Jaguar like the X-100, a prestigious sporting car, should have a bespoke Jaguar engine, despite the fact that Ford had been developing its own V8 Romeo unit. This was a lesson that Jaguar had learnt earlier, when British Leyland had tried to influence its engine installations.

Early AJ26 engine under test. (JDHT)

Development of the new AJ26 engine (which later, just prior to the launch of the X-100, was renamed the AJ-V8) was carried out at Jaguar's ex-Daimler factory in Radford, Coventry, where Jaguar engines and axles were manufactured and assembled. Though the development work was Jaguar's it had the assistance of Ford personnel and their considerable experience with V8 engines.

Radford was a very old plant, built in 1912 specifically for vehicle production, and serious consideration was given to producing the new V8 engine there. Another possibility was that Jaguar might build a new facility to produce the V8, but neither of these schemes was financially viable at the time. Ford already had its fairly new and technologically-advanced facility in Bridgend in Wales, which had spare capacity and the necessary expertise to produce the Jaguar engines economically and efficiently. The hard but necessary decision was therefore taken to move engine production away from Coventry. This would ultimately lead to the closure of the old Daimler factory in 1996, around the same time as the X-100 was launched.

Publicly, the first details of the new V8 engine to be produced at Bridgend came in *Autocar* magazine in March 1993, along with revealing spy pictures of the then still under development X-300 saloon. Even at that stage *Autocar* suspected that the new engine would make its first appearance in the X-100 sports car project, but reckoned that it would only be pushing out about 260bhp, well under the final figure.

It took only 12 months from the official go-ahead to production of the first prototype V8 engine, and very little changed after that point apart from interesting and weight-saving features such as the replacement of conventional intake manifolds by Polyamide plastic composite with integrated fuel rails, which also provided good external thermal insulation and a nice, aesthetically smooth finish to the top of the engine. Further details of the AJ-V8's technological advances will be covered in the next chapter.

The XJS and even the XJ40 saloon proved ideal test beds to try out the new engine, and at one time even Directors of the company were running around in drone cars equipped thus, no one who saw them being any the wiser that under the bonnet there lurked something entirely new.

In total £160 million was spent on the development of the AJ-V8, including the setting up of production facilities at Bridgend and all the tooling. This amounted to just short of the budget provided by Ford. Not only was the new engine delivered on time and within its financial parameters, but it was also a foot shorter than the old six-cylinder engine and 90lb lighter than the AJ-16, which permitted greater freedom when it came to designing the rest of the car. Because the engine was on target, it was decided that its launch should coincide with that of the new car.

To accompany the engine, a highly efficient cooling system was patented by Jaguar for the X-100, with low volume capacity which permitted the engine to warm up in less than four minutes, reducing engine wear and providing a more comfortable environment for the occupants in cold weather.

The new engine also got a new gearbox. Following the poor sales response to the earlier XJSs, proved later with the X-300 saloons, it was decided that the X-100 would only be available as an automatic. The work of developing the new transmission was entrusted to the German ZF company, and although the gearbox chosen was also to be used by other manufacturers Jaguar was significantly involved in its development, to ensure that it suited the X-100's specification (and those of subsequent models), so joint patents were taken out by the two companies. This was to be Jaguar's first five-speed automatic transmission, and featured the tried and tested J-gate operation first seen on the XJ40 back in 1986. The result was the fully electronic ZF 5HP 24 gearbox, specially designed for mating to V8 engines. The X-100 was to be the first Jaguar car ever equipped with a fully electronic 'box. There are more details on this too in the next chapter.

A surprise announcement came in June of 1993 from Tom Walkinshaw of JaguarSport (already committed to building the Aston Martin DB7 at Bloxham after the demise of the Jaguar XJ220), who declared his intention to produce a two-seater Jaguar to rival the E-type, costing around £30,000. It would be a real drivers' car and up to 5000 would be produced each year. Speculation followed that this would be released in 1996, coinciding with Jaguar's own X-100, but nothing actually came of the project – unless it turned out to be the later joint venture between Walkinshaw and Volvo to produce their stylish two-door coupé.

Financial support and final approval

It was now June 1993, and there had still been no formal approval of funds to build the X-100, even though Bob Dover and his team were getting to grips with the project. By this time it had come down to Ford and Jaguar seeking a commitment from the

British Government of cash to assist the project – after all, Nissan had got significant support from the Government, so why not Jaguar? But only a month later the Government gave the thumbs down to financial support, and there were strong fears at Jaguar that the X-100 would finally be cancelled. Ford also insisted on more 'clinics', using the fibreglass cars to get better feedback and evaluation on the project's viability. Fortunately the support and interest expressed at these meetings surprised even Ford.

Whilst all this was happening Jaguar's Browns Lane Assembly Plant in Coventry was closing for its summer holiday, during which time the tracks were dismantled and over £50 million was invested in new assembly technology – all, at this time, to support production of the still to be announced X-300 saloon, but which would inevitably be used for the building of other Jaguar models too, not least, it was hoped, the new sports car. However, thoughts turned to the possibility of building the new Jaguar in Portugal, whose own government had offered £23 million of financial support. This offer provided Jaguar with a gauntlet to be thrown at the feet of the British Government in the hope that it would

reconsider its position. In the meantime, the first proper prototype was completed in September using the XJS floorpan, the AJ-V8 engine, and a representation of the X-100 bodywork, which was used for high-speed testing.

By the end of the year things were really hotting up, because the British *Car* magazine had printed spy photographs of the new car taken in Jaguar's own styling studio – something Jaguar had been trying hard to avoid. Even more importantly, on 1 December the UK Government announced a grant of £9.4 million plus additional support for the project. This effectively ruled out the Portuguese offer and forced Ford to also commit itself in mid-December to £10 million of support for the X-100 programme, although even then only on the basis that commitment would not be given to any specific country for final production.

1994: X-100 is a goer

By February 1994 over 30 prototypes had been produced – most of them still substantially based on drone XJSs – for all sorts of test requirements, including hot and cold weather evaluation. Ogihara had also delivered the first 30 body-in-white shells. Even more importantly, by May Jaguar had produced two very significant prototypes (a Coupé and a Convertible) of the actual X-100, based on prototype tooling. These looked like the real

Early camouflaging attempts designed to keep prying eyes at bay, although a lot of the initial work was done using XJSs. (JDHT)

thing, could be driven, and were substantially used as feasibility studies for production. The X-100 may have been based on the XJS floorpan, but in so many other ways it was technically very advanced. Multi-plexing the wiring saved something like two hours in assembling the electrics. A reduced number of sub-assemblies was also used, many of them assembled by outside suppliers to be delivered to the 'track' as required, which cut down overall production time. Parts were sourced from the best of Ford's suppliers around the world to ensure a class-leading final product.

For the Convertible model, the work of development was again given to Karmann, who had been responsible for the XJS Convertible. Initially there were thoughts of adopting a metal frame like that used by Mercedes, but this was abandoned in favour of the lighter and cheaper approach of a conventional fabric tonneau cover. Karmann's work on the X-100 resulted in a 10 per cent lighter frame construction than that used on the XJS, yet it was torsionally stiffer.

1994 was a busy year all round for Jaguar, as it saw the launch of the X-300 saloon and the final demise of the XJ40, and thoughts were well advanced towards running-down XJS production in view of the progress made on X-100. In September the evaluation programme of prototypes was well under way, and a

NEAR MISS

The Japanese company Ogihara, which had designed and built the body tooling for the X-100, suffered damage from a major earthquake in Kobe, where their factory was based. Had it not been for the fact that the Jaguar tooling had just left Japan en route to the UK, the subsequent loss would have set the XK8 launch back some considerable time.

month later the schedule for production tooling was agreed. This included final approval to suppliers who manufactured the various components, one of which was the dashboard moulding and instrument packs produced in-house by Ford at Enfield in Middlesex.

It is interesting to compare the development of X-100 alongside the then entirely new DB7 produced by Aston Martin, another Ford-owned company. After the Ford take-over of Jaguar (and Aston Martin), Tom Walkinshaw – who had worked closely with Jaguar since the early 1980s on the XJS Touring Car Championship, the JaguarSport modified cars and, of course, the XJ220

Later camouflage. This car, a Convertible, looks more like the proverbial bread van, but it was all necessary to divert media eyes away. (JDHT)

– constructed a new prototype, code-named Project XX. Using the XJ41 base body style, XJS underpinnings, and a supercharged version of the Jaguar AJ16 engine, the running prototype was abandoned by Jaguar but taken up by Aston, and although the DB7 turned out a very different animal to Project XX, the connections were very valid. By 1994, production of the Aston Martin DB7 was already well under way at the old Bloxham JaguarSport factory in Oxfordshire. Priced at nearly £80,000, the new Aston was on the road and had been exceptionally well received. Inevitably there was to be a lot of cross-over in the development of the DB7 and X-100, but how would Jaguar's new sports car compete with Aston Martin's? We had to wait another two years to find out!

1995: a hectic year of testing

With only 5000 XJSs produced in 1995 the desperate need for the X-100 was confirmed. With development cars now undergoing even more intensive testing, X-100-clad examples received a rather Heath-Robinson, yet effective, rubberised and moulded disguise to protect the final style from prying eyes. A fair number of these cars were subjected to extensive hot and cold climate testing in order to evaluate them fully, mostly on

continuous eight-hour driving shifts. With and without cladding they were also subjected to continuous high-speed assessment at the Nardo circuit in Italy. Racing driver (and Ford consultant) Jackie Stewart was also involved in testing the X-100.

During this period production tooling for 1700 parts was established for the new model, although additional components were selected directly from the then current Jaguar parts bin. Apart from the obvious XJS connection in the floorpan, a modified version of its seat frames was also utilised, which to some extent limited the development of new seats. Apparently no fewer than 22 different styles of seat were tried before arriving at the end result. Other parts came from and/or were modified from the X-300 saloons. These included the Teves braking system, the J-gate gear-select, the air-conditioning system, upper steering column, door hinge assemblies, and even more mundane items like some of the switch-gear and the centre console arm-rest lid.

With more work carried out on the suspension, one of the advantages of utilising a new arrangement at the front was being able to accommodate anti-squat abilities, something the XJS didn't have. Also, spring rates and pitch were altered, and the rear suspension/axle mounting frame was taken from the supercharged version of the X-300 for extra stiffness. Similar enhancements were carried out to the X-300 power-assisted steering system used on the X-100.

Between 6 and 8 March 1995, Jaguar arranged seminar launches at its Whitley Engineering facility to which the technical press were invited to review the AJ-V8 engine. These were followed in April and May by press visits to the Ford plant in Bridgend, already set up to manufacture the new engine. By mid-1995 all was going well, except for the publication by *Autocar* and *Car* magazines of spy pictures of the X-100 in reduced camouflage undergoing high-speed testing at Nardo.

In October 1995 the first Evaluation Prototype was produced, which led to no fewer than 32 being built to test the effective and efficient build of the new car. These were effectively fully production-tooled cars assembled from substantially production parts on a specially prepared miniature production line at Browns Lane.

In August, *Autocar* published a reasonably accurate artist's impression of the X-100, which was followed in October by six full pages of coverage, with paparazzi pictures of camouflaged cars and a sneak picture of an unclad car. A lot of detail was revealed in the

accompanying article, where it was speculated that a six-speed manual gearbox version would also be made available.

1996: the final goal in sight

It was as late as February 1996 that the final software approval was given to ZF for the new five-speed gearbox. Moving on from this the next phase was to use some of the 30 fully functional X-100 prototypes for final testing, then for advertising and other photographic work. It was also in February that the very first AJ-V8 engine left the production line at Bridgend, while production of the gearboxes began in March.

It was also at about this time that the new car's name was settled, X-100 having been merely its in-house development code. 'F-type' was out because of its association with the previous ill-fated XJ41 project. 'XK', however, echoed past Jaguar successes in the sports car market, but XKF was felt to be too close to the MGF model insignia. 'XK160' sounded good and continued the naming style used on the 1950s XKs, but it was felt to be just too retro for a significantly new car. XK8 therefore prevailed in the end, and perhaps quite rightly so.

An evaluation prototype being put through its paces at the Mira test track in Warwickshire. (JDHT)

The media hype was building up as, in January of that year, *Autocar* produced supposedly undercover details of 100 secret cars due out in 1996, amongst which was, of course, the XK8. It targeted the car as 'the biggest launch of the year'. Less than a month later the same magazine provided more news on the XK8, declaring that it would be publicly launched at the Geneva Motor Show that March. Interestingly, at the same time it claimed to have knowledge that a supercharged version would become available, to be called the XKR8!

A small upset for Jaguar came in March, when *The Times* newspaper printed a report that the new Jaguar V8 engine was merely a re-vamped Ford unit from the US. Although Ford under-wrote the whole Jaguar engine project, apparently only two parts came from its parts bin – a woodruff key and the sump plug. Whether that was Jaguar marketing coming into play or not, the fact is that the new AJ26 engine was designed by Jaguar.

At the International Geneva Motor Show that month, Jaguar did indeed pre-launch the new car, now publicly known as the XK8. But the engine compartment was not revealed, nor were any specific details of the car announced.

One of the first batch of true production cars, still under test at this stage. (JDHT)

It was purely a pre-launch 'showcase' for the new model, meant to echo that of the E-type back in 1961. It was also in March that engine production started at Bridgend, while construction of the transmissions commenced in April.

April also saw the completed production of another 100 cars. Effectively these could have been sold to the public, but 50 were used for in-house management evaluation of how they would cope with normal everyday use.

The first batch of true production cars was made in June, with the first (Job 1) leaving the line on the fourth of that month. Of this first run of 170 cars, 20 were taken for further management evaluation, while the rest formed part of the stock build-up ready for the official launch in October.

It was also in June that the new AJ-V8 engine was publicly launched, and soon afterwards the specification details of the new car were announced. A lot of pre-launch selling took place during the summer, whilst production got up to speed. In overall

terms, while the XJS could only be built at the rate of 110 cars per week, up to 250 of the more efficently made XK8 could be built in the same time, the new car needing only 150 operatives to assemble it, and being 30 per cent quicker to build. It also proved to be 'best in class' when it came to the integrity of fitment of the component parts from the many suppliers used. By August the Jaguar Browns Lane factory had produced no fewer than 2000 XK8s ready for despatch to the dealers, with production geared at this stage to a ratio of three Convertibles to two Coupés.

Summary

Through good planning and management, early parts sourcing and a great deal of faith from all involved, the XK8 had been delivered in just 30 months from programme approval. Around 80 per cent of its parts were entirely new, with only 10 per cent carried over from the XJ Series saloons. Though it took 30 per cent fewer body panels to construct the XK8 shell than the XJS, build quality was dramatically improved and torsional stiffness increased by 25 per cent. Add a new engine, new gearbox, and new axles and suspension, and there you have it: the XK8.

Job 1 – the very first production XK8 off the Browns Lane line in 1996. (JDHT)

The XK8 had arrived. These are very early Coupé and Convertible production models in Jaguar's styling 'garden' at Whitley, with (on the left) Styling Director Geoff Lawson and Fergus Pollock. (JDHT)

The new car in detail

The heart of any car is its engine and Jaguar had, up to this time, only produced three basic engine designs: firstly the legendary XK straight six, launched in 1948 in its XK120 sports, the engine that powered every single production Jaguar until 1971 and continued in production until 1992; then the awesome V12 that powered the E-type Series 3 sports from 1971 and stayed in production for top-of-the-range saloons until 1997; and lastly the AJ6/AJ16 multi-valve straight

The AJ-V8 installation in the early XK8. This car has standard (non CATS) suspension. (Nigel Thorley)

six introduced in 1983 for the XJ-S, which powered the majority of production Jaguars until the introduction of the AJ26. It appeared to be Jaguar policy to launch a new engine in a sporting model first, and history repeated itself when the new AJ26 (from here on the AJ-V8) was introduced in the XK8.

The basic advantages of the new engine were that it was shorter and lighter, both of which had numerous advantages. Pro rata it was more powerful, refined, quiet, and frugal than previous Jaguar six-cylinder engines and was more economical and as quiet and refined as the V12.

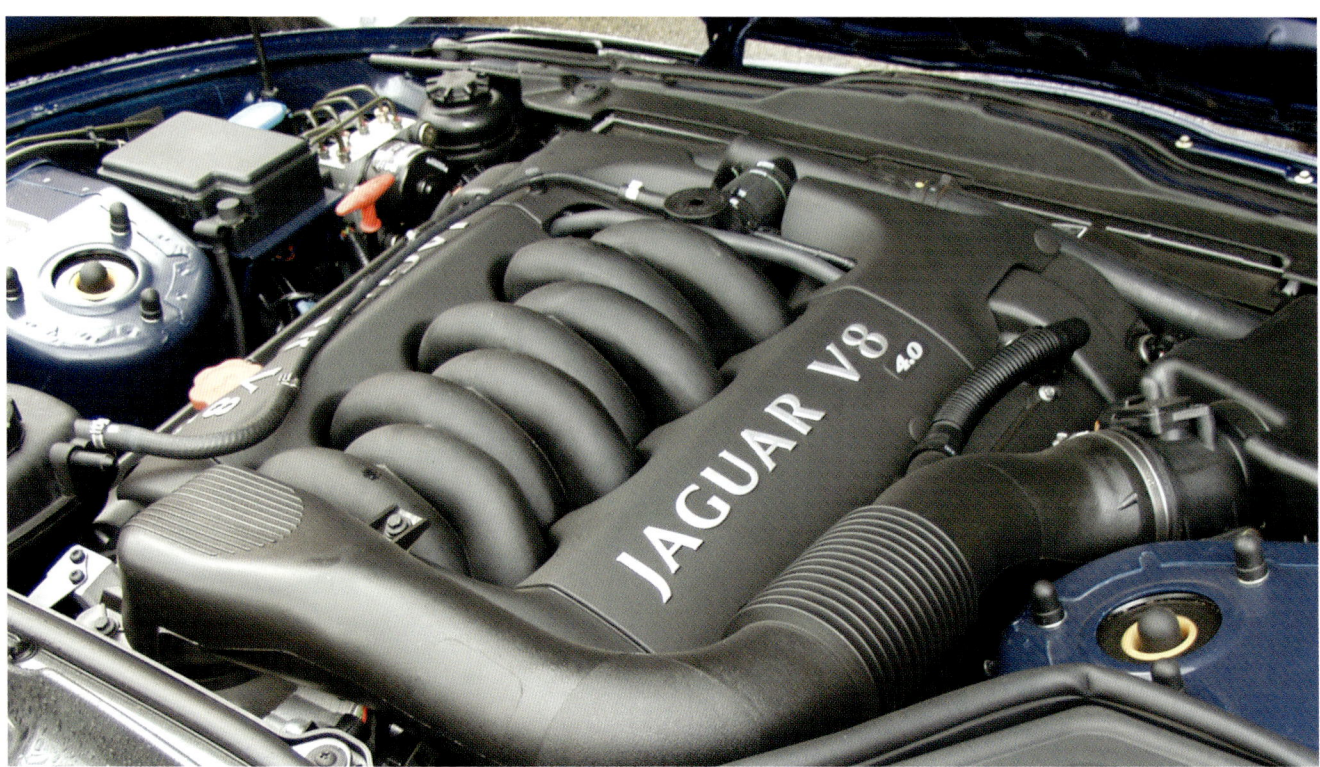

The engine is of four-cam design with a 90° V formation, apparently to minimise any out-of-balance problems normally associated with V8 engines. Of square cylinder dimensions (86mm bore and stroke), the cubic capacity is 3996cc, which Jaguar claimed provided the best compromise between the conflicts of power, torque, economy, emissions and vibration levels. Rated at 290bhp at 6100rpm, 80 per cent of the maximum torque is available throughout a range of 1400 to 6400rpm.

It is interesting to compare the performance of the early V8 engine to the outgoing Jaguar power units of the time:

	Cubic Capacity	bhp	@rpm	bhp output per litre	Maximum torque
AJ-V8	3996cc	290	6100	72.6	290lb ft @4250rpm
AJ16	3980cc	249	4800	61.0	289lb ft @4000rpm
V12	5993cc	318	5350	52.0	353lb ft @2850rpm

Jaguar claimed at the time the highest specific output of any engine in this class and the highest torque per litre in class at peak torque and high engine speeds:

AJ-V8 contemporary comparisons with the opposition

	Cubic capacity	bhp	Maximum torque
AJ-V8	3996cc	290	290lb ft
BMW 804	3982cc	282	310lb ft
Mercedes 320	3199cc	228	200lb ft
Porsche 911 Carrera	3600cc	285	251lb ft

The engine block was cleverly designed to be lightweight yet to provide significant stiffness and torsional strength from its cast ribbed-web connected banks and closed deck design. Further, in order to save weight there were no conventional iron liners to the cylinder bores, which were instead lined with nickel silicon carbide (Nikasil) to a thickness of 0.08mm, saving 15lb in weight and providing supposedly high wear-resistance because its ultra-smooth surface minimises friction. Developed for Formula One, this new technology – also adopted by other manufacturers such as BMW – meant installing a new plating plant and an all-new low pressure alloy die-casting process to ensure low porosity.

Cosworth produced the unique twin cylinder heads for Jaguar. Heavily ribbed, these provide stiffness, minimise radiated noise and are each a mirror image of the other. An 18mm offset makes for compact head design and bulk and the unusually long cylinder head bolts ensure an excellent head-to-block seal. The five-bearing crankshaft is made from spheroidal graphite cast iron, while the conrods are forged by the highly accurate Krebsoge powder sintering technique. Alloy flat top, short skirt, low friction pistons are used.

The new engine incorporated variable cam phasing on the inlet cams, with a 30° range of adjustment, which not only helped performance but also contributed towards low emission levels.

A four valves per cylinder configuration was adopted, but with more slender diameter shafts, operated by low-mass aluminium bucket tappets. Given this conventional set-up, Jaguar opted for larger valves in proportion to port size than its competitors' engines, to enhance performance. Another weight reduction came about by drilling the chilled cast iron camshafts from end to end, saving around 1lb per cam. Cam drive is by four single-row chains rather than a toothed belt, which was more common practice then as now. Chains were adopted to minimise the depth of the engine and also provided greater engine safety in service.

A 28° angle between the inlet and exhaust valves facilitates a narrow, squish-free pent-roof combustion chamber, minimising heat loss and providing for high tolerances to exhaust gas recirculation and thereby improving emissions further. A very high 10.75:1

General layout of the AJ-V8 engine heads, manifolds and cylinder block. (Nigel Thorley)

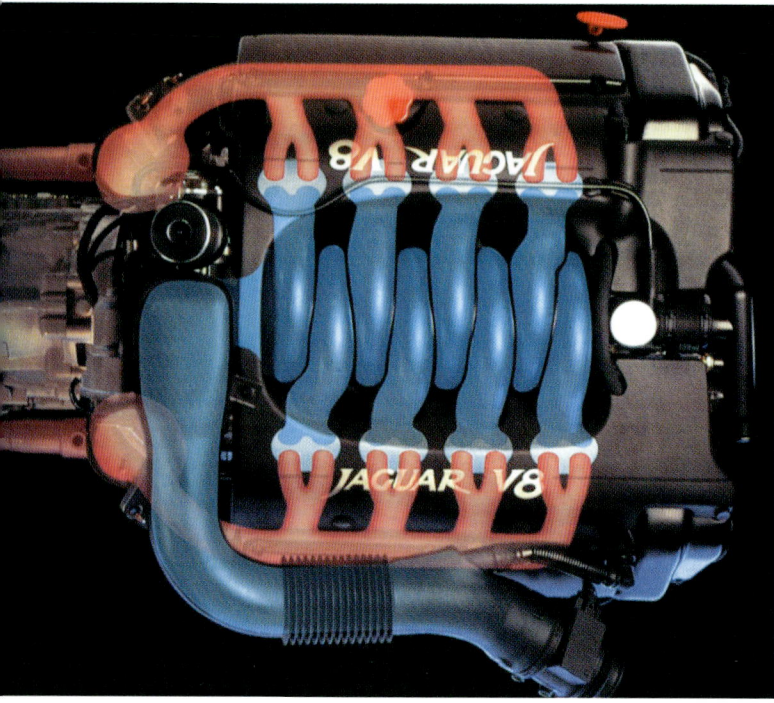

Unique attributes of the air intake system on the V8 engine. (Nigel Thorley)

Patented by Jaguar, the split coolant flow from the water pump provides best-in-class efficiency. (Nigel Thorley)

compression ratio was chosen. Yet another benefit to emissions was gained by fitting close-coupled catalytic converters and thin-wall exhaust manifolds, while a very fast from-cold engine warm-up is assured by a unique (for the time) low volume 'split block' cooling system (see below).

Plastics were used extensively, not only to save weight. The intake manifolds were moulded from Polyamide composite, which is both lightweight and has the added advantage of providing external thermal insulation and an attractive smooth finish to conventional castings. This also enabled Jaguar to accommodate an integrated fuel rail into the manifold to reduce complexity and improve injector targeting.

A new Nippondenso 32-bit electronic engine management system was adopted for the AJ-V8 engine and proved to be the best in its class. Optimising adjustment of the throttle openings, it facilitated better idle speed control and cruise control, and offered improved drivability and exhaust emissions control.

Jaguar made great play of the fast warm-up time for the AJ-V8 (less than four minutes from cold), and the Society of Automotive Engineers gave them an award for the XK8's cooling system. Using a split system, the water pump delivers water separately, with 50 per cent of the coolant delivered into a gallery bypassing the bores, delivering the flow to the cylinder heads at the rear of the engine, and then mixing with the remaining 50 per cent of coolant used to cool the bores. Jaguar also claimed that the high velocity of coolant delivery prevented localised boiling with less than 2° difference in metal temperature between the front and rear of the engine.

Manufacture of the first engines for production cars got under way in May 1996 and had built up to 35 units a day within a month.

Transferring the power

A new car and a new engine deserved a new transmission, but due to the unpopularity of 'stick shift' models for many years Jaguar opted not to offer a manual gearbox. Instead, ZF provided Jaguar's first five-speed automatic gearbox, the ZF 5HP 24 utilising advanced micro-processor control.

Using a 32-bit intelligent electronic system, the gearbox optimised gearshift points according to driver, conditions, and even temperature. The low inertia torque converter design allowed for the fitment of an advanced slip-controlled clutch, to improve fuel economy and the refinement of gear changes. The

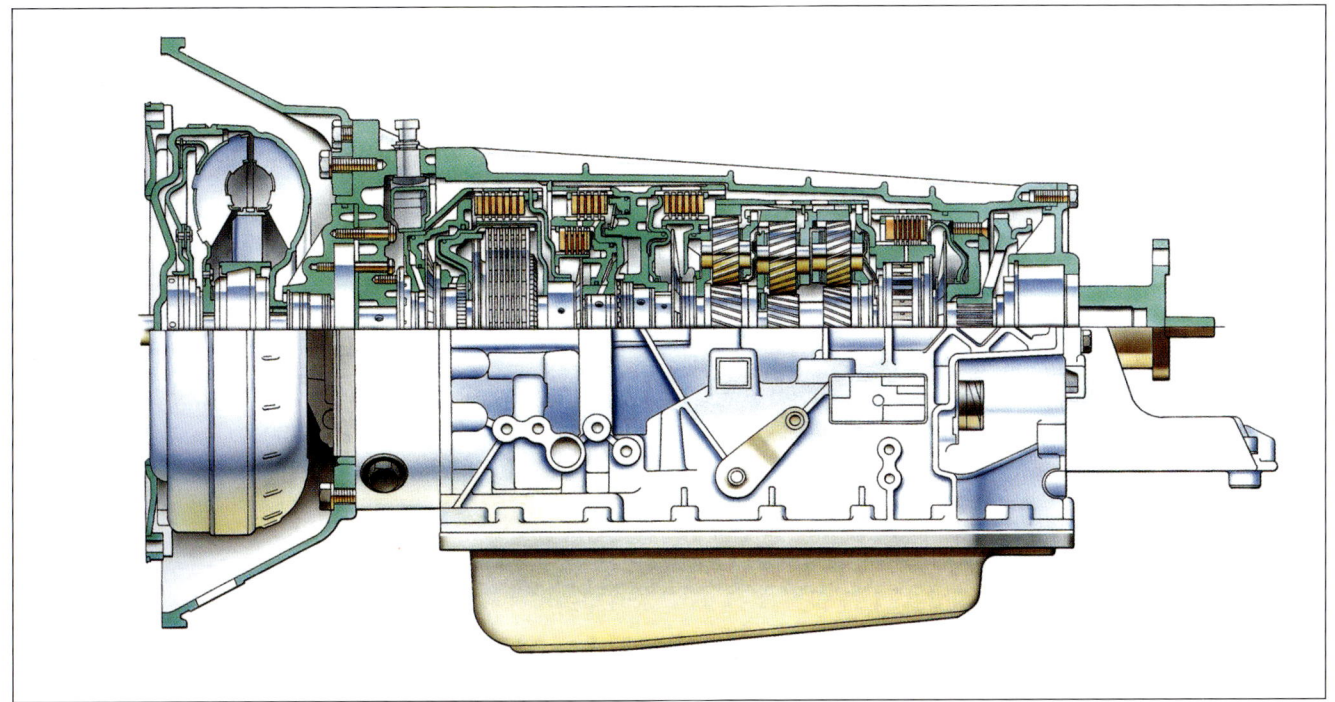

The new ZF 5HP 24 five-speed automatic transmission adopted for the XK8. (Nigel Thorley)

established J-gate operation, first seen in the XJ40 saloon, was retained for XK8 models.

Billed as a 'fill for life' sealed unit, the gearbox theoretically required no maintenance during the life of the car, but information supplied later in this publication will verify that service maintenance is highly recommended!

At the wheels

Jaguar adopted the ZF Servotronic speed sensitive rack-and-pinion steering system for the XK8, but with a special variable ratio feature to benefit low-speed

The new ZF 5HP 24 five-speed automatic transmission adopted for the XK8. (Nigel Thorley)

manoeuvring and high-speed stability, and to provide positive centre feel at the steering wheel. The system allows for power assistance to be speed-proportioned, while the positive centre feel provides stability when travelling in a straight line and in crosswinds, but at the same time doesn't increase parking effort. The variable

General layout of the drivetrain of the normally-aspirated early XK8. (Nigel Thorley)

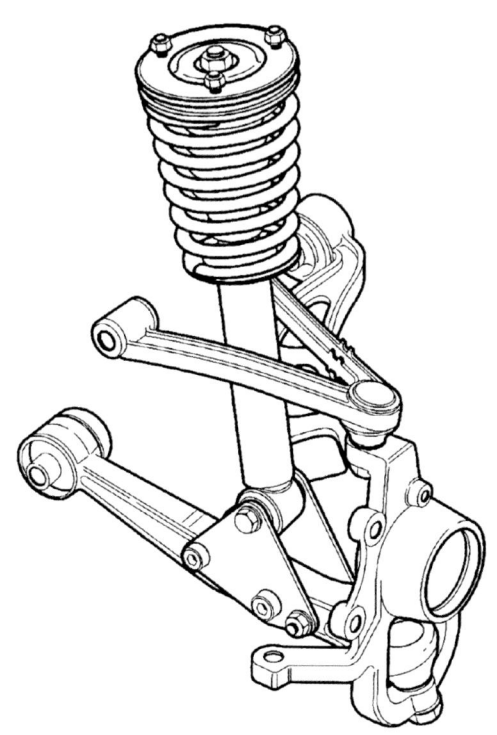

Jaguar's combined wishbone with coil spring and telescopic shock absorber design for the XK8. (Nigel Thorley)

ratio reduces the number of steering wheel turns for parking, and also reduces excessive response to driver input at high speed.

For the front suspension Jaguar opted to use a proven design but with a new departure. A double, unequal length wishbone design combined with coil springs and telescopic shock absorbers is an established concept, but in the XK8 the road springs are mounted directly to the body to improve handling and durability and to reduce suspension bush loads. Spring rates were developed to create less stress, and the hydraulic mounts (hydramounts, which are filled with oil) between the front crossmember and engine are tuned to ensure spring loads remain isolated.

The all-alloy front crossbeam identified in the last chapter, designed to aircraft quality standards, weighs in at only 15.8kg and is treated with Dacromet to guard against corrosion in contact with steel components.

As previously mentioned, the rear suspension owes a lot to the then current X-300 (XJR) saloon design. It is made up of an A-frame and monostrut design using a pendulum arrangement to allow fore and aft movement of the rear wheels at the inner fulcrums to enhance ride comfort. It also provides for good axle location.

An extra-cost option, initially only for Coupé models,

was the unique Jaguar 'CATS' (Computer Active Technology Suspension) system. This optimises the ride and handling according to conditions by means of uprated springs to increase the roll stiffness and adaptive dampers under electronic control. Sensors at the front and rear monitor the road and handling conditions and alter the electronic dampers to stiffen or soften settings accordingly. At start-up the dampers default to a firm setting, but once on the move above 5mph they revert to a softer setting. The settings continue to alter in micro-seconds when cornering, braking or on poor road surfaces.

The XK8's brakes were vastly uprated from those used on the old XJS. For example, larger ventilated discs (28mm x 305mm) are used at both the front and rear. Still using the Teves ABS system, improvements for the XK8 included the fitment of Automatic Stability Control (ASC). If a wheel starts to spin under power, the ABS control module uses the information to calculate the amount of torque reduction (eg engine power) required to eliminate the spin. Another additional aspect taken from the ABS system is Traction Control, which acts in conjunction with the Stability Control to reduce wheelspin in slippery conditions.

Wheels chosen for the XK8 at launch were the five-spoke (later known as Revolver) 8J x 17in alloy fitted with Pirelli P-Zero 245/50 ZR 17 tyres. These tyres had an asymmetric tread pattern with the outside tread area providing the best grip and the inside grooves providing good drainage. Chromium-plated versions of the five-spoke wheels were also available as an extra-cost option.

A further extra-cost option was the fitment of 8J x 18in (9J at the rear) seven-spoke (Flute) alloys, with Pirelli P-Zero 245/45 ZR 18 tyres at the front and 255/45 at the rear, the first time a production Jaguar had ever been equipped with different sized wheels and tyres front to back. The front tyres were unidirectional (different left to right), so are not interchangeable, while the rear tyres were asymmetric. These larger wheels and tyres were an integral part of the CATS suspension package on the Coupé but were also available to Convertible owners at the time. Normally a space saver spare wheel was provided in the boot area for all markets except the US.

Security and safety aspects

Security has become an important issue on cars over the last few years, so the XK8 had to accommodate the latest state-of-the-art technology if it was to be a successful seller. Taking a lead from the then current

The Sport interior of an early XK8 with cloth seat inserts, rare to find today. (Nigel Thorley)

XJ saloons, a remote-controlled key fob transmitter, operated by radio frequency, controls the locking and unlocking of the vehicle. For extra security it uses a rolling code, which changes every time the unit is operated, with over four billion combinations. The key fob controls the locking and alarm process, headlamp operation, and the electric boot lid mechanism.

Internal security was monitored by sensors. A sophisticated glass-break sensor can detect the sound of breaking glass and set the alarm off, while perimeter sensing protects the car from forced entry through the doors, bonnet and boot. It is also possible to programme the security alarm system to activate automatically if the car is left with all the doors and windows closed and the ignition key removed.

All XK8s are fitted with a supplementary restraint system involving twin full-sized airbags activated by an ECU responding to electromechanical sensing. One airbag is situated within the steering wheel centre boss and the other behind the wood-veneered facia panel on the passenger side.

Interior features

Using traditional Jaguar features of wood and leather, the interior of the early XK8s allowed two choices of finish, although the layout and controls remained the same for both. These were the Sport (or standard) trim and the Classic.

According to Jaguar at the time, the Sport was considered a more modern approach to trim finish, geared to the younger, sportier buyer – an idea poached from other marques. The seat facings were covered

The Sport interior as most were bought, with leather seat centre panels with distinctive horizontal pleating. Note the high-contrast trim colours used and the dark-stained maple woodwork, all standard features of the Sport interior. (Nigel Thorley)

This picture shows two elements of the XK8 – the unique seat style of the Sport model, and the inadequate legroom for rear seat passengers. (Nigel Thorley)

Subtle trim colours, walnut veneer and different seating style differentiate the Classic (below) from the Sport trim option. (Nigel Thorley)

in a combination of leather with cloth centre panels, the seats having three horizontal flutes with charcoal stitching. Trim colours were either charcoal or oatmeal. The conventional four-spoke steering wheel, along with the gear knob, were trimmed in partly-perforated charcoal leather to complement the black carpet throughout. The black facia top panel was co-ordinated with dark grey stained maple veneer. As an extra-cost option the purchaser could also opt for full leather seating, with horizontal flutes in charcoal, oatmeal or cream finish.

The Sport trim was not offered in the North American market and was to represent a very small percentage of sales everywhere except in the UK, where Jaguar anticipated a 60 per cent take-up.

The Classic option was decidedly more traditional Jaguar, fairly and squarely aimed at existing Jaguar buyers and those who preferred luxury and prestige. The seats were leather and featured five vertical flutes with colour-keyed stitching. A burr walnut veneer was used for the main facia area, centre console and door mounted switch-packs, accompanied by a half wood/leather steering wheel and wood grain gear knob. Seating, facia, door trims and carpets were all colour co-ordinated.

The instrument pack used on the XK8 was new at the time and was later adopted for the V8-engined XJ saloons. The main speedometer, rev counter and fuel/water temperature gauges were in front of the driver, while the analogue clock and auxiliary gauges for oil pressure and the battery were mounted centrally. The deeply in-set gauges in front of the driver were continuously illuminated and remained clearly visible even when driving in a tunnel without the exterior lights on. A development of Jaguar's onboard computer and message centre was used, and the centre console took its lead from XJ saloons of the period, and with a quieter and more efficient air-conditioning system as standard equipment than was previously used on the XJS.

All models were supplied with an 80 watt audio system as standard. This comprised multi-waveband stereo radio/cassette, four speakers (one in each door and rear quarter casings), and a power-operated rear wing mounted aerial. Alternatively, at extra cost a Harman Kardon Premium sound system could be specified, producing 240 watts, with eight-channel power amplifier and a nine (Coupé) or ten (Convertible) speaker layout. A six-disc CD auto-changer could also be specified on all models.

External attributes

Jaguar had been very clever in incorporating styling cues from previous models like the XJ220 and E-type, yet had kept the car very up-to-date in its appeal. The Coupé was undoubtedly the prettiest of the two styles, but the Convertible (nearly always a compromise) had a virtually unique styling flow for the period.

Contrary to prevailing practice in some prestige convertibles, Jaguar opted not to go for a fully retracting hood arrangement with an integrated metal tonneau cover. Instead, there was a good old studded leather tonneau, which had to be fitted manually. Cost played a part in this decision, but it also meant that space for the fuel tank and the all-important luggage accommodation in the boot wasn't compromised. At the XK8's launch, Jaguar commented that the hood standing proud with a prominent cover epitomised the English sporting car – good try, Jaguar!

Trying to design a stylish and aerodynamic sports car must always have its compromises if it is to be both practical and road legal. Jaguar had to make such a compromise at the front, for instance, with the fitment of the legally required (in the UK anyway) number plate. But other aspects of the XK8's style were characterised by clean, flowing lines. Its mix of traditionalism and good modern design is epitomised by the specially designed headlamp units, comprising a neutral lens for turn signals, a very small side light, a projection lens for dipped headlamp beam, and an ellipsoid reflector for the main beam, all encapsulated into a single unit which, in the better specified models, also included a retractable washer jet behind an extendable chromed fillet.

There was a surprising lack of chrome finish to the exterior of the early XK8s, although cars intended for the North American market were supplied with chromed door mirror backs and door handles.

What price success?

Retail selling prices for the XK8 at launch in September 1996 were:

XK8 Coupé	£47,950	$64,900
XK8 Convertible	£54,950	$72,455

These prices were for the 'base' models, so didn't include such items as Classic trim, 18in wheels, cruise control, or even a CD player. To fully spec an XK8 at this time would have set you back more than £8000 extra. Full specifications of the original models will be found at the back of this book.

Side on – a direct comparison between the Convertible and Coupé models, both of which are aesthetically pleasing and contemporary. Both are early models with the optional Flute wheels.
(Nigel Thorley)

TOP AWARD

Coinciding with the launch of the XK8, Jaguar Cars was voted 'Britain's Top Manufacturer' in the Manufacturing Industry Achievement Awards. Sponsored by *The Engineer*, the award recognised the major quality, productivity and management improvements made at Jaguar, specifically citing the work done on the XK8.

Full frontal – the XK8 displays classic proportions not that dissimilar to the 1960s E-type or 1990s XJ220. (Nigel Thorley)

The cat is back

Jaguar's marketing slogan for the new car, 'The Cat is Back', was a good ploy to revitalise its sporting car image. (Nigel Thorley)

Thirty months from plan to production is all it took Jaguar to bring the XK8 to launch – a significant achievement. Now it was time for the marketing department and Jaguar's advertising agency, J. Walter Thompson, to get to grips with the new car.

Jaguar intended that the XK8 should appeal to a broader market than the out-going XJS, attracting both luxury and younger 'premium sports car' buyers, as the marketing men called them. To set the scene, the luxury sports car sector of the market only accounted for 55,000 car sales worldwide in 1995, with almost half of that market in North America, 25 per cent in Germany and a mere 8 per cent in the UK. The company therefore targeted a first full-year sales figure of 12,000 XK8s to be sold worldwide, of which 40 per cent would be Coupés and 60 per cent Convertibles. Of this total, 60 per cent would be earmarked for the US, of which 70 per cent would be Convertibles, reflecting the strong preference for the latter in the American market.

"THE HERITAGE OF GOOD DESIGN IS LIKE DNA"

"Our goal was to create a shape that communicates integrity and a sense of honesty. The finished design must express a 'fitness for purpose' that bears a direct relationship to the mechanical components underneath. It's very easy to design a car that's a pastiche of cars, something that's trendy and hot. We worked very hard to avoid that temptation. Overall, we strove to bring obvious links with the past but without copying. The heritage of good design is like DNA, it must be traceable through history but not necessarily an exact duplicate."

– Geoff Lawson,
Jaguar Director of Styling

After achieving a peak of nearly 30 per cent of the UK market sales for this type of vehicle in 1988, Jaguar's share had taken a terrible knock due to the age of the XJS and increasing competition, particularly from Porsche, BMW and Mercedes. By contrast, in the US Jaguar had only ever achieved a total of 11.7 per cent of the market at best, and this fell considerably despite BMW being a minor player at the time, while even Porsche and Mercedes had been losing out to cars like the Lexus SC400.

Having said this, a major market research project carried out by Jaguar identified that 81 per cent of XJS owners were completely satisfied with their cars. It also confirmed that loyalty to the brand was a major reason for buying, whereas Porsche owners were more likely to target performance as their reason to buy, while with Mercedes it was style and resale value. Another interesting revelation in this survey was that the majority of XJS owners tended to be older than the average for a prestige sporting vehicle, most likely retired or female.

Two key types of potential new customer were targeted for the XK8. Firstly, those who had rejected the XJS for quite rational reasons. Research revealed these to be people who were attracted emotionally to a Jaguar but who, despite Jaguar's improvements in build quality, hadn't perceived this due to the limited changes made to the XJS over the years. The somewhat radically new XK8 could address this issue, complemented by the three-year/60,000-mile mechanical warranty that reinforced Jaguar's commitment to quality.

The Geneva launch of the XK8 rekindled the razzamatazz of the 1960s E-type launch, with a wooden crate unveiling the car to an eager media. (Reprinted from *Autocar* magazine)

The other key group consisted of those who had previously rejected the image of Jaguar sporting models like the XJS. The style didn't fit their image – they wanted something new, exciting; perhaps state-of-the-art, and here again Jaguar was confident that the new XK8 fitted that bill.

In an early statement from Jaguar's Sales and Marketing Training Manager to the dealers, he said: "The new model will revitalise Jaguar's sports car range and rebuild the company's sports car presence in markets around the world. XK8 will compete in the luxury sports car market, primarily against the Mercedes SL, BMW 840 and Porsche 911. The target customer is likely to be male, aged about 42. This is younger than XJS and reflects the more youthful, sporty image of the XK8."

Jaguar planned to 'drip-feed' information on the new car to the media and public over a period of seven months leading up to the British Motor Show in

A LEAF FROM MG

The decision to 'drip-feed' the launch of the XK8 followed the successful pre-launch of the MGF at around the same time. It worked so well for MG-Rover that Jaguar adopted the same approach for its own new sports car.

LAUNCH CAR

You can still see the original Geneva launch XK8 Coupé on display at the Gaydon Heritage Centre in Warwickshire, UK.

October, commencing at the beginning of March with the release of scant details and styling pictures to the media.

The XK8 Coupé had its first UK public airing at the Royal College of Art in London, where it was on display from 11 to 20 March as part of an exhibition celebrating the college's 100th anniversary. More importantly, however, the car soon afterwards had its first major public showing at the Geneva Motor Show. This was perfectly planned, as the E-type had been revealed to the public at the same show 35 years earlier. Following a similar 'launch' treatment to that of the E-type, the car – an Antigua Blue Coupé – revolved on a turntable, protected from early viewing by a wooden crate which was ceremoniously hoisted aloft to reveal the car in all its splendour.

It was certainly the star of the show in terms of interest and media hype, but apparently many questions were raised as to whether the car was 'right'. It was inevitably compared with the Aston Martin DB7, launched two years earlier and also based on the XJS floorpan, and there were comparisons with other cars

too, not least the E-type. Was the XK8 too retro? Were the wheels too small for the body? Was the overhang too great at the rear? Was the cabin too cramped? Was the nose right? And so on. One difference to the E-type's launch in 1961 was that there were no XK8s to drive or be driven in, and the bonnet was locked tight so that no one could view the new V8 engine.

It wasn't until April that the Convertible got its first showing, this time at the New York Motor Show, again echoing the launch of the E-type roadster at this event back in 1961. Later the same month the Coupé and Convertible were shown together at the Turin Motor Show. All of these first showings were intended to do no more than whet people's appetites, but engine technical seminars were set up for the press on the basis that information would be embargoed until 4 June.

Then in June Jaguar finally released information on the AJ-V8 engine, so that by August the motoring press was publishing the full low-down on the new engine in its magazines and declaring itself very impressed with the results. All it now wanted to do was drive a car to evaluate what Jaguar was saying – that it was class-leading and superlative, even by Lexus standards. In late June and early July what seemed like an endless programme of dealer and distributor ride-and-drives took place around the world, to hype up the sales teams for the eventual public launch.

In August, by a stroke of luck, the United States Government announced it was phasing out a 10 per cent luxury car tax on cars that cost over $34,000. With the imminent launch of the XK8, this played into Jaguar's hands.

One of the very early production cars, in this case used by Bob Dover, taken on a trip to Cambridge about four months prior to the XK8's public launch. (Nigel Thorley)

Is it a car, or isn't it? It's actually a styling mock-up, without its own power or even an interior, shown to the press before the launch to get a 'feel' for public reaction. The author was privileged to be there and take this picture at the time, and in his own comments on TV that evening said "It's a winner!" (Nigel Thorley)

The usual crop of press events now gave the journalists a chance to drive and assess the new cars in readiness for its public launch. The world dealer launch was held in Vancouver during the first week of September. Coinciding with this, around 50 XK8s were subjected to regular daily use by Jaguar managers and directors, being assessed for everything from daily commuting to long-distance high-speed travel. This was followed in late August by the US press launch in California. A world press launch took place in France from 9 to 11 October, following the public announcement of the car on 1 October.

An interesting aside, during this last-minute build up to the public launch, was the assignment of two cars, both Convertibles, to the author and Jaguar Enthusiasts' Club General Manager Graham Searle for a two-week tour of the Jaguar dealerships in the UK, to raise money for the BEN motor industry charity. Both cars set off from Jaguar's Browns Lane Plant at the end of a Factory Open Day, one going south, the other north, picking up co-drivers en route, and they remained on the road day and night until every dealer had been visited. A total of £12,000 was raised, and the run culminated at the NEC Birmingham International Motor Show on Press Day, where the cars were handed back to Jaguar and the cheque for the money raised for BEN was given to Managing Director Nick Scheele.

Although the public announcement of the XK8 had taken place on 1 October this was only to the media, to whom initial road tests and full details were released in readiness for the official UK public launch at the British

International Motor Show in Birmingham later that month. At the show, the Jaguar stand displayed a British Racing Green Coupé and a Carnival Red Convertible,

The author with others at the start of the XK8/Jaguar Enthusiasts Club 1996 BEN Charity fund-raising run, the venue being the BEN home in Rugby, Warwickshire. (Nigel Thorley)

while there was an Ice Blue Coupé on the *Autocar* stand, this vehicle having been used extensively for a three-way test (see below). From here on in there were launch events at all the dealerships, leading up to the British Motor Show.

It was announced that prior to the show customers had already placed orders for 5000 XK8s, and as Jaguar only planned to produce 12,000 in the first full year of production this effectively meant a waiting list of up to five months for anyone wanting to buy one after seeing the cars at the show. As the estimated global market for grand touring sports cars was only estimated at 55,000 a year at the time, Jaguar seemed to have hit the jackpot! Cars were finally made available to UK and US dealer showrooms during October, and to the rest of the overseas markets by November.

To top it all, at the end of the year Geoff Lawson, Jaguar's Chief Designer, picked up an Italian award naming the XK8 'the world's most beautiful car'.

Shaping up to the competition

By the time it had been publicly launched, the XK8 was not the only new and exciting sporting model to hit the market. Ferrari, for example, was showing off its fabulous (and expensive) 550, while Mercedes had its spanking new small sports car, the SLK. Another expensive supercar was the Lamborghini Diablo roadster. Nor was Jaguar the only UK manufacturer to introduce a V8 sports car that year, for Lotus had its Esprit V8, which, although smaller-engined, performed admirably. Porsche had introduced its Boxster (the first totally new Porsche sports car in 18 years), TVR had its Cerbera Coupé, and Marcus introduced its 325bhp Ford-powered Mantis. Another new car, the Spectre – made

EARLY PERFORMANCE COMPARISONS

Car	Max bhp	Max torque	0–62 mph	Max speed	Average mpg
Jaguar XK8 Coupé	290	290	6.7sec	155mph	23
Jaguar XK8 Convertible	290	290	7.0sec	155mph	23
BMW 840 Coupé	282	310	7.1sec	155mph	20.5
Mercedes SL 320 Coupé	228	200	8.1sec	149mph	25.7
Mercedes SL 500 Convertible	326	332	5.9sec	155mph	16.2
Porsche 911 Carrera	282	251	6.4sec	168mph	23.2
Aston Martin DB7	335	360	5.8sec	157mph	19.2
Ferrari 550	484	419	4.4sec	199mph	12.3
Lexus SC400 (US only)	260	270	7.7sec	145mph	23
XJS 4.0-litre Convertible	238	282	8.0sec	145mph	21.7

in the UK and powered by a 350bhp Ford V8 engine – threatened the top-end sports car market. On top of all this there was existing competition from the group's own Aston Martin DB7, which although it used the old XJ-S platform at that time would soon adopt the modified XK8 pan with suspension and steering. In addition there were the Maserati Ghibli Coupé, Mercedes SL, Porsche 911, TVR Griffith, and such American contenders as the Corvette, Camaro and Viper.

What the press and the people said

"Never mind the bollocky XJS – here's Jaguar's next sexy pistol" was the opening strapline from Martin Padgett in *Car & Driver* magazine when it first got shots of the then still to be announced XK8 in 1995. A few months later, also before the public launch, *Performance Car* magazine wrote: "Say farewell to the flabby old XJS and hello to the dynamic new V8-engined XK8, the sports car that picks up where the E-type left off."

Autocar magazine put on quite a splash in its issue of 6 March 1996. The XK8 was featured on the front cover with the strapline "How Jaguar Recreated a Legend", and no fewer than 12 pages were devoted to the new car. The carefully selected styling shots didn't reveal a great deal of detail, particularly of the interior, and no detailed specification was available at this time, but

COMPARISON PERSPECTIVE

1961	Aston Martin DB4	£4084
	Jaguar E-type Fhc	£2196 – 54% of the Aston
1996	Aston Martin DB7	£82,500
	Jaguar XK8 Coupé	£47,950 – 58% of the Aston
1961	Aston Martin DB4	141mph top speed, 0–60 in 8.5 seconds
	Jaguar E-type	149mph top speed, 0–60 in 7.1 seconds
1996	Aston Martin DB7	157mph top speed, 0–60 in 5.8 seconds
	Jaguar XK8	155mph top speed, 0–60 in 6.6 seconds

Autocar did show a number of styling drawings covering the build-up to the final design.

After the car's Geneva launch in March, the American *Road & Track* magazine got its turn to feature the XK8 Convertible in May, with an impressive six-page spread straplined "The long wait is over … and the car is worth the wait." It wasn't until November of that year, however, that it actually got its hands on a car (another Coupé) for a road test. In its opening remarks the phrases "as British as Buckingham Palace," "a Jaguar that doesn't feed off the Ford parts bin trough," and "an unqualified stunner," set the scene. Moving on to the actual driving characteristics, it found the XK8 to be unflappable compared to the ageing XJS, with well-controlled roll, although concrete expansion joints in US roads produced annoying jolts felt through the seats. Unlike the XJS, it found the XK8 positively encouraged you to press on down twisty roads. It went into raptures over the interior's wonderful textures that appealed to the eyes and fingertips. Interestingly (and in contrast to my personal experience and those of other road-testers of more than normal height), it considered there was ample headroom and seat movement for the driver. In conclusion, it felt Jaguar was on a winner!

On 3 July *Autocar* had another major feature on Jaguar. Though not primarily covering the XK8, it did seem to have inside information about the success of the Jaguar V8 engine in Ford's eyes, so much so that the company had been given permission to carry out development work on V6 versions of the power unit of 2.0-litre and 3.0-litre capacities. it also intimated that smaller V6-engined versions of the XK8 would be made available in the future. In the same issue it speculated that a supercharged V8 was under development and would appear as the XKR8 in late 1997. It also intimated that a couple of years further on there would be another all-new XK8, smaller and sportier – but such things were speculation at the time.

The British *Autocar* magazine, which has always had a close relationship with Jaguar, was first to hit the magazine-stands with its issue of 2 October containing a ten-page road test of the Coupé accompanied by a 64-page booklet on the background to the car. It favoured its brutally elegant looks, very strong engine and gearbox combination, fluid handling, grip, price, and its quietness compared to the Aston Martin DB7 it had previously tested (which, of course, still utilised a highly modified version of the old Jaguar straight six AJ16 power plant). On the other hand, however, it did initially find faults – fidgety low-speed ride,

The monthly magazines had a field day when the XK8 was launched, in some cases issuing booklets specifically about the new car. (Nigel Thorley)

disappointing interior quality, and the inevitably cramped rear seats.

In a subsequent issue of *Autocar*, after the road test, some of the comments from readers make interesting reading: "The instruments remind me of those in a 1975 Austin Princess 1800HL;" "The front and rear three-quarter angle photographs show the obvious design influence – not E-type but Mazda MX-5!;" "I have one minor criticism – the badge on the nose will make it awkward to attach a stick-on number plate;" "There is something about the performance of the XK8 that is strangely familiar. Its top speed, fuel consumption and acceleration to 100mph are all so close to the E-type that to differentiate between the two cars is superfluous. Further comparison reveals that, beyond the magic ton, the E-type has the upper hand, being 3 seconds faster to 100mph. And using the E-type price of 1961, suitably adjusted, the XK8 should cost around half its £47,000. Does this latest Jaguar demonstrate the progress that is to be expected from 35 years of automotive technological advancement. I think not, but I might be persuaded to change my mind." In April 1996 *Car* magazine commented: "Mercedes is bracing itself for a big sales attack on the SL. The Germans, like Jaguar, believe the XK8 is bound to be a winner."

At the end of October 1996 *Autocar* got to grips with the XK8 in a full-blown road-test Coupé. It was obviously impressed, particularly with the engine/gearbox relationship in terms of smoothness and refinement; the flawless gearchanges were compared to the very best from the likes of BMW. In overall terms it graded the XK8 by means of points out of five: it gave

WIN AN XK FOR A WEEKEND

In November 1996 *Autocar* magazine ran a competition for a lucky reader to win an XK8 Coupé for a weekend. All you had to do was tell it the cubic capacity of the V8 engine in the XK – pretty simple really, particularly when on the next page of the spread it told you!

The *Autocar* 1996 promotion to win an XK8 for a weekend. (Reprinted from *Autocar*)

it five for performance, only three for economy (though stating that it was better than the competition), four for handling and ride (having expected the top-end model with 18in wheels to be a little firmer), but only three

XK8 as it was launched, here seen in Ice Blue with Oatmeal Classic interior and 17in Revolver wheels. (Nigel Thorley)

for comfort, equipment and safety, because the interior was fussy and created too many reflections, there was a severe lack of rear seat legroom, there wasn't enough rearward movement for the driver's seat, and there was too much Ford switchgear! As for design and engineering, the engine got full marks, but the car only got three stars because of patchy build quality. In terms of its market and cost, *Autocar* considered the XK an undoubted success, but gave it only four stars: "Jaguar has pulled off a masterstroke with the XK8's positioning and pricing. If it can nip those last build gremlins in the bud, it'll have a winner."

In conclusion *Autocar* commented that the XK8 had one of the best drivetrains they had driven at any price, and that it was a cracking good car to drive. The fit and finish, the styling, paintwork, etc, made it every inch the class act it promised to be. However, the lack of rear seat accommodation meant it was not really a 2+2, and the mixed quality of the interior package didn't help in allaying concerns about Jaguar's ability to produce an exceptionally high quality car. *Autocar*'s final ranking was four stars out of five – 'The Best GT in the Real World'.

A few weeks later *Autocar* published another report, a direct comparison of the XK8 with the more expensive Aston Martin DB7 and, although extravagantly more costly, the Ferrari 550 Maranello. Its opening statement perhaps confirmed the reason why you would pay so much more for a Ferrari than a Jaguar: "Drive an XK8 hard enough to keep a 550 in sight and you'll soon discover weaknesses in its body control and handling, and in its brakes. Do the same in the Aston and,

although the feeling will be underlaid by a keener sense of competition, you'll still leave the arena exhausted by comparison, not to mention well beaten."

The test went badly for the XK8: "Despite being wooed by the XK8's exquisite engine and gearbox, and by its serene cabin and near effortless motorway gait, neither of us emerged at Brescia prepared to extol its virtues with anything greater than mild enthusiasm." The testers found the Aston quicker, quieter and more comfortable if more thirsty, and were seduced by the DB's curvaceous lines when directly compared to the XK8. The Ferrari had it all, down to image, outright performance, and handling, but at around three times the price of the Jag what else would you expect?

Similarly, they preferred the Aston to the Jag overall, and felt that the differences were significant enough to warrant the existence of the DB7, but they failed to consider whether the extra £34,000 of the latter was justified. In all, an interesting, but perhaps relatively inappropriate, comparison of three cars aimed at very different markets.

In November, *Car* magazine's full road-test report on the XK8 stated: "this car oozes presence and desirability. Better still it looks like a Jag and nothing else." In its closing statement, it praised Jaguar for the new car, claiming it to be a true successor to the E-type and proof that Jaguar was anything but moribund!

There were comparisons with the competition in most of the car magazines, initially against the muscular Mercedes SL500 and, of course, the DB7. *Autocar* thought the Aston to be stylistically better and dynamically a superior car, while the XK8 had refinement, superb panel fit, and more grand touring ability. But the Jaguar showed superior agility to the Mercedes, which also looked aged in the styling department. It also identified the Mercedes to have a more integrally strong structure than the others, despite the fact it was a convertible while the others were coupés.

Another joint test between the XK8, DB7 and the BMW 840i in *Car* magazine revealed the XK8 to be by far the better car overall. *Car* said: "It wins because it looks, goes, handles and rides the best (it raises the game here), and costs the least by a substantial margin. Here is a proper sporting Jaguar, which we haven't seen for so long that people have forgotten what some Jaguars once were … The BMW is yesterday's car, desirability tarnished against that of the sensual Jaguar. The Aston Martin, sad to say, is revealed as a pointless purchase at £82,500, especially when the £48,000 XK8 betters it

This XK8 Convertible is finished in the launch colour of Antigua Blue with Ivory interior and 18in Flute wheels. (Nigel Thorley)

in every way." *Motorsport* also did a comparison test of the XK8 against the BMW 840Ci, and concluded that the Jaguar out-performed, out-handled and outclassed the Beamer!

Perhaps *Autocar* summed it up best with its end-of-year review of the cars they had tested. Against the nearest comparison sports cars the XK8 came out well: the Aston DB7 was described as "better than a Mercedes SL in virtually all respects," the Lotus Esprit V8 as a "stunningly quick but curiously disappointing version of the Esprit," and the TVR Cerbera as giving "massive performance" and being "good around corners. A real giant killer." But the Jaguar XK8 was considered "the most desirable GT car in the real world, by far."

There were no complaints about the design of the hood arrangement, so often a problem for car stylists. Karmann had done an excellent job without major protrusions and, of course, the now standard and still unique feature of a full-glass heated rear screen. (Nigel Thorley)

Above: Every new car has to go through numerous crash tests and this is one XK8 that survived the ordeal very well and was subsequently used for display purposes. (Nigel Thorley)

Below: The remains of an XK8 that was subjected to a severe roll-over yet look how the centre cabin area has remained substantially intact. (Nigel Thorley)

Above: One of Jaguar's 'spaceship' mileage test car hacks, which is now, just as you see it here, in the hands of the Jaguar Daimler Heritage Trust. (Nigel Thorley)

Below: An interesting concept drawing for an XK8 Estate car. Lynx, a private company in the south of England, produced excellent Estate (Eventer) versions of the XJS, so why not the XK8? (Nigel Thorley)

Chapter **Four**

R-rated

A lot happened at Jaguar in 1996, the launch year of the XK8. Nick Scheele, the then Chairman and Chief Executive, was awarded the Midlands Businessman of the Year award, while prior to the actual launch of the new

LARGER THAN LIFE

Unipart, Jaguar's parts distributor, commissioned a special XK8 hot air balloon from Cameron Balloons of Bristol at a cost of over £100,000 for the launch of the car. This measured 69ft high and 46ft wide, with a capacity of 120,000cu ft, a top speed of 13mph, an acceleration time of 0 to 60ft in 9 seconds and a maximum rate of climb of 400ft per minute. Unfortunately, if parking were needed it would occupy the equivalent of 39 XK8 spaces!

The Unipart XK8 hot-air balloon, all 120,000cu ft of it – looking for a space to park? (Nigel Thorley)

car there occurred the untimely death of David Boole, the company's Director of Communications and Public Affairs. Joe Greenwell took David's place and saw the project through to completion. Ironically, after subsequently becoming Chief Executive of Jaguar Joe Greenwell also saw the very last XK8 come off the line in 2005.

First-hand report

As already mentioned, in the early days of the XK8 the author was lucky enough to be involved in a charity run which involved covering an extraordinary number of miles in just two weeks in one of these new cars, and the experience eventually led to me purchasing one for myself. What follows is a subjective report on my findings after driving in what was essentially a pre-production car. For example, although the standard of fit and finish was significantly improved over an XJ40 saloon or XJS, there was still some orange-peel effect to the paintwork around the boot lid area. Also, a lack of forethought meant that regular use of the boot left finger-marks all over the paintwork, and having to use the key each time to open the boot from the outside was both annoying and awkward. I was also unimpressed by the blandness of the rear end: a simple chrome finisher to the number plate area would have helped. Both this and my complaint about the boot's key operation were addressed by Jaguar later.

Aesthetically, I didn't like then, nor do I now, the exposed weld area visible on the sill below the doors – would it have been so costly to fill this in neatly before painting? At the front the positioning of the number plate seemed intrusive, another matter that both Jaguar and aftermarket suppliers have tried to rectify since.

Returning to matters of quality, very early on in the marathon one of the headlights got filled with condensation, a common problem still faced by many owners. The glovebox internal shelf rattled and the lid didn't fit very well. In the engine bay the plastic covers for items like the brake servo also didn't fit well, nor have they on XKs since! A particular annoyance involved the electric window lifts, the 'logic' failing four times, resulting in the window glass not raising at all, and every time you opened and closed the door, the glass dropped a further 15mm. Easy to reset, it was obviously a glitch in this particular car.

Finally, the retracting hood and its leather clad tonneau cover. The boot space proved very useful over the two weeks' journey, but then, on the road all the time, with varying weather conditions, the hood was up and down constantly, and to prevent ingress of dirt onto the headlining you had to fit the tonneau – a pain! However, it seemed to be made slightly too small for its purpose so never actually fitted properly (another common complaint), and some of the toggles that secured the tonneau in place under the boot lid actually fell off.

As regards comfort, I awarded the car seven out of ten. Despite being 6ft 2in in height I was able to find a comfortable position, but arguably there wasn't quite enough legroom, particularly for taller drivers than I. Certainly in my case, with the seat at its limit, no space was left at all for rear occupants, no matter how young and small they might have been. Also, although the seats had height adjustment, they didn't drop low enough for most tall drivers.

All the controls felt easily to hand and were comfortable and precise to use, although I had reservations about the deeply imbedded instruments in front of the driver that didn't quite look 'Jaguarish'. Visibility was also good, particularly with the top down, when the furled hood rested quite flat. One criticism was the fact you had to hold down the button to raise or lower the hood – I never understood why, when a one-touch operation would have been easier.

It took me a few miles to get used to driving the XK8. Initially it felt like any modern Jaguar, quiet, refined, and with that ambience of luxury. Under power, however, the car was much more responsive, and the steering more reactive. With its agility of handling and, of course, the amazing smoothness of the V8, I was sold! Two minor criticisms: not enough sound – under hard acceleration there was that slight V8 burble from the exhaust, but it needed something else to liven up the senses; and secondly there was a degree of lag when pressing the accelerator pedal to kickdown. Fuel consumption was good, averaging over 23mpg on the whole trip, which

Jaguar's obligatory 'two sets of golf clubs' boot for the XK8 worked well. The floor is shown in the lowered position with a space-saver spare wheel underneath. With a 17in Revolver wheel the floor can be raised level with the battery cover on the right-hand side, but larger wheels cannot be accommodated easily. This early car is also equipped with the CD auto-changer, on the right-hand side. (Nigel Thorley)

took in varying degrees of driving style by several co-drivers, plus stop-starts, demonstration runs, and so on. On one occasion I managed over 30mpg on a long cruise-controlled run up the A9 into Scotland.

Boom time

Immediately after the XK8's launch the dealers got their first cars for distribution to their new owners. Jaguar announced that in the first month 1825 were delivered to customers, 847 of these in the US, an all-time sales record for Jaguar sports cars in that country. Of the US cars 50 were marketed as special editions through the prestigious Norman Marcus catalogue, and all sold within 72 hours of the catalogue being produced. All this boosted Jaguar's overall sales significantly, in fact a 39 per cent increase on the same period in 1995.

AUCTION DEBUT

The XK8 made its 'used car' auction debut at British Car Auctions' Blackbush, London, auction room at the end of 1997 via a Jaguar 'closed auction' of company vehicles. A 1996 'P' registered Convertible with 12,400 miles on the clock sold for £50,000.

The first quarter's sales figures for 1997 were the best sports car sales recorded in Jaguar's history – 3977, which was 257 per cent up on 1996, when the XJS was nearing the end of its days. In March alone, Jaguar sold 248 XKs in the UK, another record for the company. By the end of 1997 the total sales for the full year amounted to 14,619, an 88 per cent increase on the previous year. A total of 49.8 per cent of these were sold in the States, and worldwide 64 per cent of all cars sold were Convertibles, a greater figure than Jaguar anticipated. Some statistics collected by Jaguar reveal a lot:

		USA	UK
Average age of XK8 buyer		55 (75% male)	49 (89% male)
Occupations	Self-employed	16%	49%
	Management	23%	19%
	Professional	26%	13%
	Retired	20%	13%
	Housewife	5%	5%

TAG Models' XK8, the first die-cast produced of the new car, coinciding with the launch of the real thing. (Nigel Thorley)

Late in 1997 this boot-lid mounted high-intensity brakelight, obligatory in the States, became standard equipment on all new XK8s. (Nigel Thorley)

Top selling exterior colour schemes at that time were: (1) Carnival Red; (2) Anthracite (black); (3) Sapphire Blue; (4) British Racing Green; and (5) Topaz (light gold).

To keep pace with demand the shifts at the Browns Lane factory were increased, and the company turned out more cars per week than at any other time in its history (XJ saloons included).

Two major service recalls were made in 1997 and 1998, the first affecting 4500 early build cars constructed between July and November 1996 after Jaguar itself had experienced three incidents of rear suspension failure. The fault, which involved a retaining ring between the differential and output shaft becoming dislocated under hard cornering, was apparently caused by supplier problems, and was rectified on all the appropriate cars by dealers. The second recall affected production between July and October 1997, and involved inspecting and replacing a potentially faulty throttle cable bracket.

With the hype surrounding the 'new' XK8, it wasn't long before modelmakers got to grips with the car, and a host of toys and detailed scale models began to appear. First on the scene, within weeks of the public launch, was TAG Precision Models from Leicestershire with its highly detailed, 10in long die-cast model of the Convertible, in the launch colour of Antigua Blue with Ivory interior. In those days this model cost a whopping £62, but that was the price of up-to-the-minute exclusivity! By the end of the year the same model (made by Maisto) was on offer for a mere £15.95.

At the British International Motor Show of 1997 Jaguar introduced its XJ8 range of saloons utilising much of the technology developed for the XK, and as time went on various aspects of the two model ranges merged to clean up the parts bin. The biggest news at the time was the announcement of the new Supercharged V8 XJR saloon, and although denied at the time, it was inevitable that this engine would eventually go into the XK8, just as magazines had been predicting.

A Police XK8?

Not quite, but almost. The picture says it all, and anyone contemplating breaking the speed limit might well reconsider their actions after seeing one of these Police cars! But the truth of the matter is that not only was the XK8 too expensive for a Police vehicle, but it was hardly practical either, with lack of interior accommodation or places to install all their hardware (although that large boot could arguably take a few cones). This car, a standard Carnival Red

Coupé, was dressed up as a Police car and loaned to the Metropolitan Police by arrangement between Ian Jackson from that force and Jaguar's Special Vehicle Operations Department. It was used for a trip to Europe for the annual European Police Motor Clubs Conference.

Into 1998

This was the year in which the first public announcement was made of problems with the Nikasil coating used on engine bores – though not with Jaguar, but with BMW. The latter admitted to over 600 engines being changed in six months due, it was felt, to sulphur damage, thought to occur when acid generated during cold starts attacked the nickel base of the coating. Jaguar at the time denied it was a problem in its own cars, as its engines were designed for fast warm-up. However, as many now know, Jaguar suffered as well, and this is covered elsewhere in this book.

Up to this time, demand and residual values of XK8s had been remarkably high – in fact, the best figures Jaguar had achieved in many a year. But with the car approaching two years of age, and after the

Caught on camera: not something the average motorist would want to see on the roads in 1997, this is fortunately a mere 'mock-up' for the European Police Motor Clubs Conference. (Nigel Thorley)

successful introduction of the big V8-engined saloons (particularly the XJR), it was inevitable that more secondhand XKs would come onto the market. By early 1998 this had resulted in a significant downturn in used car prices by up to £3000, particularly on Coupés, and there became a strong differentiation in demand for particular specifications. In each of two consecutive months the British used car guides reduced XK prices by 3 per cent.

Enter the R

It had long been known that, eventually, a more powerful version of the XK8 would be made available, in order for Jaguar to keep abreast of the competition. Once the XJ8 saloons had been announced in 1997, including the XJR 4.0-litre Supercharged V8 model, it was inevitable that the same engine would make its way into the sports car – which went on sale in May 1998 as the XKR, available in both Coupé and Convertible forms. Its fastest-selling sports car was set to also become the

fastest performing sports car in Jaguar's history. The first announcement of the XKR was made a few weeks before the Geneva Motor Show, the long-established launch pad for sporting Jaguars, where it arrived just in time to commemorate the 50th anniversary of the XK120, Jaguar's first postwar sports car.

As with the XK8 at the Geneva event of 1996, a special launch colour was chosen, then only available for the R models. This was Phoenix Red, echoing, although not exactly the same hue as, the Carmen Red used on E-types in the 1960s. The complete range of XKR exterior colour schemes was very limited at first, and didn't even include Spindrift White, a popular colour in overseas markets, because there were fears that

The XKR at launch, both Convertible and Coupé being in the special XKR-only colour (at the time) of Phoenix Red. (Nigel Thorley)

The special bonnet louvres – a throwback to E-type days – had a purpose: helping to keep the engine cool. Initially, you couldn't buy them or an XKR bonnet pressing unless you already owned this model. (Nigel Thorley)

For the supercharged model, out went the chromed splitter bar and in came a mesh grille. A subtle badge change on the nose also identified this model. (Nigel Thorley)

the heat generated under-bonnet would discolour the exterior paintwork over time.

At a casual glance the XKR looked little different to a conventional XK8, but there were subtle changes. Starting at the front, a stainless steel mesh grille occupied the nose area, reminiscent of that used on XJR saloons from 1994, a feature that has become the norm on all Jaguar high-performance vehicles since. A new badge adorned the nose, now reading 'Jaguar Supercharged', the same treatment also appearing on the boot lid.

The bonnet pressing, although the same as the XK8, carried two inset louvred panels to aid airflow and keep the under-bonnet area cool. Strategically positioned for the best low pressure airflow, they also reflected the style of the E-type bonnet. The bonnet pressing had to be adapted to allow for the movement of stiffeners and a new sound-deadening liner was fitted to accommodate the louvres.

On the boot lid a small and discrete spoiler was fitted which was apparently not only for adornment but also aided airflow, compensating the aerodynamics for the addition of the bonnet louvres, all the aerodynamic aspects being tested in a wind tunnel. Finally, new 'XKR' badging appeared at the rear. An interesting aspect was that Jaguar would not supply the rear spoiler or louvred bonnet as aftermarket parts except for bona fide XKR cars.

New wheels and tyres were adopted to handle the increased performance. The alloy wheels, called Double Fives (ie ten spokes), had 8in rims at the front and 9in at

the rear. All the wheels were fitted with red background growler centre-cap badges, at that time unique to the XKR. Pirelli P-Zero System tyres were again used, this time 245/45 ZR 18 at the front and 255/45 ZR 18 at the rear. Of a revised construction, they suited the car well, improving both handling and grip and providing a new linear response to steering inputs.

Mechanically the XKR was significantly based on the new XJR V8 saloon announced earlier. With much of the development work done and the saloon in

Easy to miss at first glance, but the XKR benefited from a separate rear spoiler on the boot lid. Note too the extra badge, which was deleted a little later. (Nigel Thorley)

The new Double Five alloy wheel with red centre for the XKR model. (Nigel Thorley)

engine first seen in the XJ8 the year before. Essentially the same unit with minor changes to accommodate the different location, the ECUs were recalibrated to the sports car specification. With the Eaton M112 supercharger fitted and a compact air-to-liquid intercooling system with twin intercoolers, it generated the same 370bhp, providing an excellent 28 per cent increase in power over the normally-aspirated XK8 engine with a 33 per cent increase in available torque.

An even more efficient radiator and condenser were fitted and a modified exhaust system, to meet legislation and cut down noise levels. A new run of pipework to suit the gearbox (see below) fitted to supercharged cars and the downpipes and heatshields were also unique to R models. Unlike the normally-aspirated cars, with one fuel pump, XKR models used two fuel pumps with revised pipework, an installation again taken from the equivalent saloon model developed earlier.

With the extra power output from the supercharged V8 engine, Jaguar chose a new heavy-duty transmission, the Mercedes W5A 580 five-speed, electronically controlled, intelligent automatic. Beefier than the ZF XK8 unit, it required revised mountings.

The XKR was the first car in the world to feature the new ZF Servotronic Mark 2 speed-sensitive power assisted steering system. Its variable ratio rack was

production (and selling well) it was a straight carryover of technology into the XKR. It featured, for example, a variant of the existing 4.0-litre AJ-V8 supercharged

The supercharged engine installation in the XKR. (Nigel Thorley)

recalibrated to provide a greater degree of weighting at medium to high speeds, improving steering response and precision and providing more feel during cornering. Steering response under all conditions was also improved by the use of stiffer mounting bushes. A new rack was mounted on a revised crossmember.

As the XJ8 owed a lot of its suspension and brake development to the XK8, the enhanced systems used on the XJR were followed through to the XKR. This included the fitment of a two-piece propshaft and upgrades in the suspension to cope with the increased performance. All XKR models were fitted as standard with the Jaguar CATS electronically controlled suspension system. Upgraded front disc brake pads, of lead-free construction, were fitted to cope with anticipated higher working temperatures.

Unseen changes included many modifications to the wiring harnesses and allied systems to accommodate the new engine and transmission. A new cross-brace had to be used at the front on Convertible models, to ease the fitment and removal of the radiator and condenser. To improve torsional rigidity, B/C post braces were also added.

Internally, little changed for the XKR model except that, even at this higher price level, the Sports pack trim

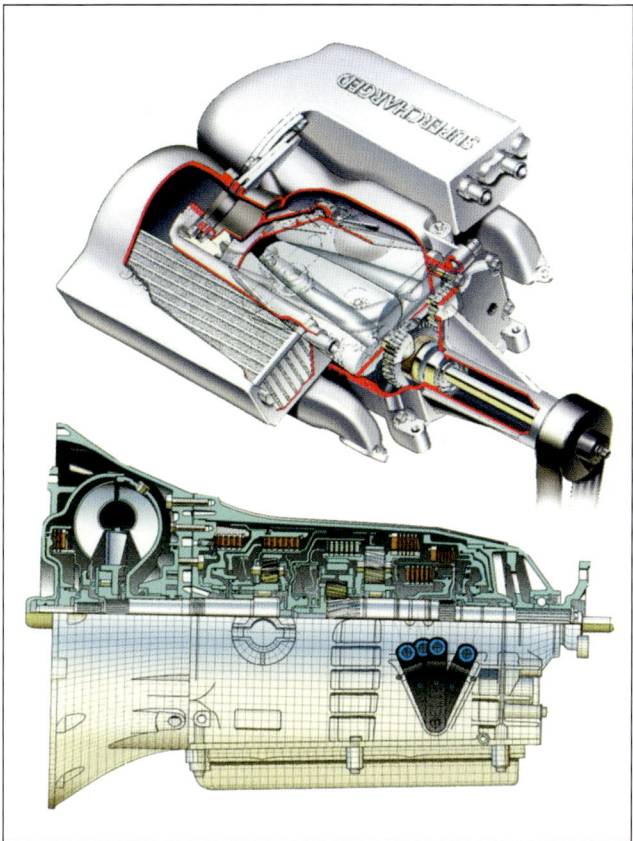

Important new elements of the XKR – the Eaton supercharger and the Mercedes gearbox. (Nigel Thorley)

At first glance there was little difference between XK8 and XKR interiors. But all XKRs had Sport trim as standard and carried the 'XKR' insignia emboss on the steering wheel. (Nigel Thorley)

Look a little closer and the rev counter has a revised red line calibration and carries the 'Supercharged' logo. (Nigel Thorley)

finish was standardised. However, all XKR owners got a CD auto-change, cruise control, all-leather faced seats, memory mirrors and headlamp power-wash in the standard specification, and to differentiate the R from the 8 the 'XKR' logo was embossed into the half wood/leather steering wheel centre and there was a discrete 'Supercharged' legend in the main instrumentation. The rev counter was also recalibrated to match the increased performance of the engine.

In the UK the XKR Coupé cost £60,005 and the Convertible £67,005. The extra £9350 over the equivalent

Leather seat pleating took on a different style for the XKR models. (Nigel Thorley)

normally-aspirated engined XK8s did include a £4000 value of additional equipment, an extra cost on the other models.

With the increasing popularity of the Jaguar marque in Germany – in fact Jaguar had experienced an incredible 2000 per cent increase in sales there since the introduction of the XK8 – a celebration saw the first 50 lucky owners of XKRs flown over to the UK to personally collect their cars. Arriving at the Jaguar factory, they were given a tour of the production facility, wined and dined, before collecting their cars (over £3 million worth) to drive back to Germany the next day.

Comparative performances

	bhp	Torque	0–60 mph	Top speed	Price
Jaguar XKR Coupé	370	387	5.1sec	155mph	£60,000
Porsche 911 Carrera	296	251	5.6sec	171mph	£65,000
Honda NSX	276	220	5.7sec	170mph	£69,500
Lotus Esprit V8	349	295	4.2sec	172mph	£59,950
Nissan Skyline GTR	280	271	5.0sec	155mph	£50,000
Chevrolet Corvette	339	356	5.7sec	171mph	£39,000
Chrysler Viper GTS	378	454	5.3sec	151mph	£68,800
TVR Cerbera V8	420	380	4.3sec	185mph	£45,000
Aston Martin DB7	317	337	6.9sec	155mph	£82,500

More press comments

In 1997 *Autocar* magazine took two examples of the XK8 to RAF Coltishall for a photo-shoot with the Jaguar GR1 jet fighter planes based there. As if anyone needed confirmation of the success of the XK8, all the RAF personnel were totally seduced by the cars (a matching

Coupé and Convertible) – as their Wing Commander put it: "It's simply stunning, prettier than a DB7, and yet classic Jaguar. I want one."

A little later Steve Cropley enjoyed a Convertible in Wales, commenting that it was one of the finest top-down cruisers to glide off a production line anywhere in the world. After reporting earlier on the Coupé version he was apprehensive about the structural rigidity of the Convertible and its practicalities. Given that the weather was terrible and the car was not equipped with CATS suspension or the larger 18in wheels, he was exceptionally pleased with it. He further stated there was no downside to a Convertible, even if it cost another £7000 (which you got back in resale value down the line).

Autocar also had a long-term loan XK8 Coupé from Jaguar, and in August 1997, after 7500 miles, reported that it was 'truly special' and that 'dynamically our long-term Jaguar XK8 has never failed to impress'. Criticisms amounted to the lack of interior space: it felt it really wasn't a 2+2 at all because they couldn't get two people of the correct size and shape to fit the rear seat. It would also have liked Jaguar to drop the variable ratio steering, and didn't like the accelerator pedal, which required lots of prodding to get the best out of the performance: even in kickdown the response was slow. Just two months later the car had covered 15,000 miles and their respect for it continued to grow. Fellow journalist from *Motorsport* Andrew Frankel got hold of the car for a European trip and managed to notch up an indicated 161mph on the speedometer, probably very close to the 155mph maximum speed that Jaguar publicised, and he found it perfectly stable and could still carry out a normal conversation in the cockpit.

Throughout the total mileage the only problem thus far had been the loss of one of the headlamp pressure wash covers. Their summing up said: "Great shape, fine engine, suspension, performance, handling, effortless mile-eating ability with surprising fuel consumption. A fine car which gains stature with the miles and underlines Jaguar's new reputation for building cars well. Rakish looks go with top-drawer road ability but belie XK8's easy to own nature. Great value against the competition."

At 20,000 miles new brake pads and new front brake discs were called for because of a slight judder at slow speed; this was done under warranty. Jaguar also replaced the rear tyres. Another 5000 miles down the

On the docks: a lucky German XKR owner taking his new car home. (Nigel Thorley)

SALES COMPARISONS 1996-98

	UK	USA	Europe	RoW	Total
1996	945	2183	789	356	4273
1997	2817	7223	3412	1049	14,501
1998	2913	6189	3210	607	12,919
1999	1912	6449	3032	447	11,840

line the front tyres had also worn down and a brakelight bulb needcd replacement.

At 35,000 miles the car came in for replacement, and the other problems experienced were summarised. These, in the main, were very minor, from an intermittent front suspension clunk, to the headlining drooping, the wipers stopping working, a facia rattle, and a boot lid that at one time didn't or wouldn't close. Other than these they had nothing but praise for the car, and the total costs incurred over 35,000 miles only amounted to £1701.47 for service and parts.

Autosport also had the opportunity, for a week, to compare the XK8 Coupé with the equivalent Mercedes SL500, and its comments are worth reproducing in full: "The Jag has a more rigid, better-riding body. Its facia is simpler, better laid out and – surprise – its switches and controls have more of a quality feel. And I liked its driving position better. The Benz, on the other hand, had a truly brilliant powertrain. No smoother or quieter than the XK8's, but torquier, more responsive at low revs, and driving through a slicker, quicker-acting transmission."

Views of the car were, as always, somewhat subjective. For example, *Car Trends* magazine said after testing a Convertible that it thought the steering was heavy and vague, but praised the brakes. When *What Car?* magazine first tried the XK8 it concluded that it wasn't an aggressive muscle car welcoming boastful driving, nor was it the last word in handling and performance, but it was seductive, nimble and quick, and nothing remotely came close in price. *Top Gear* magazine got its chance to try the XK8 in 1997 in a direct comparison with the BMW M3, Porsche 911 and Mercedes SL320, driving all three on the Continent to establish their 'grand touring' abilities. It obviously favoured the Porsche, but stated that the Jag had the

grand touring balance right, while both the Porsche and BMW supplied the better driving fun.

Autocar got first crack of the whip with the XKR Coupé via Mark Hughes, who commented early on in his report that "the sheer thrust from 2000 to 6000rpm is not only awesome and untemperamental, but also relentless', and finished with the comment: 'combines XK8's refinement and comfort with truly fearsome performance." Later that year the same magazine carried out a head-to-head between an XKR Convertible and the equivalent Porsche 911 Carrera Convertible. Similarly priced, the Jaguar had the edge in performance, comfort, ride and boot space, but the Porsche was decidedly the better drivers' car.

In an *Autocar* ranking of 1998 cars the XKR came a lowly 47th out of 100, supposedly based on its fuel consumption, brakes and handling. *Autocar* also carried out a Britain's Best Drivers' Car test at around the same time, in which the XKR came woefully far down the list because it felt it was more of a grand touring car than sports. It was, however, in good company at the bottom, with the Prodrive Imprezza. The Jaguar managed a lap time around Silverstone of 1min 15.15sec compared to the Porsche 911 at 1min 12.12sec and the Lotus Esprit at 1min 11.60sec. Problems with the XK related to the brakes (again), lack of control from the automatic transmission, and even the traction control.

Car magazine also did a major head-to-head, with the XKR pitched against the DB7, BMW 840Ci, Mercedes SL60, Porsche 911, and the Nissan NSX and Skyline, a formidable bunch. Looking for the best all-rounder, it straight away ruled out the SL on the basis of cost/value for money and lack of driver feel. The Skyline was dropped for its brashness and cheapness! The BMW felt like an old car, was too big and wasn't the best at anything. The Aston was a good all-rounder, but too expensive and apparently flawed in many areas. The second Nissan was then discarded on the basis of style and steering, which left the Porsche and Jaguar. They loved the Porsche and thought it a very exciting car, but the XKR won the day for so many reasons, not least because "the Jaguar handles the drama for you so your drive will be more relaxing … The Jaguar's monstrous, relentless torque is wholly addictive and completely thrilling, but you can arrive at your destination unshaken even though you have been stirred."

Chapter Five

Ongoing development and excitement

With sales buoyant after an upsurge resulting from the addition of the two new XKR models, Jaguar and the XK were flying high. The production figures up to the end of 1998 were the same as sales, as Jaguar was selling every XK it produced:

	1997	1998
XK8 Coupé	5141	3319
XK8 Convertible	9765	7662
XKR Coupé	11	1402
XKR Convertible	12	838
Totals	14,929	13,221

Rumours abounded during 1998 that Jaguar was up to something in the form of an even quicker version of the XKR, a new car that would appear at one of the international motor shows. The press and public were not to be disappointed when, at the Paris Motor Show in September 1998, Jaguar unveiled the XK180 to rapturous applause. Although at the time a non-runner (later it would actually run, and still does), Jaguar boss Nick Scheele stated that within months a street-legal version would be built.

The XK180 is definitely a part of the XK8 story, as it is significantly based on the then still new XKR, and

To create a concept car like the XK180 required many hours of hand crafting and finishing, to achieve what turned out to be a superb result. (Nigel Thorley)

many of its features were later incorporated into XK production. Although very much a concept car it paved the way for later XK development and led to its eventual replacement by the aluminium-bodied car.

Special Vehicle Operations

The XK180 story started with the formation of a new department within Jaguar, Special Vehicle Operations, a spin-off from the Limousine Department that used to manufacture the Daimler DS420 at Browns Lane. Rather than lose such expertise following the demise of that model, the SVO Department was set up, primarily to provide bespoke modifications to existing models and carry out development work and support in the provision of specialist vehicles like Police cars, one-off prototypes, and such things as armour-plated cars.

To give the department greater exposure, the idea developed – with approval from Jaguar's directors – that it should also work on other projects, such as special trim adaptations to customer specifications, and out of this came the Insignia project, which offered interior and exterior trim mods on the XJ40 saloons and XJS sports models that were relatively successful in their own way. Later the department worked on the Daimler Corsica concept two-door drophead coupé, based on the X-300 saloon, built to commemorate 100 years of Daimler motor cars. The scene was therefore set for SVO to get involved in other projects based on current vehicles.

The most powerful AJ-V8 engine up to that time, installed in the XK180. (Nigel Thorley)

The XK180 was originally conceived in 1997, when it was envisaged as a mildly modified XKR but with a vastly uprated engine and some styling add-ons from Jaguar's D-type racing era. However, with the help of Keith Helfet, from the Jaguar styling team (who had previously been involved in such diverse projects as the XJS facelift, the XJ220 supercar and, of course, the XK8), this idea soon developed into producing the ultimate XKR sports car. Once that was agreed the decks were cleared and the opportunity was taken to lighten the car – effectively to totally redesign it, designing and building an entirely new body structure from aluminium.

Using the 1950s D-type as inspiration and the production XK8 as a base to produce a viable modern car, not just a rehash of something that had gone before, work began in earnest. It was felt important that the origins of the XK8 should show through, but the project gave the team the opportunity to shorten the relatively long-wheelbase and rear overhang and incorporate modern styling ideas which would also be functional.

A hack of an XK8 Convertible was chosen for development. SVO cut the shell to remove 5in of wheelbase, fitted a strong roll-over cage, and set to work on the other aspects of design with the help of Jaguar's Whitley Engineering facility. From Helfet's original drawings, Abbey Panels Limited in Coventry (who used to produce the Jaguar E-type bonnet, XJ220 shells, and much more) built a clay styling buck onto which the aluminium body was hand rolled and beaten. Meanwhile back at the SVO department at Browns Lane, an XKR platform was prepared, shortened by 125mm, onto which the hand-built body was fitted and the rest of the car was built up. The end product turned out to be actually 345mm shorter than the production XK because of other styling changes at the front and rear. There had not been sufficient time or money to go in for any stringent testing – even the body wasn't wind-tunnel tested.

As for the mechanics, the XKR parts bin was raided, but racing-style adjustable Bilstein aluminium shock absorbers were mounted inside the uprated adjustable coil springs. The enhanced braking system came from Brembo, with larger cross-drilled ventilated discs and aluminium four-pot callipers. The anti-roll bars, all bushes and the rear A-frame to support the suspension were also strengthened. Steering was pure XKR but with higher gearing.

The standard five-speed Mercedes automatic transmission from the XKR was fitted, but not with the

From any angle the proportions of the XK180 look right, and the XK8 connections are obvious. (Nigel Thorley)

usual J-gate operation. Instead, Jaguar opted to fit a 'slick-shift' type of button gear change system via the steering wheel. An indication on the dash alerted the driver to which gear was selected.

The biggest news came with the engine installation. The then current 4.0-litre V8 Supercharged engine found in the XKR and XJR models was again used as its base, but with modifications to the Supercharger gearing speed (increasing it by 10 per cent), a bigger intercooler, improved induction, and big-bore exhaust system. Jaguar was able to extract a whopping 450bhp out of the engine with approximately 445lb of torque. The rest of the drivetrain was pure XKR. To transmit that performance to the road, massive 20in split-rim alloy wheels were fitted, 9in wide at the front, 10in at the rear, with Pirelli P-Zero tyres.

The end result of the XK180 styling was and still is quite amazing, particularly considering that the whole project was built and brought to launch in just 12 months without formal technical drawings and with such a small team involved. Externally the car still owes much to the XKR – the imposing front with obligatory mesh grille – but the revised bonnet design (opening à la E-type, with enlarged louvres to dissipate the heat) and the slightly 'stubbed' nose makes it look more purposeful. The smooth side lines, without door handles, and the upswept nature of the doors leading into the rear wings, are clean and pleasing to the eye yet retain much of the XK in their design. The shortened

wheelbase also suits the car well. The sculptured treatment to the rear deck, echoing the seat headrests, looks wonderful, and the rear spoiler does its job so much better than the D-type's fins of the 1950s. Helfet even chose an evocative, yet technologically advanced metallic paint finish for the car, apparently taking cues from the 1957 Le Mans winning Ecurie Ecosse D-types and the traditional British Racing Green.

Although the team started with a slightly modified XKR set-up, the internal styling also developed into something exciting but always functional, with strong use of aluminium and leather and the reversion to toggle-type switches and, not least, the lovely red starter button. Front seats are Recaro with proper full racing harnesses, but there is no room for rear seating because of the reduced wheelbase, and the car is all the better for it.

Yes, the XK180 was a pure concept car meant to stir the imagination and generate excitement about the Jaguar brand, something it did remarkably well. But it is also fair to say that every part of the concept was viable for a production car had Jaguar the time and money to have addressed the legislative and technical issues when it originally designed it. Indeed, many features from the XK180 found their way into later models. For example, the shortened wheelbase and reduced rear overhang

A very functional approach to the interior, with instrument layout taken from the 1960s Jaguar style. Note the red starter button near the gearlever. (Nigel Thorley)

The XK180 was the first Jaguar to have paddle-shift gearchange controls on the steering wheel, this very tactile gearlever change and quadrant being a theme only just coming to production in the all-alloy XK. (Nigel Thorley)

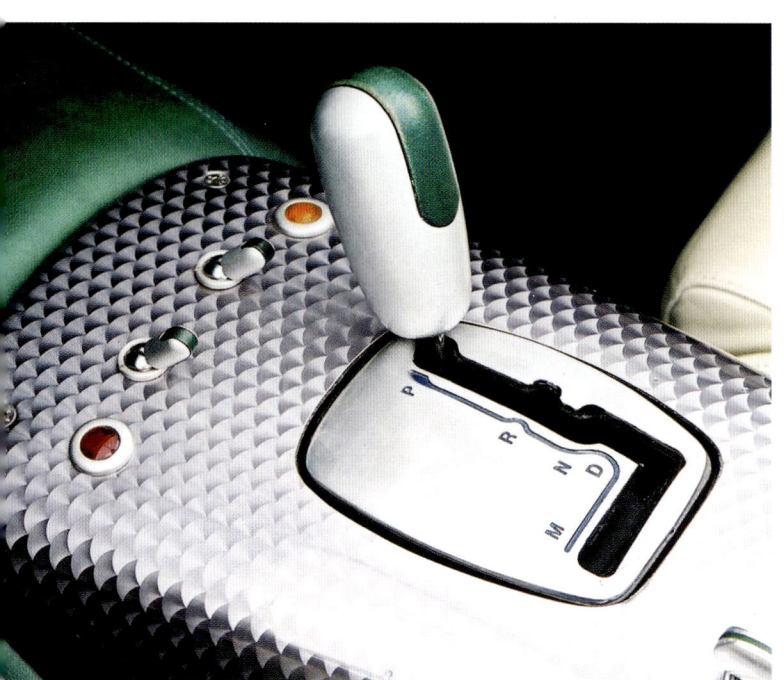

is found in the very latest (aluminium) XK models. The improved engine performance also benefited later cars. The use of digital rear lighting found its way into the S-type saloon in 1999 and later into other Jaguar models too. The beefed-up braking system and alloys turned up on XKs not long after in the form of R-Performance options, and even the alloy dash is now an option on cars as diverse as the X-type and XJR.

Public reaction to the car was incredible, with many defying Jaguar not to build it as a production vehicle, but it was not to be. Whether because of budgetary factors, fears of another XJ220 situation, or simply a lack of sufficient resources, the project was prevented from going further.

The ultimate driving experience

Though this is a phrase used by BMW, it is one your author cares to use in relation to the XK180, having had the opportunity to drive this fabulous motorcar. The seats seem to fit every driver perfectly and there is no loss of room compared to a standard XK. The small leather clad steering wheel falls easily to hand and you have just enough controls to worry about without the cockpit being fussy – in fact it takes you back to earlier days when cars were much simpler.

Pushing that evocative red starter button bursts the engine into life, and the sound from the enlarged

exhaust system needs to be bottled for permanent appreciation (TVR eat your heart out). The car feels easier and lighter to drive than the XK8 or XKR (it is 200kg lighter anyway) and you quickly feel a part of it. The seats hold you firm, the smaller diameter steering wheel gives you excellent control, and the whole car feels solid and exceptionally smooth, but the sound of that exhaust note urges you on to use the power under your right foot.

The steering is nice and sharp, much more so than the production XKs (probably because of the shorter wheelbase), and the car feels more manoeuvrable despite the massive 20in wheels connecting you to the road. The performance is excellent – better, in fact, than you actually realise – and there are no vices in the form of knocks, groans, or harshness. The XK180 is a fantastic drivers' car, and surprisingly refined as well.

You have the choice of full automatic transmission or moving the selector to 'manual', which gives you total control over gear changes via the steering wheel mounted buttons. The ease and smoothness of gear changes is a credit to the car, and judicious use of the gears enables the car to rocket to speeds unthought-of. But you have to be careful: remember that there's a lot of horsepower under the bonnet, the wheelbase is short, and you're not a Formula One driver!

All in all a fantastic experience I shall always remember, and it's easy to see why most enthusiasts

This was arguably one of the finest designs that could have been generated from the production XK8, and it's a shame it never entered production. It stole the hearts of many Jaguar enthusiasts and led to many XK8 improvements over the years, and even today elements of this design are reflected in the current aluminium XK. (Nigel Thorley)

were demanding that such a beautiful car should have been built.

XK 180 performance

Top speed	180mph
0–60mph	5.0 seconds
0–100mph	10.0 seconds

1999 model year changes

The launch of the S-type and the XK180 Concept took the spotlight somewhat off other production vehicles, including the XK, despite the still comparatively recent addition of the XKR range. However, two new colour schemes were introduced for all models, Alpine Green and Emerald Green displacing Sherwood and Aquamarine from the XK range. Also, by popular demand the XKR launch colour, Phoenix Red, now became a standard production colour available on any XK model. To complement the somewhat restricted range of colours for the XKR cars, Meteorite Silver and Topaz (gold) were offered as additional schemes. The original Stone colour option for the Convertible hood on both XK8 and XKR models was supplanted by Light Beige. (A full list of all XK colour schemes by year will be found in the appendices.)

The XK Convertible models came in for some revision. To structurally improve the integrity of the Convertible shell a stiffening brace was fitted between the seatbelt pillar and the B post. To do this involved the movement and modification of quite a few ancillary items, right down to heatshields and audio speakers. This was an adaptation of the stiffening brace already fitted to XKR models. In addition an X brace was fitted at the front to aid the removal and fitting of the radiator and air-conditioning condenser. Again this followed XKR practice and rationalised the production changes for all cars.

More happened 'under the skin'. Firstly, due to changing legislation over European impact requirements, the bodyshell had to be further strengthened to sustain front offset body deformation in an accident. Reinforced panels extended the driver and front passenger toeboards back towards the transmission tunnel, along with internal stiffening to the adjacent side members. On Coupé bodies additional plates were welded to the side members to further reinforce the toeboard area, and an extra stiffening panel was welded to the inside of each outer sill. In October 1998 the Mark 2 Servotronic steering system, originally adopted for the XJR and XKR, became standard fitment on all XK models.

The AJ-V8 engines of all models also came in for revision. Now coded AJ27 (the original engine was AJ26), they featured air-assisted fuel injectors that gave improved performance and reduced the time for catalysts to reach operating temperatures. On the normally-aspirated engines the previous two-stage variable cam phasing gave way to a continuously variable system, which provided for a linear valve timing pattern to improve torque at low speeds and optimise emissions, while modified pistons with increased skirt length improved refinement. Finally, a more responsive electronic throttle controlled the engine management system. All the 4.0-litre engines benefited from the fitment of dual-tipped platinum sparkplugs, which provided nearly 70,000 miles of service life before they needed to be changed. All these modifications were necessary to satisfy ever more stringent regulations regarding emissions, particularly in the US. In addition the oil cooler was deleted from the specification of the normally-aspirated engines.

On the supercharged engines, a new kickdown control switch gave improved response. The braking system was also enhanced for supercharged models by the fitment of larger discs and lead-free Textar brake pads. The ZF gearbox also came in for revision, with a recalibration to improve gearshift quality on non-supercharged engines.

Customers ordering new XK8 models with CATS suspension henceforward benefited from the fitment of stiffer steering bushes and Bilstein shock absorbers, like the XKR models. Similarly, if the optional 18in alloy wheels were specified the XKR-type Pirelli P-Zero tyres were fitted.

Hardly anything had changed with the external trim except that the relatively new badge on the boot lids of XKR and some overseas XK8 models was finally deleted at the end of 1998. Internally, Sport trim cars got an Ambla door trim instead of cloth finish, while the legends on the instrumentation for all models changed to make them more legible. A boot stowage net became a standard fitment in all XK models to secure small items.

As the British International Motor Show readied us for the 1999 model season, things began to hot up for the Jaguar XK. Although not direct competition, the limelight was switched to cars like the new Audi TT, Jaguar's own S-type saloon, and even the Ford Focus

SHAPING UP TO THE COMPETITION

A comparison of the XKR with its rivals, in terms of performance and price, now read as follows:

	bhp	Torque	0–60 mph	Top speed	Price
Jaguar XKR Coupé	370	387	5.1sec	155mph	£60,010
Porsche Carrera 4	300	258	5.2sec	174mph	£67,850
Maserati 3200GT	370	362	5.1sec	164mph	£60,765
Lotus Esprit GT	349	295	4.1sec	171mph	£49,950
Chevrolet Corvette	339	356	5.3sec	165mph	£40,425
Chevrolet Cam Z28	280	332	5.4sec	158mph	£22,725
Chrysler Viper	378	454	5.3sec	172mph	£68,800
TVR Cerbera Speed 6	350	330	4.5sec	180mph	£41,100

NB: The top speed of all XKs has always been electronically limited to 155mph. However, it is known that on test at MIRA standard production XKRs have achieved up to 175mph.

At the British International Motor Show the XKR helped to boost sales for the XK range to level out the losses – particularly from the XK8 Coupé – of 1999. (Nigel Thorley)

and Rover 75. Actual competition for the XK included the newly imported Porsche Carrera 4 Cabriolet and four-wheel drive models, Jensen's new (but stillborn) Interceptor, the AC Ace and Aceca Coupé, the entirely new Maserati 3200 GT, and Aston's Vantage, so it was a good place to show off the XK180 and attract attention to the XKR.

Depreciation was starting to finally take its toll on the XK8, a worry for both Jaguar and its dealers, for whom it was going to prove a rough winter. Values of early XK8s had dropped by over £1000 per month. Sales had been so buoyant that it was obvious the market had to cool down as more and more secondhand cars became available. The XKs, though, held out much better than some of the competition, with long-term price-drooping models like the Range Rover suffering twice as badly as Jaguar.

Despite this, Jaguar made strong progress for the second year in succession in the annual JD Power US survey on vehicle reliability. Jaguar improved its position to become second to Subaru, although the main beneficiary of this was the XJ saloon. The XK8 still came well down the list, but JD Power awarded Jaguar the Most Improved Brand award.

XK6?

After the excitement of the XK180, news leaked from Jaguar in 1999 relating to the possible development of a new, smaller sports car as an addition to the XK8 range. Sources claimed it would be launched around 2001 and would be based significantly on the then still new S-type saloon platform (also shared with the Lincoln LS in America). Using the S-type's 3.0-litre V6 engine, and possibly the 4.0-litre V8 as well, it was estimated that the new XK6 would be much smaller than the XK8, have design cues from the S-type, and be designed alongside a new Ford Thunderbird to cut costs and development time.

This was, at the time, a very logical development following the success of the XK8. Jaguar needed something with which to attack the competition in this field, where cars like the Porsche Boxster, Mercedes SLK and BMW Z3 M prevailed. There were even fears that BMW (now owners of Rover) might resurrect the Austin Healey name with a car for this market. Although, as

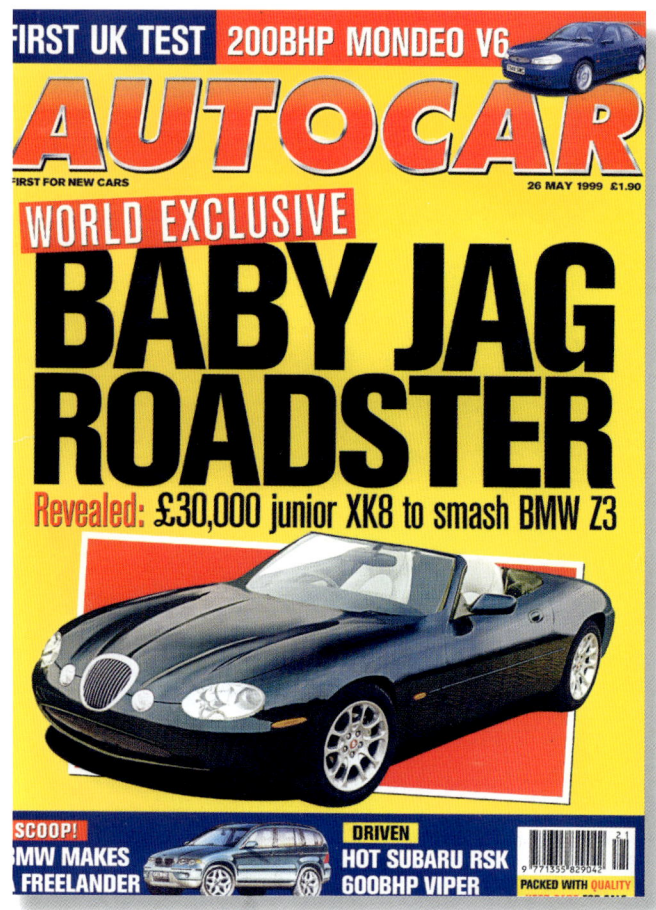

Autocar's impression of a new XK6 sports car, back in 1999. (Reprinted from *Autocar*)

Burberry, the clothing manufacturer, had previously created special XJ-S cars using their well-known materials. An XK8 Convertible followed in 1999. (Nigel Thorley)

we now know, the XK6 came to nothing, development was under way for something even better – the F-type, a project we'll return to in the next chapter.

Key personnel changes

Early in 1999 Jaguar announced that Nick Scheele, its Chairman and Chief Executive, was leaving to take up a new position with Ford as its Senior Vice-President Europe. Nick had joined the company back in April 1992 and had worked hard to see the X-100 project through. He had always been a strong supporter of the model, and of Jaguar Cars, and would again take some responsibility for Jaguar as a whole after becoming Ford's Senior Vice-President World. He was instrumental in bringing Joe Greenwell back to Jaguar as Chief Executive.

Chief Stylist Geoff Lawson died suddenly in June the same year, and was succeeded by Ian Callum, the man behind the Aston Martin DB7 who was later to design the aluminium XK that would replace the models covered in the first half of this book.

R-Performance

In readiness for the Frankfurt Motor Show in September 1999, and coinciding with Ford's decision to brand its Formula One team as Jaguar, the company finally introduced some of the add-ons first seen in the XK180 and developed under the Special Vehicle Operations banner. Primarily intended for the XK8 and XKR models, but also made available for some of the XJ range and S-types, these performance-related options by SVO were identified by the name 'R-Performance'. They were available on new cars by special order, but customers with older cars would have to wait until 2000 to get them as aftermarket add-ons from a Jaguar dealer.

BBS designed and supplied the R-Performance alloy wheels, which for the XK were either 18in Milan or 20in Paris or Detroit (named after the launch venues for the XK180 concept car), all of the two-piece, split-rim make-up. The 20in wheels were the largest ever to be fitted to a Jaguar car. All wheels were fitted with very low-profile Pirelli P-Zero tyres of the correct size. The 20in wheels necessitated the fitting of rubberised rear wheelarch extensions to meet the construction and use regulations criteria.

Also available were much improved brakes based on racing technology. Brembo designed them with two-piece, cross-drilled, ventilated discs, 355 x 32mm at the front and 330 x 28mm at the rear, with aluminium four pot callipers bearing the Jaguar name. There was

The massive 20in Detroit R-Performance wheels, a feature of the XK180 that finally made production on the XKR. (Nigel Thorley)

Rubberised wheelarch extensions are required for the fitment of 20in wheels and tyres to an XK. They are glued and screwed in position. (Nigel Thorley)

also a Handling Pack, which could only be fitted to cars with CATS suspension. This was made up of your choice of wheels plus the Brembo brakes, uprated springs, anti-roll bars, and retuned variable ratio steering and dampers. With this option ride-height was reduced by 10mm.

Mid-term XKR model with R-Performance Detroit alloy wheels showing the wheelarch extensions and wider track generated by the larger wheels. Note also the removal of the 'Supercharged' boot badge by this time. (Nigel Thorley)

Prices for the R-Performance enhancements ranged from £1450 for the Milan 18in wheels with Pirelli 245/45 and 255/45 tyres, to £5900 for a fully kitted-out XKR Handling Pack. A full breakdown of the components can be found in the appendices.

1999 Press reviews

Autocar carried out an interesting comparison road test between the XKR – the car it rated as the best front-engined grand tourer – the TVR Cerbera Speed 6, and the Maserati 3200 GT, a very close and new rival to the Jaguar. From the appearance standpoint *Autocar* still commented on the XKR's high stance with loads of space between wheels and arches and the enormous rear overhang. The Maserati was commended for its uniqueness and purposeful style while the very low, long TVR wouldn't win any awards but was instantly identifiable, more so than the Maserati.

Internally it found the Maserati the most comfortable and roomy, with many Fiat 'hand-me-downs', the Jaguar cramped with fussy instruments, and the TVR claustrophobic and over-stylised. In contrast, the XKR was mechanically the smoothest and deceptively fast because of its cosseted feel and behaviour. The Maserati was harsh and difficult to control and had a heavy clutch, and the TVR, with an even heavier clutch, was noisy and uncomfortable for long-legged drivers, and had a longwinded gear change and over-light throttle.

In conclusion it decided the Jaguar was, overall, the best of the three but in need of better brakes, a larger fuel tank, and more space inside. The Maserati could have won the contest but lacked development in its dynamics, and the TVR was just a raw basic sports car for a specialised market.

When evaluating the relevant costs and benefits of owning a £35,000 used sports car with 2+2 seating in mid-1999, there seemed a clear choice between a 1996 P-registered XK8 Coupé, a 1995 M-registered Porsche 928 GTS, or a 1997 P-registered BMW 840Ci. *Autocar* considered the XK8 was let down by its interior. The BMW was old and had a cramped cabin area but had superb build quality, while the aged Porsche offered rock-steady reliability, performance, and top resale values. However, could either the Porsche or BMW offer the street cred of the Jaguar?

Another *Autocar* road test appeared in October 1999, this time featuring an XKR Convertible with the latest R-Performance additions. Tested at an all-in price of £66,000, the car had the total Handling Pack with big brakes, and uprated and lowered suspension. *Autocar* still waxed lyrical about the car's long-legged cruising ability and mid-range overtaking capabilities but was even keener to write about the improved braking system. It apparently took the tester five consecutive full-bore stops from 130mph to induce any brake fade, and stopping the car from 70mph required two metres less space than the standard XKR. It also identified far better feel from the brakes under all conditions.

Unfortunately it didn't have the same opinion of the handling. Despite the SVO improvements the steering still let the car down and the handling was not up to the standard expected from drivers of Porsche 911s and the like. Body control was noticeably tauter and the bigger tyres and wheels and stiffened suspension didn't have too adverse an affect on the ride, which improved with speed. *Autocar* concluded that the additions had done an excellent job but that the Jaguar still needed more, and many would have argued that the extra £6000 the R-Performance options cost should have been on the car from the start, as an inclusive package.

Chapter **Six**

The millennium and beyond

2000 model year changes

For the 2000 model year Jaguar had to keep abreast of increasing competition and newer and more sophisticated technology. So first off it provided the XK with the Adaptive Cruise Control system (developed for Jaguar by Delphi Automotive Systems), which later became a standard fitment on XKR models and optional on XK8s. This has at its heart a microwave sensor about the size of a shoebox and weighing 1kg, which is mounted in the nose section and acts as a detector system, monitoring what lies ahead of the car by means of a radar aerial and proximity sensor, and relating the information to control units for the engine, transmission and brakes. It is activated by a button alongside the Sport-mode button on the centre console, with a readout in the speedometer.

Activating the console button allows settings to be made via push-buttons on the steering wheel: you set the speed the car is to maintain (exactly the same as with a conventional cruise control, except that you can control it by 1mph increments indicated on the speedometer readout), and then set the trailing distance you wish to maintain from the vehicle in front. Once on the move, you select 'cruise' and the car does the rest. It detects moving traffic and carries out a mathematical evaluation compared to the car's speed and makes the appropriate adjustments smoothly and in plenty of time, dependent on the speed differential. If the vehicle in front turns off or moves into another lane, the system identifies this and increases the speed accordingly back to the pre-set cruise figure. Alternatively, if the vehicle in front continues to slow, perhaps for a junction or hazard, the ACC continues to recalculate the necessary action. It does not, however, take regard of stationary objects, nor will it bring the car completely to a halt. At a safe distance it sounds a warning, coupled with an indication in the speedometer display that the driver must take control.

Next, although satellite navigation had been around for a few years – and, indeed, Jaguar had introduced a CD system for its S-type in 1999 – it wasn't until 2000 that the XK sports models became available with a fully integrated system. This was a much faster DVD based system which integrated well into the car, with the appropriate equipment in the boot and the colour screen situated in the centre dash area below the air-conditioning vents, occupying the space usually taken by the auxiliary gauges. The analogue clock also

The integrated satnav system replaced the auxiliary gauges in the centre of the dashboard. A clear display, concise and easy to understand controls and clear voicing made it a very good DVD-based system. The only downside to the original design was the small digital clock in the bottom left corner; later changed. (Nigel Thorley)

disappeared, being replaced initially by a small digital readout on the satnav screen.

Rain-sensing wipers became a standard fitment on all XK8 models the same year, controlled via the usual steering-column mounted stalk in the 'auto' position. At the same time the anti-lock braking systems were upgraded with 'ABS Plus', designed to recognise the difference in wheel speed and distribute brake pressure accordingly during high-speed braking.

The normal audio system was upgraded with six speakers, and the CD six-disc autochanger became standard equipment on all models. The Premium sound system was also changed to a more impressive Alpine unit providing 320 watts of power, compared to 80 watts from the old system. The Alpine unit also allowed independent adjustment of the sub-woofer bass speaker.

It should also be mentioned at this point that, for the 2000 model year, Jaguar redesigned the engine to accommodate conventional steel cylinder bore liners which, although increasing the weight, eliminated the embarrassing problem of the Nikasil lining wearing away and leading to premature failure of the engine. Further information on this aspect of pre-2000 cars can be found in Chapters 8 and 9.

With the above changes Jaguar had improved the value-for-money aspect of the XK range. With no price increases in 2002 they would, in fact, add around £4900 of value.

Competition in 2000

Though Lexus – who had long been a threat not only to Jaguar but also to Mercedes and BMW – lacked a degree of street cred, they were busily working on improving this in 2000 with a concept car (later to go into production), the Sports Coupé. As Toyota put it at the time, this was strategically aimed at customers who purchased cars like the Jaguar XK8. Strictly a 2+2 of similar proportions to the Jaguar, they even tried

to emulate the Spitfire-style dashboard of the XK. But the big advantage came from its fully-retractable metal roof, which folded away into the boot à la Mercedes SLK, although it left no room for luggage when down!

The year 2000 saw an interesting development in the secondhand market for XK8s. After a period of alarming price mark-downs by the trade and a so-called 'glut' of used cars for sale, things changed for the better. An upsurge occurred in the demand for prestige coupés and convertibles, and the XKs benefited from it. Strong demand from customers who were realising the value-for-money of used XKs, compared to the likes of Astons, Porsches and Ferraris, actually forced prices up, and Jaguar dealers in particular were very keen to acquire good low-mileage examples at above 'book' price. Strangely, though, the right specification was still vital to a good sale, the car ideally needing 18in wheels, the right colour, and Classic trim.

It was a testament to where Jaguar had got to in improving their build quality and reputation – nothing like this could have been said for the likes of the XJ-S, the E-type, or even the XK120 after a few years in production.

The F-type unveiled

Mention was made in the previous chapter about the strong possibility of a smaller version of the XK, perhaps an XK6, based on the mid-sized S-type platform. Those rumours turned into reality at the Detroit International Auto Show in January 2000, when Jaguar gave the world its first sighting of the F-type Concept (coded X-600), the spiritual successor to the E-type and more of a true sports car than the XK8.

Ever since announcing the XK180 Jaguar had been debating the possibility of another sporting car to their line-up, in addition to, rather than instead of, the XK8. Meetings had been held with Ford in the US and focus groups had been organised with the owners of rival cars like the BMW Z3, Porsche Boxster and Mercedes SLK. The feedback was so positive that Jaguar and Ford were encouraged to commence work on the X-600.

Given another clean sheet of paper, Keith Helfet (who

was behind the XK180) was given free reign to produce the F-type 'in the flesh', from which Jaguar could gauge public reaction in a different marketing environment to that currently satisfied by the XK. The final result owed nothing to existing Jaguar or Ford floorpans but was unique, which, in itself, presented problems for those who had to work on the feasibility of turning

If the XK180 concept car was pretty, then the F-type was positively beautiful. Extremely well proportioned with an ease of line and compact dimensions – everything a Jaguar sports car should be and an ideal little sister to the XK. (Nigel Thorley)

The F-type's lines showed off to their best advantage, perhaps. The family connection with the XK180 can be clearly seen. (Nigel Thorley)

The F-type's interior bore a very close resemblance to the XK180: alloy dashes are back in fashion. (Nigel Thorley)

the concept into a production vehicle. The concept had no weather protection, and didn't have a tall enough windscreen or proper side windows to provide protection from the wind and other elements. Nor was it a runner, so adaptations would need to be made to allow for the engine. And as for that inevitable floorpan – if bespoke, it could cost millions, if used from the existing S-type or the still-to-be-announced X-type smaller saloon, that might compromise the purity of the original concept design.

The reader might therefore consider that the F-type Concept bears no resemblance to, nor need be of any concern to devotees of, the XK8 and XKR, but that would be a little unfair. The F-type would have ridden on the back of XK's success and would undoubtedly have become the offspring of the bigger car. The anticipated style would have echoed, in many respects, that of the XK, and despite initial comments it would have to have shared some items from its parts bin to be economically viable. Had it been produced, the F-type Concept would have been significantly smaller than the XK (25in shorter and 4in narrower), would have been strictly a two-seater, and would have cost around £30–35,000.

Subsequently the F-type Concept became the subject of a detailed 12-month feasibility study at Jaguar and Ford, and this, plus the overwhelmingly positive

public reaction to the car, convinced them to give the go-ahead. An official announcement was made at the Los Angeles International Auto Show in January 2001 that it was 'go', and that it would take about three years to bring the F-type Roadster to production 'to complement the XK range'.

Despite its dealerships accepting deposits in advance of seeing an actual car, bad news followed in 2002 when Jaguar announced that it was shelving the F-type project as a result of being overstretched with work on existing models such as the S-type, the X-type, and the then still to come Diesel development and the alloy XJ.

I personally remember visiting Jaguar's Public Affairs Department and being shown an A4 ring-binder stuffed full of complimentary comments, letters and even offers to buy the F-type, and indeed many Jaguar dealerships reported having extensive lists of customers' names in readiness for an official order book. Its cancellation was a sad day, which left the mantle of Jaguar sporting models with the XK8.

Silverstone special edition

In April 2000, in time for the British Grand Prix at Silverstone and coinciding with their commitment to Formula One racing, Jaguar announced the launch of a special edition XKR, appropriately called the Silverstone. Just 100 examples were to be sold, 50 as Coupés and 50 as Convertibles, all of which would be finished in Platinum Silver exterior finish with a black hood on the Convertibles. The only external difference to standard

XKRs was the unique bonnet and boot badges carrying the words 'Jaguar Silverstone', with the growler image on a black background with grey surround.

Silverstones were fitted as standard with the 20in Detroit split-rim R-Performance alloy wheels, with matching Pirelli P-Zero ultra low profile tyres. The Coupés were further enhanced with the R-Performance Handling Package with bigger brakes, uprated anti-roll bars and springs, and recalibrated steering and dampers. Internally the sill tread plates also carried the 'Silverstone' inscription, and all the cars were trimmed with Sports seats in Warm Charcoal (black) leather with red stitching, matched to similar carpeting and a leather sports steering wheel. The woodwork chosen for all these special editions was grey smoke-stained birds eye maple with the 'Silverstone' insignia laser-etched on the passenger side. As befitted the high standard specification of these cars, they were also equipped with the Jaguar Alpine Premium Sound System with stacker CD system in the boot. Prices for the Silverstone models were: XKR Coupé £66,785, XKR Convertible £72,185.

2001 and more updates

For the 2001 model year Jaguar made a number of changes to the XK range which, in the main, tidied up the look of the car and enhanced the specification. This was managed without any price increases at all at the time – in fact there were actual reductions in the XK range. 2001 prices were:

The bespoke interior of all Silverstone models featured Warm Charcoal trim piped in red with black carpets with red stitching, matching red stitching to other trim areas, and 'Silverstone' markings. (Nigel Thorley)

XK8 Coupé	£48,700 (down by 6.5 per cent)
XK8 Convertible	£55,350 (down by 6.3 per cent)
XKR Coupé	£56,700 (down by 7.4 per cent)
XKR Convertible	£63,350 (down by 7.2 per cent)

Starting at the front, the fog lamps were changed to a flush mounted style, with a new bumper to accommodate them. This gave the fog lights more prominence and imparted a cleaner look to the front of the car. The chrome splitter bar on the XK8 model also came in for slight revision.

The only changes to the side view involved the wheels. On XK8 models the original 17in Revolver wheels were replaced by a new 17in Lamina design, while on cars supplied with the CATS suspension package another new wheel, the 18in Impeller, replaced the original 18in Flute wheels. Double Five 18in wheels remained the norm for XKR models, with the option of 19in Apollo wheels, unless R-Performance options were fitted.

Following on from the S-type saloon, at the rear the XK models took advantage of the new 'jewelled' style of rear light units, also sporting chromed surrounds. Much brighter than the old style, the rear wings were subtly altered internally to accommodate the new lighting.

Better news, and long overdue, was the fitment of an

The main frontal difference from 2001 was the revised style and fitting of fog lamps (revised lamp on right), which also affected the nose itself. (Nigel Thorley)

The restyled bumper showed less of the underside and incorporated a clip-on cover concealing the towing hook. Jewelled rear lighting, now surrounded by chrome trim, and an S-type style plinth with push-button operation, were all 2001 XK features. (Nigel Thorley)

external electrically actuating unlocking button to the boot lid. The button, with a growler emblem, was fitted in the centre of a chrome-plated boot plinth above the registration plate embossed with the name 'Jaguar'. Of the same design as used on the S-type saloons, this also incorporated the registration number lighting unit. The conventional key lock within the XK8 badge remained. Another change at the rear was the bumper style, which now had a small under-spoiler that was deeper, to hide more of the boot floor and underside of the car. This also incorporated a hidden cover under which a towing eye was concealed, different to the exposed eye on the earlier cars. Larger chromed exhaust tail-pipes were fitted to XKR models, bringing this car into line with the same treatment given to XJR saloons of the period.

Technology having moved forward for the 2001 model year, all XKs benefited from further safety features like the fitment of side airbags for the first time on XK models and the latest Adaptive Restraint Technology System (ARTS), the first time this was fitted to a car. This system uses an ultrasonic detector to gauge the position of the front passenger, which is linked to other sensors (situated in the A and B posts, the centre console and the seats) to determine the weight of the passenger, the position of the driver in relation to the steering wheel, and whether one or both parties are wearing a seatbelt. Every ten milliseconds the sensors react to determine whether or not and at what level to deploy the airbags in an accident. This means that if there is no passenger in the front seat, the side airbag is not deployed at all, and if someone is in too close proximity to the dashboard or steering wheel, the airbags are deployed at a lesser level, for safety reasons.

Another safety aspect involved modifying the bodyshell to include reinforced front side-members for added rigidity. This had the added benefit of accommodating various sensors required for the ARTS system. At the same time, to meet new legislation child safety restraints were built into the body-in-white.

A change to the fairly new Adaptive Cruise Control (ACC) enabled the set speed on the cruise control to be always displayed in front of the driver. In the event of the radar sensor in the nose becoming blocked with mud and dirt a 'sensor blocked' message now appeared to alert the driver.

The interior too underwent changes at this time, with a major redesign of the seating. With stronger and more pronounced bolsters for better support, the opportunity was taken to revise the style of pleating. For XK8 models the Classic five flutes were used, while the XKRs had a Sports embossed style with horizontal curved pleating, which was an optional extra on XK8s. All XKs, regardless of specification, now came with electric 12-way adjustable front seating, with separate adjustment for height of the front seat cushions/backs and separate, electrically adjustable head restraints. When a front seatback was folded forward for access to the rear compartment, the head restraints

All-new seating in 2001, the first major interior change since 1996: separate and adjustable head restraints, revised pleat style and thicker seat backs with better adjustment, all at the expense of rear seating accommodation. (Nigel Thorley)

automatically retracted to their lowest position, and reverted to their chosen position when the seatback was returned.

Modification of the seatbelts meant that when the buckle was connected, an electrical contact was made which allowed a 'comfort spring' to come into operation, making for a more comfortable seatbelt fit. On Coupé models the seatbelt height adjusters were redesigned to be more ergonomic. A final interior change saw the addition of 'mood lighting', which emits ambient light to the interior of the cockpit at night.

A new extra cost option was the availability of a dual band, fixed in-car telephone system in the XK. This enabled the phone to switch between networks to ensure the best reception with a lesser chance of losing a call. A revised filtering system cut out unwanted background noise, providing better hands-

BIRTH CONTROL

In 2001 Jaguar's Director of Communications and Public Affairs, Stuart Dyble, was driving his pregnant wife to hospital in his silver XKR. Within minutes his wife Vanessa had given birth to their new daughter Sophie in the car. So those road testers who may have complained about lack of room — think again!

Dual band telephone systems also became available for the XK in 2001. (Nigel Thorley)

free reception. The dual band phone system, although expensive, also incorporated Voice Activation for the dialling of up to 20 pre-programmed telephone numbers.

A data port could also now be fitted to allow information to be transferred to and from a laptop and a memo recording device. As a further accessory an

Another XK special edition, the XKR 100, just 100 of which were made. (Nigel Thorley)

owner could specify a mobile phone charging point, sited inside the glove box.

Up to this time owners of XKs who wanted a reverse park aid fitted had to arrange this with a Jaguar dealer as an aftermarket fit. From 2001 this could be specified on the original order for a car and fitted during assembly.

Exterior paint schemes changed again, with Spindrift (white) and Alpine (green) being deleted and a standardisation of the colours available on XK8 and XKR models.

Centenary car

Jaguar announced a limited special edition of the XKR in 2001. This was the XKR 100, commemorating the 100th anniversary of the birth of Sir William Lyons, the founder of the company. Just 50 Coupés and 50 Convertibles were produced, all finished in black with matching black leather interior and contrast piping. They were fitted with the R-Performance Handling Pack, alloy surrounds to the instruments and gearlever surround, drilled alloy pedals, special commemorative plaques signifying their uniqueness and, of course unique exterior badging.

Flying the flag

Jaguar prepared a special Union Jack-adorned XK8 Convertible for the Austin Powers movie *Goldmember*. This was also used for promotional purposes in North America when Jaguar announced their 'London Calling' advertising campaign. Subsequently a number of Jaguar dealers 'dressed' other XK8s in the same style for promotional use. The original Austin Powers car is now in the hands of the Jaguar Daimler Heritage Trust.

Production figures

At 14,929 cars 1997 was the peak year of XK production, with a drop in overall numbers to 13,221 in 1998 and 11,421 in 1999. After a slight increase in 2000 to 12,241 production fell again in 2001, to the lowest figure yet for a full year of 10,735.

In the 2001 JD Power survey Jaguar again achieved good results, enjoying a third consecutive year in the top ten for the XJ saloon. The XK sports achieved better results with a fifth place, behind the Audi TT in first, Porsche Boxster second, Porsche 911 third, and Jaguar's own XJ fourth. The XK managed sixth place in the sound system class behind Lexus, BMW and the Jaguar XJ again, and fifth in the best heating and cooling category. It scored consistently high in most categories except for ownership costs, mechanical and exterior problems. The general comments were: "The JD Power debut reveals real strengths, especially its road ability, cabin assembly and style. However, the cabin is too impractical, seats are prone to faults and bodywork is iffy."

Press comparisons

The American *Road & Track* magazine had run an XK8 Convertible from 1997 until towards the end of 1999, and after nearly 50,000 miles it rated the car very highly. Apart from a minor accident necessitating the replacement of the front bumper, it got 31,500 miles out of a set of Pirelli tyres. Based on depreciation at that time, taking into consideration the mileage, *Road & Track* estimated that the XK8 had taken a $21,570 'hit' in value, making the price per mile running costs about 89 cents – expensive. Out of pocket maintenance involved replacing the brake discs, a new foglamp, a gearshift rubber and, of course, tyres. But it was sorry to see the car go back!

At numerous times the motoring media have compared the XK range with the opposition or even with Jaguar's previous model, the XJS. In 2002, *Jaguar World Monthly* magazine even compared the XK against a choice of two other pre-owned Jaguars and a new X-type 2.0 litre, all offered at similar prices. The choice between a 1997 XK8 Coupé, a 1998 XJR saloon, a 2000 model year S-type and the new X-type seemed automatically to favour the XK8 but, as it pointed out, at that time it was very hard to find an example within this price range and then not necessarily to the specification and colour you might desire. One also had to bear in mind the practicalities of the issue. Though £20,000 may have seemed a reasonable figure and the choice one-sided, was the XK8 the most suitable vehicle for your requirements? This is an argument that still carries weight today, especially when compared to the practicalities and performance of, say, the XJR.

Jaguar World Monthly carried out another comparison at the end of 2004 between a used XK8 and a BMW 840ci, the former having the looks, while the latter provided better driver well-being, with firmer suspension and solid build quality.

The Austin Powers 'Shaguar', now part of the Jaguar Daimler Heritage Trust collection of vehicles. (Nigel Thorley)

The muscular XKR-R doing what it does best – perform. (Nigel Thorley)

XKR-R

And now onto the fastest XKR of them all – the XKR-R, a one-off experimental Jaguar that came out

Full racing seats and harness, Alcantara trim and an adrenalin rush when you rev the engine! (Nigel Thorley)

of the Special Vehicle Operations Department, which had been responsible for the XK180 and later R-Performance options. The idea was to create the ultimate XKR sports car, stiffer, more agile, and with improved performance and more macho. This is what Jaguar wanted, to compete with the likes of the Mercedes AMG cars and the BMW Alpina.

The project started with a completely conventional XKR Coupé. The whole bodyshell was strengthened to

increase stiffness in order to take a different drivetrain. The front end was seam welded for strength, with the front crossbeam solidly mounted with aluminium instead of rubber mounts. The beefed-up steering rack devised for the XK180 was also fitted. At the rear a half roll cage was welded into place replacing the rear +2 seating arrangement of the conventional car, and the rear end of the bodyshell, aft of the floorpan, was cut away and an S-type rear end carefully welded into place.

With these changes carried out, a complete S-type rear suspension/axle assembly was fitted. With technology moving on so fast, even the XK's set-up, derived from the XJ saloon, was not practical for higher performance, the S-type's offering a greater range of ride and handling capabilities.

Competition-style spring and damper units were fitted with individual reservoirs and spherical top mounts, and the whole car was lowered to improve the centre of gravity, becoming 30mm lower than a conventional XK8 and 20mm lower than an XKR. It was fitted with 20in R-Performance split-rim wheels and ultra-low profile tyres. With the added benefit of the then still new revised front and rear bumper treatment, and the addition of straight over-sills (shades of revised production XK still to come), the end product looked aggressive and powerful even when standing still.

Under the bonnet, the engine was still the 4.0-litre AJ-V8 unit, but fitted with twin carbon fibre air intakes. Like the XK180 engine the crankshaft pulley size was increased to raise the boost level and a bigger intercooler and radiator also helped. The end result was an engine achieving up to 450bhp at 6200 rpm. To push the gases through, a massive straight-through exhaust system was hand-crafted, with four tail-pipes.

SVO opted to fit a six-speed manual gearbox, using a Tremec T-56 mated to the engine via a two-plate clutch, as fitted to cars like the Aston Martin Vantage, Chevrolet Corvette and Dodge Viper. Finally, the handbrake was an electrical/hydraulic system operated from a rather elongated handle by the driver's seat.

Internally, all the wood veneer was replaced by carbon fibre, new to the XK at that time. Alcantara was used for some of the trim, along with racing-style Recaro seating with full harnesses – no shopping car this!

This one-off car is now in the hands of the Jaguar Daimler Heritage Trust and although never put into production for cost reasons, elements subsequently found their way through to production XKs and also to the new aluminium XK replacement.

Over 450bhp from the modified 4.0-litre engine fitted to the XKR-R. (Nigel Thorley)

The 2001 model year XKR Convertible finished in Platinum Silver with 18in Double Five wheels. (Nigel Thorley)

The new generation XK

Falling sales

Although, as a company, Jaguar was doing quite nicely, the XK wasn't doing so well. From a production high of nearly 15,000 cars in 1997 sales had deteriorated to under 11,000 by 2001, and got dramatically worse from there on. The total production figure for 2002 was a mere 6861 cars, and that reflected in sales, as

A new, highly sophisticated six-speed gearbox, later standardised for all XK models. (Nigel Thorley)

it was now pretty easy to find new XKs in the dealer showrooms awaiting customers.

This should, of course, be put into context, as after being Jaguar's bestselling sports car ever it was inevitable that after six years sales would drop, and even then they remained favourable compared to some of the later XJS models. Another 'hit' on XK sales may well have been the publication by the motoring press of 'spy' photographs of what was supposedly the next new XK, but was in reality no more than a revamp of

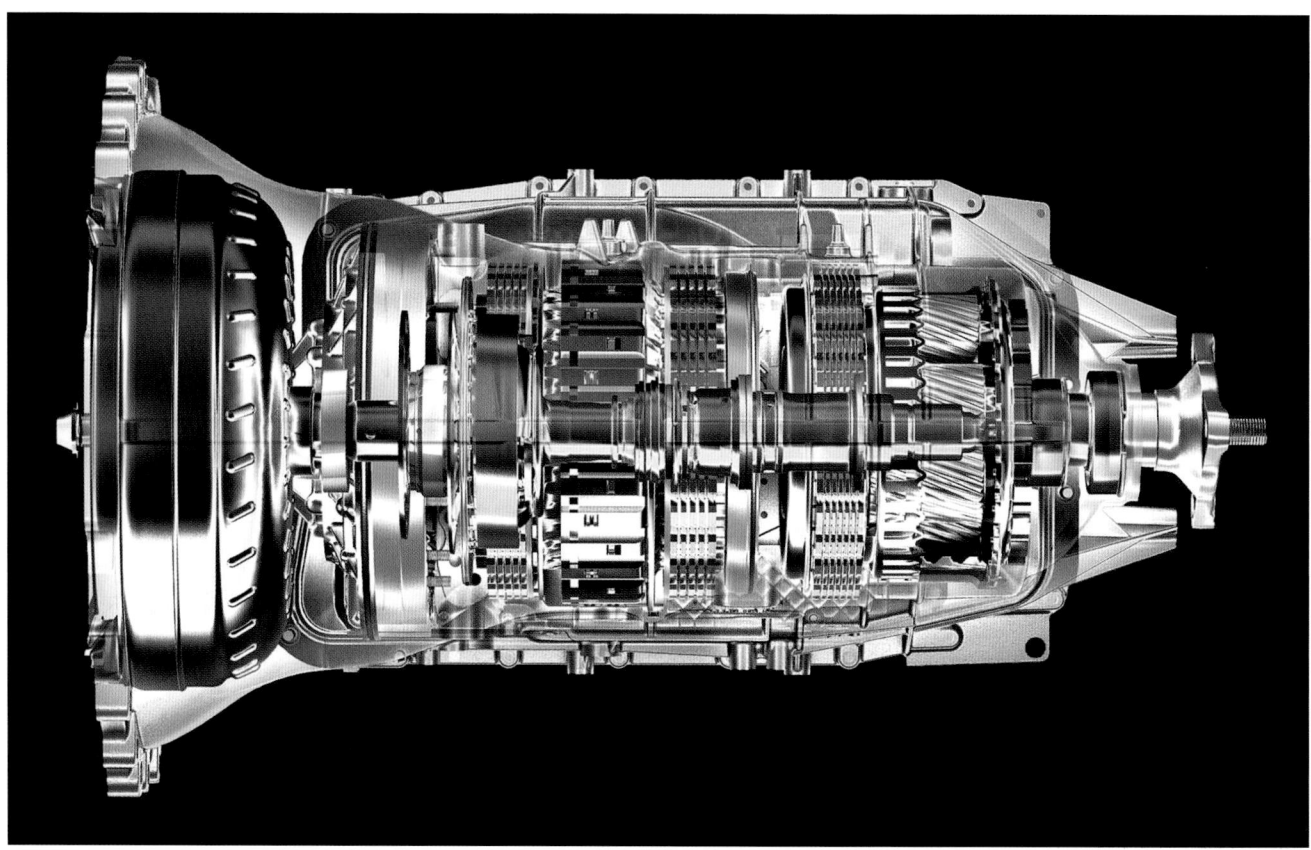

the existing model. Jaguar therefore needed to revitalise interest in the XK, and more changes took place for the last phase in its lifespan.

Six-speeder

Late in 1999 ZF announced the forthcoming introduction of their first six-speed automatic transmission, Model No 6HP 26, specifically designed for rear-wheel drive performance cars. This was to eventually replace the ZF 5HP 24 five-speed unit used in the normally-aspirated XK8 models and the Mercedes W5A 580 box in the XKR cars.

The big advantage, apart from more gears, was that with improved technology the new gearbox was 12 per cent lighter and 50mm shorter than the old five-speed unit, but with a greater torque capability. Although a die-cast casing, the new gearbox used a glass-reinforced plastic sump to keep weight down. It also incorporated a new Bosch TCM (Transmission Control Module) integrated into the main gearbox housing with cable and plug connections. The use of six gears provided a wider spread of ratios and, of course, a taller top (sixth) gear which ZF claimed would result in improvements of between 1 and 5 per cent in acceleration and 5 to 7 per cent in fuel economy.

Another innovation with the new gearbox was a torque converter that cut off at idle so that the engine wasn't under load when the car was stationary. ZF also integrated the 'mechatronic' electronic module into the gearbox housing to improve the quality of gear shifts.

This new gearbox was produced in 2001, when Jaguar became one of the first customers to use it, though at that time only on the S-type mid-range saloon. But its use in the XK soon followed.

2002 changes

New Jaguar buyers (of any model) benefited from a revised policy on new car warranties. From now on all new Jaguars (including XKs) received a comprehensive three-year, unlimited mileage warranty (previously 60,000 miles). This had a two-fold effect on the reputation of the company and its cars. Firstly it only came about from the fact that Jaguar had improved its build quality and longevity significantly in recent years; and secondly it sent out important signals to those contemplating buying a Jaguar.

More importantly, however, big changes were in hand for the 2003 model year XK range. Dubbed by the company 'The New-Generation Jaguar XK', these were

Jaguar's new 4.2-litre engine for the 2003 model year, codenamed AJ-34. (Nigel Thorley)

to be the most significant changes to the model range since its introduction in 1996. They revolved around an enlarged engine, the new gearbox, better brakes and chassis, improved electronics and revised trim. At the heart of these changes was the adoption of a new version of the AJ-V8 engine (coded AJ-34), enlarged to 4.2-litres (4196cc) capacity, first seen in S-type saloons. The logic behind the redesign was to improve performance and economy.

Many internal changes took place and the whole engine was claimed to be stiffer than the version it replaced. Indeed, the pistons, for example, were forged from single billets of aluminium and had jet cooling on the underside of the crowns. The new engine also benefited from variable camshaft phasing, in which an hydraulic actuator on each inlet camshaft is operated by a pair of electronically-switched oil pressure control valves, actuated by the engine control module, which contains maps of engine speeds and loads. This produces faster engine response and optimum performance at all engine speeds, which in turn helps emissions. The induction system was also amended with multi-hole injectors to refine the spray pattern in the combustion chamber, and the block and bed-plate were redesigned for extra lightness (6kg lighter than the outgoing 4.0-litre).

For the supercharged installation, an Eaton unit was again fitted, with an industry first on a production car: helical rotor gears for low noise. The supercharger

From 2003 on, XKs received new badging, in the XKR's case directly from R-Performance. Similarly, the higher performance models got their rear plinth finished in body colour. (Nigel Thorley)

therefore spins 5 per cent faster than the one used in the 4.0-litre engine.

In the XK8 installation the new engine produced 300bhp at 6000rpm in standard form. Fitted to the XKR model with supercharger, it boasted 400bhp and significantly improved torque up to 408lb ft. Compared to previous models, the 4.2-litre engine improved performance all round by 3.5 per cent in the XK8 and 8 per cent in the XKR. Jaguar claimed not only better performance, but also improved refinement and fuel economy, as demonstrated by the figures given here.

Adopting the ZF 6HP 26 six-speed automatic transmission for all XKs at the same time as the introduction of the new engine eliminated the necessity

2003 car with the then new standard equipment Gemini 17in alloy wheels for the XK8. (Nigel Thorley)

for two different gearboxes. A final change in the drivetrain involved a revised rear axle ratio to suit the new gearbox and the increased torque of the engine.

Engine comparisons

With improved performance came improved brakes, the Brembo now being adopted with larger ventilated discs (355mm x 32mm front and 330mm x 28mm rear), four pot callipers and steel braided flexible brake lines as standard on XKR models. Non-supercharged models had the enlarged standard discs (325mm x 28mm front and 305mm x 20mm rear). Another standard fit on all

	4.0-litre	4.0-litre s/c	4.2-litre	4.2-litre s/c
Engine capacity (cc)	3996	3996	4196	4196
Bore x stroke (mm)	86 x 86	86 x 86	86 x 90.3	86 x 90.3
Maximum (bhp @ revs)	290 @ 6100	370 @ 6150	300 @ 6000	400 @ 6100
Maximum torque	290 @ 6100	387 @ 3600	310 @ 4100	408 @ 3500
Compression ratio	10.75:1	9.0:1	11.0:1	9.1:1
Top speed (limited)	155mph	155mph	155mph	155mph
0–60mph (seconds)	6.7	5.3	6.1	5.3
Av fuel consumption (mpg)	23.9	22.6	24.9	22.6

models was the new EBA (Emergency Brake Assist) technology, which automatically applies additional braking pressure if the driver has not provided it under extreme conditions.

The Adaptive Restraint Technology mentioned earlier also became standard equipment on all XK models.

Two-tone upholstery was a limited feature available on later XKs. Also note the change of gearknob style. (Nigel Thorley)

CATS suspension remained a standard fit on XKR models but was an extra cost option on XK8s. Yet more standard fit features on all models were DSC (Dynamic Stability Control) and cruise control.

Externally the changes for the 2003 model year were more subtle. Following Jaguar practice with all its other models, new rear badging was of a cleaner style and the R-Performance logo was adopted for XKR models. The boot finisher above the number plate was from then on body-coloured for XKR models.

Front light units changed, all cars featuring black surround recesses to the headlamp units, with Xenon gas headlights standard on XKR models along with automated headlamp levelling. An 'Autolamp' mode was added, to automatically switch them on in poor ambient light. Also, within 20 seconds of turning the wipers on the lights would also switch on.

More alloy wheel changes also took place at this time. Gemini 17in became the standard fitment on XK8 cars, while two new 18in styles – Hydra and Centaur – became available for the XKR and optional at extra cost on the XK8. With these additions Jaguar offered a comprehensive range of alloy wheels from the base 17in size up to R-Performance split-rim 20in.

The final external change came in the range of paint finishes. New paint schemes were Adriatic Blue (metallic mid-blue), displacing Sapphire; Jaguar Racing Green (darker metallic green with lighter under-tones); Ebony (solid black); and Midnight (Metallic black), displacing Anthracite. Other displaced colours were Emerald Green, Platinum Grey, Mistral Blue, Roman Bronze, Titanium Grey, and Westminster Blue. As can be seen, the total range of exterior colours was thus dramatically reduced.

Internally a new style leather and alloy gearknob featured on XKR models, all dashboards now featured an etched leaping cat emblem on the passenger airbag door, and there were quite dramatic changes in the trim style and colour schemes. The choice now included themes first seen in the small X-type saloons of single or even dual colour options, like Heritage Tan with Warm Charcoal and Cranberry with Warm Charcoal. For the traditional finishes, Dove Grey was added to the popular Cashmere and Ivory.

The extra-cost Recaro seating. This car is also equipped with polished alloy instrument surrounds. (Nigel Thorley)

In addition there was the option of having factory-fitted Recaro sports seating trimmed in soft grain leather in a choice of three colours, plus an aluminium pack based on instrument bezel and J-gate surrounds, door release levers, pedal pads and sill tread plates (standard on XKR models). The instruments were amended on all models anyway, with a new domed style of finisher.

New accessories for all XK models at this time included an electronic compass display within the self-dimming electrochromatic interior rear view mirror and a DVD-based satnav system with additional country coverage in Spain, Portugal, Sweden and Denmark. A digitally generated analogue clock could now be displayed in the navigational screen as well. The previously discussed ACC (Adaptive Cruise Control) could now be fitted to XK8 models as well as the XKR.

Prices were increased for the 2003 model year to the following:

XK8 Coupé	£48,700	$69,995
XK8 Convertible	£55,350	$74,995
XKR Coupé	£56,700	$81,995
XKR Convertible	£63,350	$86,995

Jaguar made a slight stylistic change to all XKs a few months later when the exterior side rubbing strips were removed to clean up the line of the car.

The competition

Jaguar XK sales were still tailing off, with a total production figure of just 5656 in 2003. This was nearly 18 per cent down on the previous year and the trend looked likely to continue in 2004. Despite all the upgrades, improvements and enhancements, the XK, although still looking the part, was falling behind the competition in many ways.

For example, the Mercedes SL looked more contemporary than the XK, and Mercedes' AMG-modified SL550 showed the company's commitment to enhanced versions of standard production cars. TVR had their new T350 Coupé along with other models offering sheer grunt and an incredible presence in style and sound, if less refinement than the Jaguar. Chrysler's Crossfire had been joined by a very attractive, and much cheaper, full Convertible model, and Lexus were

2003 model year XKR Convertible in Platinum Silver with xenon headlights and 18in Hydra alloy wheels. (Nigel Thorley)

now promoting their new SC430 Convertible, a very creditable combination of legendary Lexus quality with a sporty and economical 3.2-litre V6 engine, for less money than the equivalent XK Convertible.

Some attractive proper four-seater coupés were also stealing the limelight, including the Mercedes CLK, which with its 5.0-litre V8 engine and full spec came in well below the price of a Jaguar XK8. Oh yes, and the Maserati Spyder (and Coupé) were by now much improved. And let's not forget Porsche, which was offering an incredible 15 sports cars in its range and was still the bench mark by which other manufacturers, even Jaguar, were judged. And lastly, just around the corner was the new BMW 6 Series.

Another special edition

With sales tailing off in the valued United States market Jaguar decided to broaden its appeal with another limited edition car, specifically for that market. Called the Portfolio and only available with the supercharged engine and in Convertible form, it boasted unique colour schemes and interior trim and production was limited to just 200 cars.

The unique exterior paint finishes of blue or red were echoed by matching Boxmark leather centre panels in the seating, door trims, and even the steering wheel, all in the same colours. The seats were of special Recaro design with integrated headrests. The cars were also treated to 20in Detroit R-Performance wheels and tyres as standard equipment. One hundred examples were built in Jupiter Red and the other hundred in Coronado Blue, all with a

US Portfolio special edition, this one finished in Coronado Blue. Note the lack of side rubbing strip applicable to all later XKs, and the chromed door handles, a standard feature on US models. (Nigel Thorley)

black Convertible roof. All sold in 2004 at a price of $93,995 ($6000 more than a conventional XKR Convertible).

Typical uniquely finished interior of the US Portfolio model. (Nigel Thorley)

A deeper mouth and new splitter bar at the front for the 2004/2005 XK. (Nigel Thorley)

And the new treatment for the XKR model. (Nigel Thorley)

The last chance Coupé and Convertible

Another year went by and Jaguar was experiencing unequalled growth in new car sales around the world, but this was down to the other models in the range, particularly diesels. In order to maintain that edge it needed to keep the XK competitive on the street for just a little longer. The XK therefore received yet another upgrade, this time more cosmetic than technology-based.

Building on all the changes and updates made over the years, the exterior styling came in for the most significant alterations for this last revamp. In Jaguar's own words, this was to give the car a more contemporary feel. The front got a revised nose section with a deeper mouth for the front air intake and a lower front, which gave the car a more aggressive stance. Jaguar also claimed a performance benefit, as the lower front end improved the aerodynamics. The enlarged mouth necessitated a change in the design of the 'over-riders', the chromed splitter bar and even the number plate mounting on the normally-aspirated cars, and a new mesh grille on the XKR models.

To complement the new nose, additional sill covers lowered the sides of the car to match the front and were completely flat in section, 'hiding' the previous sculpted nature of the sill shaping, while at the rear a new bumper and boot spoiler gave the car a slightly more squat appearance. Enlarged exhaust tailpipe trims were used on XK8 models, and a larger rear spoiler and quad tailpipe exhaust finishers on the XKR.

More new wheels completed the external update, with three new multi-spoke options becoming available – the 18in Aris, 19in Atlas, and 20in BBS Sepang – alongside the carryover designs from the previous update, comprising the 17in Gemini (still standard fitment on XK8 models), 18in Hydra (standard on XKRs), and 20in BBS Montreal and Detroit R-performance wheels.

The main body structure and exterior panelling remained unchanged, but the new 'treatment' certainly changed the way the car looked. There were also changes to the choice of exterior paint finishes. A solid black, Ebony, joined the existing Midnight metallic black; Quartz was an additional metallic grey; Radiance and Salza replaced Carnival red; and Ultraviolet (metallic purple) and Zircon (pale metallic blue) were further additions to the range. Black window surrounds were now used on all models, replacing the previous Dorchester grey colour.

Interior alterations

The interior was also refreshed, with the introduction of two new wood veneers. Elm – a lighter hue than the traditional burr walnut – was supposedly a more modern alternative to walnut (which was still offered), while an entirely new finish was Piano Black, a very high-gloss black provided as a no-cost option for XKR customers. The grey stained birds eye maple finish also remained available as the standard finish on all models.

An R-Performance option of aluminium surrounds for the facia instrumentation, J-gate gear selector and pedals could now be chosen for an ultra-modern appearance

Side view of the 2004/2005 XK8 Coupé, in this instance finished in Zircon Blue and sporting 18in Aris wheels. The revised shaping to the front nose section and rear bumper, along with the 'clip-on' sill covers, clearly differentiate this model from previous XKs. (Nigel Thorley)

when ordering a car new. The number of interior trim finishes was reduced, and out went the two-tone finishes described at the beginning of this chapter.

The only slightly revised exterior rear view of the later XK8. Note particularly the larger exhaust tailpipes. (Nigel Thorley)

Jaguar's later Piano Black interior treatment for XKs. (Nigel Thorley)

ASL is activated by the button that replaces the normal Cruise Control. (Nigel Thorley)

The 2004 Jaguar XK also introduced, as standard, a further key electronics feature in the form of ASL, or Automatic Speed Limiter, standard on all models. The ASL system enhances the security of drivers and passengers by preventing the car from exceeding a pre-selected maximum speed. When the driver has programmed a speed beyond which they don't wish to exceed, the Automatic Speed Limiter will constantly monitor the throttle inputs and engine speeds. Once the selected maximum speed is reached, ASL will maintain it even if the throttle pedal is depressed beyond that point.

However, to ensure absolute safety, ASL is automatically cancelled if the driver applies full kickdown via the throttle pedal and the automatic transmission. This new feature is operated by a switch on the gearshift surround and steering wheel, and has a readout display on the speedometer.

Birds eye maple veneer in an XKR with Recaro seating. (Nigel Thorley)

The speed set is shown in the speedometer in front of the driver. (Nigel Thorley)

Special option packs

Coinciding with the introduction of these latest XKs, Jaguar announced a range of what it called "value for money option packs," which were available in all markets except Japan and North America. There were three packs to choose from: separate Premium Packs for both XK8 and XKR, and a single Technology Pack for both, the object of which was to upgrade their specification significantly.

The XK8 Premium Pack comprised 18in Aris or 19in Atlas wheels; reverse park radar control; heated front windscreen; aluminium J-gate and bezel surrounds; elm wood veneer; sports seats; Xenon headlights; heated mirrors; a seat and mirror positioning memory pack; and cupholders. The XKR Premium Pack comprised 19in Atlas or 20in BBXS wheels; reverse park radar control; heated front windscreen; Recaro seats; cross-drilled brake discs; sports steering wheel and Momo gearknob; seat positioning memory pack; aluminium J-gate and bezel surrounds; Piano Black veneer (with Burr walnut veneer also optional); and cupholders. Both these packs were also available with a reduced number of items for other world markets (but still not Japan and North America). The Technology Pack comprised Adaptive Cruise Control, Premium sound system, and satellite navigation.

The 'new' XKs went on sale in March 2004 at the following prices:

XK8 Coupé	£49,920 (£49,995 from August 2005)
XK8 Convertible	£56,720 (£56,795 from August 2005)
XKR Coupé	£58,120 (£59,995 from August 2005)
XKR Convertible	£64,920 (£66,795 from August 2005)

Despite falling sales, in September 2004 Jaguar announced that it had sold its 40,000th XK in the States, its most important market. The XK was still the company's most successful sports car ever, despite its production in 2004 reaching only 4413, an all-time low. However, Jaguar stated that sales of XKs were apparently 30 per cent up on the same period in 2003, which proves that the 'new' models must have had some effect overall.

Introducing carbon fibre

Jaguar was by now quite used to presenting special edition XKs, and late in 2004 another was to appear, this time – initially, at least – exclusively for the UK: the Carbon Fibre car. Just 100 were produced, marketed as the most well-equipped XK to date. Based on the XKR

and available in either Coupé or Convertible form, this special edition even got a unique and comprehensive full colour brochure of its own, complete with a mock carbon fibre sleeve. The 100 lucky buyers not only got a unique, extremely well-equipped car but also got a short-break holiday in either Scotland or Dartmoor, paid for by Jaguar.

It is easier to list what Carbon Fibre models did *not* include as standard features, but items it did come with included, for example, an integrated compass in the rear view mirror, a dual band telephone, a first aid kit and a warning triangle. Buyers could choose any colour they liked from the existing XK range and the same for trim, but – obviously, to match the name of the model – all came with a carbon fibre finished dashboard instead of conventional veneer. What price such opulence? £64,650 for the Coupé and £71,450 for the Convertible, or in the latter case over £4500 more than an equivalent 'standard' XKR Convertible.

As it turned out another 200 Carbon Fibre cars were subsequently produced and sold into the US market to commemorate Trans-Am racing successes (see later). Slightly different to the UK car, the owners didn't get the option of a weekend break and the seats were fitted with Alcantara inserts and matching door panels.

2005 V for Victory and S for Superb

At the NAIAS Motor show in Detroit on 10 January 2005, Jaguar unveiled their stunning new sports car concept, the ALC (Advanced Lightweight Coupé), a car that would form the basis of the replacement for the XK8 and XKR, due to be phased out of production that year. This was followed by the announcement at the Geneva Motor Show in March of a European Special Edition XK called the 4.2 S, available in both Coupé and Convertible form with upgrades; and the announcement at the Los Angeles Auto Show in June of the Victory special edition for the US market, supposedly built to celebrate the four Trans-Am championship wins by Rocketsports, who campaigned XKRs.

STILL HALE

The Jaguar XK was still in the running as far as many were concerned, despite being eight years old at the end of 2004, when the Spanish car magazine *Sabre Ruedas* voted the XKR Convertible the best Convertible of the Year. A jury of 15 automotive experts called it 'a true milestone in automotive design'.

Carbon Fibre by name, carbon fibre by trim – the telltale of one of these special edition cars is the unique dash treatment. (Nigel Thorley)

Available in both XK8 and XKR variants, the Victory had quite a production run, 1050 cars being manufactured in Coupé and Convertible form. Though it was actually no more than a rebadged 4.2 S, it constituted the last XK model prior to the latter's deletion from the Jaguar range. The only differences

Victory and S models shown in two of their special colour schemes – Satin Silver and Bay Blue. (Nigel Thorley)

between the Victory and the 4.2 S are the Victory badges and insignia on its sill tread plates: all the other information given below applies to both models.

Mechanically these cars were standard, up to the latest specification announced the previous year. Externally they are identifiable by the revised badging on the boot and the growler badges incorporating a chequered flag emblem. Standard wheel fit was the 19in Atlas for the XK8 (the largest standard fit wheels ever offered on an XK8) and 20in split-rim BBS Perseus for the XKR. Although buyers could specify any of the existing Jaguar exterior paint finishes for the 4.2 S, four unique colour schemes were also offered – Copper

Black Metallic, Front Blue Metallic, Bay Blue Metallic, and Satin Silver Metallic. Darkened rear light clusters were fitted to all models.

Internally, upon opening the doors the first recognisable change came with the sill tread plate

Last of the line, in this case a 4.2 S model with Elm wood veneer. (Nigel Thorley)

US Victory model with carbon fibre dash. (Nigel Thorley)

Final badging style, which applied to both the 4.2 S and Victory models. (Nigel Thorley)

Detail carpet treatment for the 4.2 S and Victory models. (Nigel Thorley)

design, highly polished with the chequered flag emblem either side of the model identification. Dash and allied trim areas were finished in Elm on the XK8 or Carbon Fibre on the XKR (with the no extra cost option of Elm), in both cases with alloy edging to the instruments as

standard. As well as the standard range of interior trim finishes a new Dove carpet colour was provided for the 4.2 S, with standard fit 'Jaguar' embossed leather edged over-carpets.

Soft grain leather seating was used on all these cars and other, normally extra-cost fitments – like power fold-back mirrors, headlamp power-wash,

US Victory model in Copper Black with chromed alloys. (Nigel Thorley)

New badging for the final European models. (Nigel Thorley)

heated front windscreen, rain-sensing wipers, heated seats, Xenon headlamps and Bluetooth connectivity – were standard on both the XK8 and XKR versions. A 320 watt, eight-speaker Premium sound system was also standard equipment. Prices for the XK 4.2 S models were:

XK8 Coupé	£50,477
XK8 Convertible	£57,995
XKR Coupé	£59,995
XKR Convertible	£66,795

So lavish was the price and specification for these cars that Jaguar produced a very attractive and unique hardbound brochure for the car, as a fitting tribute to what would be the last XK8 and XKR produced.

Closing comments

Howard Walker from the States passed the following comments in *Jaguar World Monthly* magazine leading up to the demise of the XK. He said: "I've just been driving one of the last-of-the-last XKR Convertibles and I'd forgotten just how drop-dead gorgeous, just how sensuous-like-Catherine-Zeta the thing is ... And to my eyes the car still looks as sexy as hell ... See

Last variant of the XK8, the 4.2 S in Convertible form finished in Zircon Blue. (Nigel Thorley)

The very last XK off the line, an XKR 4.2 S, now part of the Jaguar Daimler Heritage Trust collection of vehicles. (Nigel Thorley)

one cruising the boulevards of Beverly Hills and it will still turn heads. The last XKR to me will always be the coolest cat around."

Final US prices for the XK models as they finished production were:

XK8 Coupé	$70,495
XK8 Convertible	$75,495
XKR Coupé	$81,995
XKR Convertible	$86,995

These prices exclude the USA's usual $1000 Gas Guzzler tax.

The very last XK rolled off the production lines at Jaguar's Browns Lane factory on Friday 27 May 2005, the last Coupé being handed over to the Jaguar Daimler Heritage Trust. Final production figures for the XK were:

XK8 Coupé	19,748
XK8 Convertible	46,760
XKR Coupé	9661
XKR Convertible	13,895
Total	90,064

Chapter **Eight**

Buying an XK8

If you are considering the purchase of one of these 1996 to 2005 XK models, reading this book will give you a good grounding in the background and development of the model. You can compare specifications, the changes that took place over the ten years of production, and even check out aspects of maintenance and modification, but you need more. In this chapter I plan to give you guidelines regarding what to look for in these cars, but before we go further, we should emphasise general pointers to set the scene which can also be referred to in relation to the later New XK models, featured in this book.

Decide on your budget

This is an important issue and will help you narrow the field when looking for a suitable car. There are ample used-car price guides around, which you should study at the time you intend to purchase. This will help you target a particular range of model years or even the type of car.

For ultimate value, an early XK8 Coupé with 17in Revolver wheels and few additional goodies can make an ideal entry into XK ownership. This example is finished in Carnival Red with Oatmeal Classic interior. (Nigel Thorley)

If an X-150 is more to your liking and budget, an early Coupe in Liquid Silver with 20" wheels can now make a very attractive buy. (Nigel Thorley)

When budgeting do not just ascertain what you are willing to spend on your acquisition: go a little further and think about the on-the-road costs. Your age and driving experience will dictate insurance premiums, but you should consider the number of miles you intend to cover a year and not only the general maintenance costs, such as the normal 10,000/15,000-mile interval

Accumulated dirt and moisture can cause corrosion between the floorpan and reinforcing plates, leading to swelling and eventually cracking as shown here. If the cracking becomes severe, the work involved in rectification is intensive because of the removal of all the interior trim. (Nigel Thorley)

servicing, but also, probably, unplanned major repairs, or even the cost of replacing a set of tyres – all of which can turn out to be somewhat daunting to the uninitiated.

Jaguars are expensive cars when new and therefore deserve good, regular maintenance. Normal service intervals are not extravagantly pricey, particularly if you use a Jaguar independent specialist as opposed to a franchised dealership, but check out the service schedule data in Appendix D and you will see that at various intervals these services increase both in man-hours and the work required, which will increase the maintenance costs considerably.

The choice of car

As these first generation cars were only in production for less than ten years, the choice is quite restricted. Once you decide on a Convertible or Coupé, normally-aspirated XK8 or supercharged XKR, your field is significantly narrowed. The same applies to the later New XK models.

Coupés will always come cheaper than equivalent Convertibles, since the latter are very popular (particularly, surprisingly, in the UK). XK8s will also always be cheaper than equivalent supercharged models, so this choice is purely down to you and what you want from the vehicle.

For normal everyday driving performance (and economy), the normally-aspirated XK8 is perfectly adequate, and you could save a lot of money by opting for this choice. If you want extra performance, 'kick-in-the-back' enjoyment and cachet, and don't mind the slight drawback in economy terms and refinement, then you must go with your heart and choose an XKR.

Similarly, the choice between Convertible and Coupé is down to personal preference. Arguably one could say

A medium mileage, seven-year-old XK8 that had been supposedly well wax-protected – but peeling back the front wheelarch inner panel reveals the start of corrosion! (Nigel Thorley)

Removing the panel will reveal this, looking back towards the cockpit of the car from the nearside front wheelarch (right-hand drive car). Look at the number of places where damp can fester and eventually cause corrosion if not protected. (Nigel Thorley)

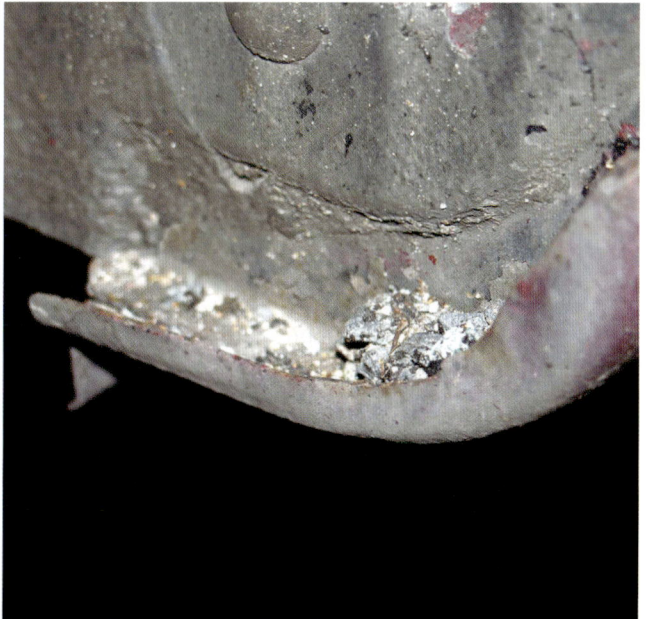

The rear sill lip could almost have been designed to collect debris, which will eventually cause corrosion. It is a simple matter to keep it clean and dry. (Nigel Thorley)

The unsightly weld mark along the visible face of the sill can cause problems if the paint cracks like this. (Nigel Thorley)

the Coupé looks the more attractive in exterior style, has marginally better visibility and is less vulnerable than the Convertible, but on a warm summer's day, on an open country road, what could be nicer than to drive around in a superbly smooth XK with the top down?

This also applies to interior finish. The Classic trim with conventional walnut veneer is always a good seller, whereas the earlier Sports style with dark stained maple and high contrast trim finishers is never as popular, so this may dictate a price difference. Likewise, many will prefer the more contemporary alloy finishes to traditional woods in the New XK range. Specification too will play its part in the price you pay.

For example, a car equipped with the Premium sound system and cruise control is going to cost more than one without. Compare the specifications in this book to identify what was and wasn't standard on these models over the ten years. In some cases the aftermarket cost of fitting an extra is prohibitive – items like cruise control should not be considered a viable option for retro-fitting, for example.

I will cover many of the service aspects and known problems with XKs in the next chapter, and some of these should be borne in mind when buying. A service history is essential, though these days that doesn't necessarily have to have been with a Jaguar franchised dealership, as long as you have good solid evidence of the work being regularly done by someone who knows the model well.

SPECIFICS – 1996 to 2005 models

Body and trim

XK bodies were well protected, but bear in mind that the earliest cars date from 1996 and without regular attention may well have suffered from corrosion somewhere. The XJS-based floorpan can be particularly vulnerable if damaged in any way – it has been known to crack due to swelling caused by corrosion between the floorpan and reinforcing plates. Areas around the joins between the floorpan and the sills can also cause problems. Removing the rubberised inner wheelarch panels from the front will reveal areas that, although originally painted, are prone to ingress of dirt and mud, and corrosion will eventually start here too: these areas are best treated regularly with a wax protective substance.

Whilst looking underneath the car, see if the nose or front crossmember or even the radiator may have been damaged by speed bumps. Another important area to check is the rear edge of the sill, where it folds under to join the floorpan in the inner wheelarch area and forms a curved lip which will naturally gather dust and

Although dealers don't recommend the steam cleaning of engine compartments these days because of the level of electronics used, there is no reason that an engine and ancillaries should not look presentable and clean. Note the semi-matt finish to the suspension turrets at either side of the engine bay signifying the original paint finish on these cars, not to the same high standard as the exterior panels. (Nigel Thorley)

debris thrown up from the rear wheels. This debris in turn collects water and eventually corrosion will start. Cleaning out this area regularly and treating it with wax will prevent long-term damage.

Still looking at the sill area, halfway along (below the door aperture) there is a welded join which can stress, eventually leading to cracking in the paint, particularly on Convertibles. This should be checked and if identified cleaned back to metal and repainted.

Typically, as with any other car, debris can build up in the lips of the wheelarches, so look for this and for rust bubbles appearing where damp has begun to eat into the paintwork. The rear wheelarches themselves are vulnerable, as they carry no protective rubberised panels like the front. Painted black from the factory, this 'ordinary' paint wears off over time revealing little beneath except the scantily-applied body colour.

Paintwork generally is very good on these cars. You may notice a slight difference in the colour between the plastic nose section and the metal bonnet – this is normal, but if excessive can mean that one or the other has been repainted. This may not be an issue, as all XKs will at some time suffer from pebble rash across the bonnet caused by debris thrown up from the road or other vehicles skimming across it. This is normal and can only be rectified by stripping the bonnet back to bare metal and respraying. Because of the curved nature of the front and rear and the vulnerability of the bumper and nose facings, look for previous or current damage or even badly stone-chipped lights, all of which can be expensive to repair or replace.

As with all modern cars, the factory painting of Jaguars is carried out in a very different manner than it was years ago. This means that the outer panels are well finished whilst the inner faces may not be finished with a topcoat at all. Interior panels such as the interior of the bonnet or inner wings being nicely gloss finished will therefore indicate a repair/repaint at some time.

Paint chips can also be a problem on the screen surround, a grey painted affair on most models. This seems to collect chips and marks which easily fester into corrosion. It is actually more cost effective to replace the surround rather than to remove it, repaint it and refit it – another, although small, cost to consider when buying.

All XKs were equipped with alloy wheels (see Appendix C), but what was supplied originally may not necessarily be on the car now; changing or updating the wheels is normal practice and is no detriment to the car providing the correct type and style of wheel is fitted

Check the condition of tyres and wheels and ensure the correct size is on the correct wheel. It is not unknown for front wheels (narrower on most XKs) to be fitted at the rear! The condition of split-rim alloys is particularly important, as they tend to be more vulnerable to kerb damage and more costly to repair. Nigel Thorley)

to Jaguar specification. You should particularly beware aftermarket non-Jaguar wheels.

All alloy wheels deteriorate over time either because of minor corrosion from the hot dust off the brake pads or by damage from kerbing. This is particularly important with the larger split-rim R-Performance wheels, as these are very expensive to replace; repair being a limited option dependent on the amount of damage. All alloys can be refurbished professionally these days but this is another cost to consider when buying one of these cars.

Similarly, look at the tyres. The majority of XKs were fitted with Pirelli or, latterly, Continental tyres. Other tyres can be fitted, of course, provided they fall within the guidelines of size and profile for the car and wheel used. Uneven wear on the tread will give an indication of poor driving, wear in the steering/suspension of the car, or just lack of regular attention to tyre pressures – all signs of a poorly maintained vehicle. Again, tyres don't come cheap with any XK model.

Finally on tyres, remember that the larger wheels

Modena Yellow may not be everyone's idea of an XK colour, but it is not unusual to find XKs in unique colour schemes chosen to suit the original owners. (Nigel Thorley)

(18in and above) normally have asymmetric tyres fitted, which means you must ensure that the direction of rotation as marked on the tyre wall is followed. Check this out, because if they are incorrectly fitted not only will they be unsafe to drive on at speed, but they will also contravene current legislation.

Lastly, the exterior colour scheme should be mentioned (the full range is given in Appendix E). The specific colour chosen by the original purchaser may not be ideal for second and subsequent owners, and this can affect the price, as contemporary fashion plays a major role in the choice of cars and colour schemes. For example, a white XK used to curry little favour in the UK, but was extremely popular in the States and hot countries like South Africa. These days, white is back in fashion in the UK. Black was a fashion colour, particularly popular in the London and Home Counties area of the UK, yet not popular at all in the

North of England. Statement colours like Aquamarine are niche market for many, and more mundane finishes like Topaz appear not to be suited to the secondhand market for older XKs. Greens are still considered an unlucky colour by many, but most blues are very popular, as is silver these days.

When examining an impending purchase, check that there are two sets of keys and key fobs. If not, keys are very expensive to replace, and if one of the fobs doesn't activate the locking and arming system it could be that there is no battery in it. If one of these batteries has to be changed, it must be done within a ten-minute period, otherwise the vital link is lost and it can be very expensive to get reprogrammed.

Interior trim

Internally, these cars wear well. The first area to check is the seat facings. Always leather (though some Sport cars have a cloth inset), the driver's seat will say a lot about how the car has been used or abused. Seat coverings are not cheap to repair or replace these days unless you buy a secondhand set from an accident-damaged car (some are available). Many XKs featured lighter-coloured upholstery, which shows marks and stains more than darker colours.

Similarly carpets will damage, particularly on the driver's side, from constant use. Overmats were always available, so if they were not used it is another sign of lack of care by a previous owner.

The woodwork does not suffer too much, although the veneer can sometimes start to split, particularly around the instruments. This is not normally due to bad ownership but merely to the passage of time. You can buy complete wood sets for these cars either direct from Jaguar or from other sources, but this is again another area of cost to consider when buying.

The hood on Convertible models should be checked. With constant use the external covering will scar whilst the interior headlining will stain and mark easily. Regular cleaning should rectify this sort of thing. On the mechanical side mention is made in another chapter about the gelling of the hydraulic fluid used in the earlier models, which will either slow down or prevent the function of the hood mechanism. If this is the case when you check out a car, you should certainly demand that it is rectified before you buy.

Electrics

The electrics are far more long-lived than on previous Jaguars, but when looking to buy a car check that everything works, and correctly – though it may not necessarily be the item that doesn't work properly that is at fault: with modern multiplexing the source of a problem could lie anywhere within the car's electrical system and might require specialist advice to put right.

Normal problem areas relate to indicators double-flashing, instrument bulb failures, seat mechanism failures, electric window lift settings, and the multi-function steering column stalks becoming unable to adjust the onboard computer readouts. Only the last is a bit expensive as it usually entails replacing the speedometer instrument pack.

The headlamps are renowned for collecting and holding condensation. A dealer 'fix' has been to drill a very small hole in the rear side of the lamp unit and plug it with a vented grommet.

Mechanicals

The first major concern affects the pre-2000 model year cars carrying specific VIN numbers (see Chapter Nine for full information). The earlier engines used a Nikasil cylinder bore lining which has been known to degrade,

eventually leading to total loss of compression and the need for a new engine. If buying a car equipped thus, you should carry out certain checks:

1. Is it still the original engine as identified on the registration document (which can be checked with a Jaguar dealership)?
2. If so, has the car recently had a blow-by test to check the engine compression?
3. If it is a replacement engine, does it have the correct identification tag (see next chapter and the picture below), or can you see that the engine block is painted grey?

If the answer to question 1 is yes, and even if it has had a blow-by test, it is reasonable to ask that such a test be carried out again, with written documentation to prove the figures, even if you agree to pay the small cost involved if the test results are satisfactory. Again, see the next chapter for further information on what the blow-by test should indicate.

If it is claimed that the engine is a Jaguar direct replacement, it may have lost its tag or the colour of the block may be difficult to determine – in which case you should enquire about proof in the form of an invoice, or details about the Jaguar dealership that carried out the change. Again, if this is not forthcoming then a blow-by test should be carried out.

The correct replacement engine tag fitted by Jaguar if an engine has been changed. The tags sometimes go missing, and even the colour of the engine block won't always help, so paperwork is vital if buying a car with a supposed engine change. (Nigel Thorley)

As a general rule the car should start easily first time, hot or cold, and run evenly and supply good performance without hesitation. If any of these characteristics don't apply to a car you are testing, then further investigation should be carried out before purchasing.

Similarly, listen for rattles from the engine, particularly on start-up, which could be attributable to a failing timing chain tensioner, another common problem with these engines and covered in the next chapter. Also, check that the cooling system is in good condition and that there are no acrid smells of coolant or signs of leaking (the water pumps are prone to disintegrating). Rattles from underneath at the rear on earlier cars nearly always relate to handbrake cables, easy to rectify but annoying to hear.

A good solid service history should relieve a lot of concerns, and it is worth checking with previous owners or the appropriate Jaguar dealership about a car's past history before you part with your money. Concerning mileage, it is still generally considered that a low-mileage car is best for the obvious reason that it has had less wear and tear, but with today's highly sophisticated vehicles this is not necessarily the case. A high-mileage car, in constant use, can provide superb transport for many miles without trouble. The longer an XK remains unused, the more likely there are to be minor, and in some cases major, problems through flat batteries (which on being recharged bring up more major issues), tyres going 'square' through the constant weight standing on one area, corroded brake discs through lack of use, etc, etc. A higher mileage car, with a good service history, can often be a much better buy and, of course, will cost less than a very low-mileage example. Worth thinking about!

Many early cars suffered from a worn bush in the throttle housing caused by the cable being dislodged and causing unnecessary wear. A factory 'fix' was to fit a cable tie, and by now this should have been carried out on all cars.

Then there is the issue of the timing chain tensioners, which can often be heard on earlier cars as a slight rattle on start-up (not always the case, though). It is a good idea to establish if the top tensioner has been changed, which should be substantiated by an appropriate invoice for the work.

Look for irregular tyre wear too, particularly at the front which could be indicative of worn ball joints, a very common fault on these cars which can result in other major repair work. It is also usual for the steering to be knocked out of track more easily than with other cars. This can be determined by the feel of the steering (it will pull to one side) and, of course, by uneven tyre wear.

Bushes and shock absorbers will cause the most common problems with regular use – all easily dealt with, although you should bear in mind that if the car is equipped with CATS suspension then special and expensive shock absorbers are the order of the day.

In conclusion

There are always plenty of cars for sale. Have a clear idea of what you are looking for, let your budget dictate, learn as much about the car(s) as you can, take expert advice, and take your time.

Chapter Nine

Owning, running and caring for your 1996-2005 XK8/XKR

An overview

Although the technology in most earlier Jaguar models can be attributed to conventional engineering, electrical practice and construction, things started to change dramatically for the company after the Ford takeover. The X-300 saloons (1994 to 1997) saw the introduction of new technology and improved build quality, and when the AJ-V8-engined cars came along they had a major impact and caused somewhat of a technological revolution.

The V8-engined cars are therefore very different to previous models in virtually all areas. For example, there is very little component interchangeability between the XK8 and any previous Jaguar models except for the floorpan (carried over from the XJS). Front suspension, steering, etc. are all very different, although the rear axle and handbrake mechanism owe their origins to the XJ40 saloon introduced in 1986. The first generation XK8/XKRs are therefore a product of the technology from the 1990s, much better in many respects but nevertheless built to price, lightness and ease of replacement parts, and not so much for repair.

The concept of construction has also changed dramatically since the early 1990s. Safety issues relating to impacts and emissions controls, etc. have all played their part in forcing Jaguar, like other car manufacturers, down a route which complicates matters for enthusiasts wishing to work on these cars. Certain equipment areas are now compartmentalised for safety – for example, the vacuum brake servo booster, the reservoir plus appropriate ECU, the relays, etc. are all housed within plastic cases with covers. These make the engine bay look cleaner but inevitably mean more work at repair time.

One of the first things that XK enthusiasts must realise, therefore, is that these are not the easiest vehicles for a DIY mechanic to work on. Whilst servicing and some other maintenance work is quite possible, other, more involved work is not only very complex but awkward, requiring specialist tools which, by virtue of cost, don't make it viable for the average home-maintenance mechanic to buy them on the rare occasions they may be needed. The factory equivalent of workshop manuals don't exist for XK models, and although the Jaguar Daimler Heritage Trust now offers CDs of parts and service supplementary information, this material is rather scant and, at the time of writing, covers only the earlier models.

Alternatively there is the Jaguar Global Technical Reference website at www.jaguartechinfo.com, a subscription website which is quite comprehensive

SAFETY ISSUES

Before commencing any work on a car, certain measures should be taken to ensure maximum safety:

- Never work underneath a car supported only on jacks.
- If working underneath, ensure the car is located on solid level ground and supported on sufficiently strong axle stands situated in the correct positions under the vehicle.
- If only raising part of the car, ensure that the wheels still on the ground are secured by chocks.
- Only use equipment suitable for working on a specialist and heavy car like the XK.
- When carrying out any electrical work, disconnect the battery earth terminal in the boot.
- Wear effective clothing that is both safe for you and unlikely to cause damage to the vehicle.

and includes technical information on the XK range. Service schedules, instructions and other worthwhile information can be found there.

Engines

Modern technology and construction methods, however, have their advantages. The engines are very

Examples of early (1996) and late (2005) XK8 engine bays, the latter, of course, of 4.2-litre capacity. (Nigel Thorley)

compact, making for ease of access. Even fitting a supercharger on XKR models does not hinder access too much, and indeed, the R engines are essentially the same as the normally-aspirated versions in so many ways that one should not be afraid of buying an XKR just because it 'appears' more complex. The engines are designed and assembled well, but some of the execution is probably not as good as with earlier, more basic units.

These well thought-out engines are built to facilitate economy and weight-saving, so in construction the lower section is actually a complete cross-cast web, milled to form the main bearing housing. This entire 'web' bolts to the underside of the cylinder block, like prewar cars with a separate crankcase, blocks and heads. Items such as the valves and springs are lighter and a fraction of the size of traditional engines of similar capacity, so engines rev higher pushing less weight around which means more power.

Extensive use is also made of plastic components, which have strengths and weaknesses. Very light and easy to mould into weird and wonderful shapes, they are economic to produce and fit and are better insulators against noise. Even items like the inlet manifolds are plastic. On the downside, the longevity of plastic parts has sometimes been called into question, particularly as regards regular wear in items like timing chain tensioners, or where plastic covers and parts have to be frequently removed and replaced.

The interchangeability of V8 engines in later life is fraught with problems. If you need a replacement it is vital you get hold of the exact type of engine for the exact XK model. It isn't, for example, easily possible to fit an S-type 4.0-litre unit to an XK8, or even to fit an XK8 engine not built to accept an oil cooler into a car that has one. Even items like the sump changed according to model application.

Modern engines are also full of electronic equipment and sensors. The days of the simple distributor and HT leads has long gone. Instead, AJ-V8s have eight individual ignition coils, one above each sparkplug; there is no distributor and all ignition mapping is done through ECU inputs. This is where the sensors come in, such as the Crankshaft Speed Sensor (assessing engine speed), the Camshaft Position Sensor (at the back – some have two), the Knock Sensors (one per cylinder bank), the Engine Coolant Sensor, the Air Temperature Sensor, and the various other emissions control components, dependent on which world market the car was originally built for.

Items like the throttle body assembly are also to some extent over-engineered and very complex compared to previous models and require care when handling or attempting to work on them. Then there are the exhaust systems, gases passing through catalysts in the downpipe assemblies with one or more oxygen sensors – and so it goes on.

Regarding the supercharged engines, again the whole design and installation has been very well thought out and engineered, so these shouldn't frighten anyone. Jaguar chose the gear type of supercharger, essentially a gear pump, rotating one set via the engine which in turn drives another set, all of which are superbly machined. The system works by forcing air into the engine, compressing it and giving it greater density and therefore greater mass. Put very simply, a greater mass of air forced into the engine allows for more fuel to be injected and therefore a bigger 'bang' is created, so the car goes faster. The air becomes exceptionally hot so intercoolers (one per inlet manifold) are there to cool it – so hot, in fact, that it relies on the engine coolant itself to keep the air 'cool'. Finally there is one electric water pump pumping coolant around the intercooler circuit. It sounds complicated but it is, in fact, a very simple principle that has been used many times before in motoring history and is a very reliable way of extracting more power from the engine.

It must be pointed out that the compression ratio for the supercharged engines is much lower than a normally-aspirated unit, which again means that you can't replace an R engine with an 8 unit, or vice versa.

There are also a couple of strategically vital issues concerning the longevity of the earlier V8 engines fitted to both XK8 and XKR cars, so important that they are featured separately and in detail here.

Nikasil engine linings

As the new AJ-V8 engines were built for lightness, a new Nikasil (nickel silicon carbide) coating was used instead of conventional cylinder bore sleeves in order to save weight. BMW had experienced some problems with this type of lining earlier, but Jaguar felt that with its new-technology engines with fast warm-up times similar problems would not apply. Also, they had not experienced problems during the extensive testing of V8 engines in the XK8 prior to launch.

However, it later became evident that the Nikasil lining could degrade, which was primarily put down to the use of high levels of sulphur in the fuel. In these circumstances sulphur is converted into a corrosive

substance during the combustion process, which then causes erosion to the bore lining. Jaguar then identified that the problem was only associated with the UK market (although cases have since been recorded elsewhere), and even within the UK there were 'hot-spots' which led to worse problems than elsewhere. But of course, the movement of cars through different owners and countries cancels the geographical aspect out somewhat.

Since January 2000 the sulphur content in fuels has been eliminated, but the problem nevertheless still crops up in earlier engines after a time. It can also be aggravated by the type of use the engine is subjected to. For example, a very high mileage example, driven for consistently long periods, is a less likely candidate for problems than a car that merely covers a minimal mileage (mainly on a cold engine).

The symptoms relating to this problem show in poor cold-starting and/or a general lack of performance, both of which can be attributed to low compression, a sure sign that the bores are worn. The ultimate test is to have a blow-by (airflow) test done by a specialist, who can determine and then compare the degree of engine breathing with the factory standard. Connecting an airflow meter to a warm engine determines the flow in litres per minute, the upper limit being 40 litres per minute; at this level or above it is considered best to change the engine, although in practical terms any figure above about 30 litres per minute should give cause for concern. In the region of 9 to 19 litres per minute is about normal for a good condition AJ-V8.

A very quick point of reference which can also highlight the incidence of premature bore wear is to remove the air filter assembly, and if this is found to contain oil then this can be attributed to the same problem.

Many early cars have already had replacement service-reconditioned engines fitted by Jaguar, and all post-2000 engines have conventional cast iron cylinder liners so this problem can never arise again. If your car doesn't have substantiated documentation to prove the fitment of a new engine, there is usually a special tag fitted to the nearside of the engine block to identify it and, of course, if the engine is a replacement then this number should be different to that shown on the original log sheet. Lastly, all reconditioned engines from Jaguar were apparently spray-painted a grey colour, though this may be difficult to determine on an engine in situ.

There are only a few viable rebuilt AJ-V8 engines available at the time of writing, outside of the Jaguar network, so the main source of supply is still Jaguar themselves, in the form of a replacement service exchange unit via a Jaguar dealership. Or you could purchase a used engine from one of the several Jaguar specialist breakers now taking in accident-damaged cars. But remember, the correct type of engine should be fitted to each specific XK model, or you may get involved in many problems that will take a considerable amount of time, and perhaps money, to rectify.

As the cars concerned are now getting older, there are fewer opportunities to gain redress from Jaguar Cars over the cost, or part cost, of engine replacement. This depends on previous ownership, mileage, and service history, and the only way to find out is to contact the Jaguar dealership from whom the car came or by which it has been maintained.

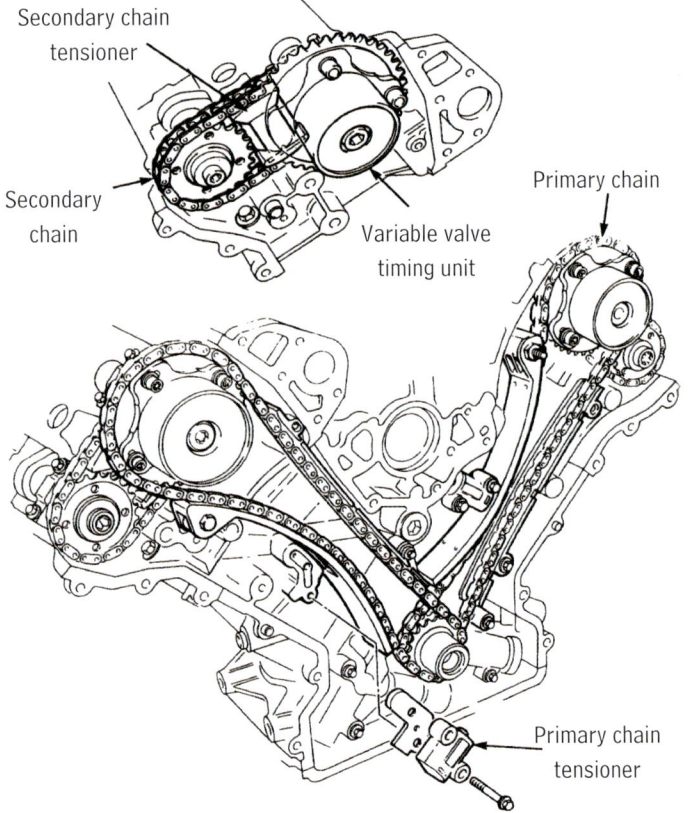

Chain and tensioner layout in the XK engine. (Nigel Thorley)

Typical example of a damaged secondary tensioner, with the covering breaking away from the metal shoe. (Nigel Thorley)

Timing chain tensioners

The engines suffer from breakage of the upper timing chain tensioners. Any cars that have received replacement engines supplied by Jaguar should already have been modified to a later style of tensioner, but probably of the plastic type. It could also be that the tensioners themselves have already been changed by a previous owner, but the only way to tell (without documented service history to support this) is to remove the cam covers and physically check.

The problem takes the form of either the main casing splitting and/or the plastic material over which the chain runs parting from the metal shoe itself. To make matters worse, as the plastic parts from the metal the shoe will break up. This will immediately cause the piston to extend further from the cylinder, so creating more side loading onto the housing body and increasing the propensity and speed at which it will crack. If the plastic comes away from the shoe the chain will run in the metal backing, and if allowed to continue the tensioners can break up completely, with disastrous results – the chain becomes jammed and breaks, at worst rendering the engine uneconomical to repair.

To add further complications there are also lower timing chain tensioners and plastic dampers which are far more inaccessible. These, however, tend to be more reliable, particularly as the chain does not ride directly over the lower tensioner. However, failure of these lower tensioners will create a pronounced rattling noise from the engine and when this occurs these tensioners must be replaced, as breakage of the chain is possible.

This is a much more involved job with obvious financial implications.

The only way to check the condition of these is by removing the camshaft covers, when the upper tensioners become easily visible. The lower ones require the use of a slimline torch to illuminate them from above. Generally speaking, if the primary chains (tensioned by the lower tensioners) are taut on both the tight and slack sides, the lower tensioners can be considered to be good, assuming there are no visible signs of mechanical damage.

It is possible to change the upper timing chain tensioners without removing any of the chains at all, which means that the job is a relatively inexpensive affair, consuming typically two to three hours of labour plus the cost of two new tensioners, plus a set of cam cover gaskets and seals. However, if the lower tensioners are also to be changed it becomes more than a full day's work, and including parts the cost will be considerably more.

Even though the secondary chains may be running on the metal of the upper timing chain tensioners, if after careful examination the chains appear to be alright, it is acceptable to merely change the tensioners. However, if the chains have become damaged – exhibited by a wearing of the surface of the chain where it meets the metal of the tensioner – it is possible (with the correct tools) to split and remove the damaged chain and replace it with a split-link unit. This negates the need to remove the primary chain and the obvious costs associated with such work.

If engine rattle is noticed on start-up, or there is resonance throughout certain speed bands, it is prudent to consider having the lower tensioners checked. It isn't

The various types of timing chain tensioner used on the V8 engines. The two at the top – both of which are damaged in some way – are examples of the original type fitted by Jaguar. The third is the first generation replacement, which was stronger and incorporated a useful clip-pull to release the spring when fitted. At the bottom is the very latest type, made of metal, which is likely to prove a better option all round for longevity. (Nigel Thorley)

Alternatively the tensioner main casing may split like this. (Nigel Thorley)

that difficult to do this work at home although some special tools are required (camshaft position setting tool, sprocket retaining tool, suitable short Allen key socket with an appropriately slimline torque wrench (reading up to 125Nm), plus a quality socket set), and when fitting the replacement tensioners it is important to realise that they are different for each side of the engine – if you fit the wrong tensioner to the wrong side, the engine will be damaged.

The work involves the removal of the electrical coils, air filter box, coolant expansion tank, and camshaft covers from both banks. With the top tensioners and timing chains in view, the engine has to be turned over by hand to a position allowing a special locking tool to be inserted over the camshafts. The exhaust camshaft sprocket is then removed, and after unbolting the tensioners they just lift free.

Tensioners have been upgraded over the years, the latest type, introduced in February 2005, being an aluminium-bodied version of the secondary (upper) tensioner. It is advised by many specialists that all engines equipped with plastic tensioners should really have them replaced with the new aluminium version as a matter of preventive maintenance.

With the cam cover off, using a long screwdriver, you can check the tension of the lower timing chain. If slack, this will need to be addressed.

In the overall scheme of things, looking after the tensioners is a moderately inexpensive job – particularly when compared to the cost of major engine repairs should a breakage occur.

The fuel system

A common occurrence with these engines relates to flooding. This is normally down to starting a car cold and moving it a very small distance before turning the engine off again. It is a problem with many modern cars and engines, and results from excess fuel in the bores flooding the engine. In many cases this can be overcome by flooring the accelerator, which informs the EMS to disable the fuel injectors momentarily so that when you crank the engine over (with the pedal depressed) the cylinders are vented and eventually the car will fire naturally. Alternatively, go to the fuse box in the boot and remove fuse No. 7, which disables the fuel pump. You can then crank the engine over at half-throttle, building up oil pressure to the point where the engine will momentarily fire for a few seconds, using

Thermostat and seal for the V8 engine. Note the bleed hole jiggle pin, which must be set to the 12 o'clock position when fitting. (Nigel Thorley)

up the fuel it has. Then, on reconnecting the fuse the engine will re-crank with the aid of a light throttle.

To avoid the problem, leave the car running for about five minutes to warm up before turning it off.

Cooling system

One of the Achilles heels of the V8 engine is the cooling system. It is actually a very efficient system, but there are some important issues with it and its construction. It could be said that modern lightweight materials let it down.

On the expansion tank there is a small Low Coolant Temperature Sensor at the bottom, so if the 'low coolant' light appears on the dashboard it is vital the level is checked immediately, because this warning doesn't come up quickly enough. The electrically controlled design of the temperature gauge provides for a midway point for 'driver comfort', so again is far from accurate. Also, by virtue of the temperature sensor's placement, some parts of the engine can get very hot whilst other areas (like the thermostat housing) can remain quite cool.

The expansion tanks bolt onto the inner wing and there are small bleed pipes that push-fit. It is not uncommon for these pipes to get caught, pulling them free, particularly as they become brittle on older engines. If detached, then again temperature readings will be affected.

Given all of this, there are two reasons for the engine to overheat: either the water pump or the thermostat will have failed. Signs to look out for (because of the inaccuracy of the warning systems) are the cooling fans staying on for long periods regardless of temperature, and/or one of the top hoses blowing off – particularly on normally-aspirated cars – causing a sudden severe loss of coolant.

The thermostat housing has water outlets made of plastic which can cause problems with hoses blowing off. The hose clips used on these cars are actually spring clips, which require a special tool to undo them. Used for ease of manufacture and because they are quicker to undo and fit, on plastic housings they tend to lose tension, causing the hoses to blow off. The housings on supercharged engines are aluminium and therefore don't necessarily present the same problems.

The thermostat is of the conventional style thermos type with its own seal supplied. The thermostat has a bleed hole (giggle pin) to allow air to purge, so it is essential that this pin is set to the 12 o'clock position when fitting into the housing.

The water pumps have plastic impellers which disintegrate over time. A quick way to check is not to take the water pump off but simply, with a cold engine, take the filler cap off from the expansion tank, then run the engine at approximately 1200rpm. If the pump is working correctly, water will be circulating quite briskly, causing a swirl of fluid from the bleed pipes back into the tank. If the pump isn't working, there will be little circulation and therefore hardly any swirl.

The water pump sits right at the front of engine below the pipes and housing. The seal beneath the bleed housing can also leak. The pump is fairly easy to change. The pulley is held in place by three 8mm bolts and it is best to undo these before de-tensioning the drivebelt, as the one holds the other in place. When removing the belt it is best to inspect it for wear. The belt on supercharged engines doesn't actually need to be de-tensioned, but if it needs to be changed it is easier to remove the fan cowl as well.

With the belt removed, use a screwdriver or bar to ease off the water pump pulley. This will give access to five 8mm headed bolts that hold the pump in place. Undoing them allows the pump to be pulled out, being simply an O-ring fit into the aperture in the cylinder block. Once removed, the remains of the impeller blades will be seen and replacement is necessary. Replacements still have plastic (but improved) impellers and come with a modified gasket and no O-ring. A new thermostat should always be fitted if changing the water pump.

Severe overheating problems with these engines can lead to major bills, and the resultant damage can be amazing. Every care should be taken to prevent overheating. For example, the heater return and feed hoses pass underneath the manifold. They cost little to purchase but can take between one and three hours to replace dependent on the model. An unexplained coolant loss can often be attributed to the failure of one of these. It is not unknown for an engine to become so hot that it will melt a breather pipe.

Whilst not a common occurrence, these engines are in later life beginning to blow head gaskets. Any signs of heavy steam from the exhausts or a slight misfire on start-up (usually when cold) must be investigated further.

It is worth noting that from about the 2001 model year different compounds of antifreeze were used. Mixing this later type with earlier antifreeze can cause the coolant to gel, with inevitable consequences.

The all-important water pump for the V8 engine, clearly showing the plastic impellers which are the cause of many overheating problems. (Nigel Thorley)

Gearboxes

The gearbox used up to 2003 in normally-aspirated cars is a ZF five-speed unit, whereas the supercharged models use a Mercedes 'box as fitted to many larger-engined Mercedes cars. Both are very smooth in operation and don't usually give any problems up to 60,000 miles. However, beyond this point they can cause problems, ultimately resulting in expensive replacement.

The ZF 'boxes have a forward clutch pack with a retaining clip that wears through the pressed steel housing and eventually falls away. The initial symptom of this is a slippage between gears. Later, after a normal journey, upon restarting and selecting drive, the box will not engage. Applying some throttle, the gear will engage and 'bite' harshly. Often reverse gear is still available. Not everything may be lost, however, as the same symptoms could be brought about by a blocked oil filter preventing oil passing through the gearbox.

The Mercedes gearbox on the R models has a problem with its output shaft assemblies and planetary sets breaking up. Early 'boxes had an alloy housing with little support, and over time the gear set started to move, the bearing eventually boring its way through the housing and dropping away, allowing the gears to lock up and break through the casing. This could also lock up the differential. So much debris is created during the wear process that the gearbox filter will clog up. This causes the gearbox to produce a whirring noise and/or slippage in some of the gears, which can be taken as an early warning of impending doom.

The gearboxes are supposedly a non-serviceable item, which means 'sealed for life'. However, you can buy – either from Jaguar or other suppliers – both gearbox sump gaskets and oil filters. Entirely new gearboxes from Jaguar can cost several thousand pounds, but many gearbox specialists now offer remanufactured units.

The normally-aspirated 'box does not have a conventional dipstick or filler plug. Instead there is a small plug on the side through which oil is injected via a syringe pump (done when the engine is cold) until it overflows. This has to be done from underneath with the car on level ground, so it can be awkward for anyone to carry out at home without a pit or ramp. Also, the oil needed is quite special (Esso LT7 1141) and expensive, although it is possible to buy exactly the same oil for less money from specialists. It is vital, however, that only this oil is used to avoid unnecessary damage to the 'box.

Whilst the supercharged gearbox does have a dipstick tube, there is no dipstick. It is supplied as a special tool to Jaguar dealerships (and any independent specialists who purchased one), and it is by the use of this that the gearbox level is ascertained.

It is strongly advised that at around 50,000 miles the oil is drained, the sump pan removed, and the filter and oil replaced along with a new sump pan gasket. This will decidedly help to prolong the life of these gearboxes, at little expense.

Bearing in mind the high cost of the major 60,000-mile service, it is a good idea to opt for the gearbox work at 50,000 miles, which will save some expenditure later. By regular servicing, however, the life expectancy of both gearboxes can be much improved.

The normally-aspirated ZF transmission has a range sensor switch, which sends signals to the engine control modules indicating what gear is selected and relates this to the ECU. These switches can be affected by water ingress creating erroneous signals that may show up on the dashboard message centre, such as 'overheating', 'gearbox failure', 'restricted performance', etc.

This is not necessarily the terminal problem the message would indicate. Often £200 spent on a new switch can cure the symptom, but initially a Jaguar dealer or good independent's diagnostic equipment will identify the source of the problem. The Mercedes gearboxes do not have a rotary switch on the gearbox. Instead a linear switch within the gear select quadrant is fitted, inside the car.

Another problem affecting the ZF gearboxes is the need to remove oil cooler pipes with threaded unions, which are made from aluminium and can easily seize, making them difficult to remove. They can shear, or it may be necessary to cut the pipe from underneath. It can take up to three hours to change these and there is the possibility of damage to the gearbox casing. Again, the Mercedes 'boxes use conventional banjo joints, so preventing the above problems.

There are no known problems at present with the very late six-speed ZF boxes.

Front suspension

The XK uses a very special aluminium subframe arrangement, different to any previous Jaguar. One of the problems here is that the steel bolts used to fit it to the car can seize in position. The XK also uses a different style of subframe mounting, with a 'V' mount at the rear and round one at the front. The former is known to split, but a set of long Torx-headed sockets is required to undo the bolts – access is difficult.

The lower wishbone arm is an integral unit with the ball joint. A new arm from Jaguar is very expensive, but they can be reconditioned. However, because of the angle at which the ball joint is pressed into the arm specialist equipment is needed to replace it. As a matter of course it is suggested that if changing the ball joints and bushes, then the front bushes should be changed at the same time.

The bushes are unique and need care in replacement. Note that there are two different part numbers, those ending with the suffix CA fit on the front lower wishbone, while those ending with BB are for the rear lower wishbone. Beware: they look exactly the same but are subtly different. The top wishbone bushes are of the slip-flex type, similar to but not interchangeable with those used on many earlier cars, such as the XJ Series.

The shock absorber and spring arrangement is also an integrated part, but uniquely the diameter of the spring is different top to bottom. There is a bush at the bottom of the shock absorber which is easily changeable when worn.

Wheel bearings at the front are very difficult to change because of the need for special tools, but their maintenance is a very important issue. When they start to deteriorate and cause excess noise they should be changed immediately. The longer the worn bearing is left the harder it will be to change, and it could ultimately lead to other more expensive repairs. You can identify a worn wheel bearing by a constant drone at the front of the car accompanied by the feel, even

The ABS rotor nut securing the hub and the special tool needed to undo it: the only means to remove it without damage. (Nigel Thorley)

This is no joke – the amount of leverage that can be required to remove the rotor nut to replace the front wheel bearing of an XK8! (Nigel Thorley)

through the steering wheel. The noise gets worse as you turn the steering, as well.

Although the wheel bearings are easy to assemble from the manufacturer's point of view, being a one-piece housing with integrated bearing, when it comes to later replacement they are difficult. Removing the wheel housing appears to be a simple matter of removing the upright, undoing the nut, removing the calliper and disc to get to the hub, and taking out the bearing. However, the bottom ball joint taper fit is very tight – extremely so – and in the worst cases has to be cut off. The ABS rotor nut has to be removed, which secures the hub through the bearing and has a series of castellations on it for the wheel speed sensor to pick up. The sensor has to be removed, which is very expensive to replace. The rotor nut also requires a special socket to undo it. This is a non-wear item, so should clean up well.

The leverage required to undo the very tightly-fitted bolt is enormous. On reassembly it is tightened to 220Nm – imagine what a few years of use, water ingress, etc, will do for the loosening torque required.

After all this the bearing has to be pressed out of its carrier – again, in principle not difficult, but some force is required, and a special cradle is helpful to secure it in position. Two special circlips hold the bearing in situ, which should always be replaced and fitted to the same orientation, that is, pointing down.

Another area to check is the power steering cooler, which fails regularly. It is not difficult to change, but on the feed side there is a high pressure union, like a bayonet fixing, which requires another special tool to separate.

Rear suspension

Though based on a design going back to the XJ40 saloons of the late 1980s, the differentials are of a different construction, and are far longer-lived and mostly trouble-free. But unlike earlier models there are complications due to the revised construction and installation of the new axle. For example, if you need to change the rear shock absorbers you have to unbolt and lower the rear suspension completely a few inches, and require a special (slim) spring compressor in order to release the shock absorber from its integrated spring. To do this necessitates undoing the rear tie bar, removing the A-frame safety plate, and unbolting the nuts holding the top plate of the shock absorber spring pan.

Then, with the spring compressed, the fulcrum pin must be removed, which can also be problematic as they seize in situ. In worst-case scenarios the bolts have to be cut off. Being difficult to access as well means you need a small angle grinder to do this work.

There is another issue relating to those cars fitted

with the CATS active suspension system. Each shock absorber has an electrical connection which goes to the main wiring loom. Over time the shock absorbers actually 'rotate' in service, which can cause these electrical connections to wind and eventually pull off, in some cases necessitating their replacement, which again means dropping the rear suspension as a complete item.

When fitting new shock absorbers, the liberal use of copper grease will prevent squeaks when back in service. The lower section of the spring terminates in a pigtail, which must seat correctly with the end of the wishbone forging. If not done correctly, the ride height is affected and the spring can dislodge when on the road.

This leads us to the issue of the A-frame bushes, which will deteriorate over time. It is vital when replacing these to 'lock' them in with a suitable adhesive or they will work loose and deform, allowing the A-frame to rest metal to metal in its mountings.

Again, safety precautions *must* be adhered to. Although a very slim coil spring compressor is needed for the rear of the XK, it is vital that it is of a substantial design fit for its purpose. (Nigel Thorley)

As mentioned in the text, removing the fulcrum pin at the rear is hampered by lack of space, particularly with a spring compressor in the way. Here a small angle grinder has to be used to cut it free. (Nigel Thorley)

Brakes

Like most modern cars, all XK8s feature all-round disc brakes, which these days are more prone to wear due to our driving habits, greater reliance on brakes, and even the harder materials used in the production brake pads. As such, the discs rarely last for more than 30,000 miles and, dependent on model, they can be expensive to replace.

Symptoms of the discs being in poor condition are a vibration through the steering wheel under braking, a juddering or pulsating through the brake pedal, or the brakes just being less effective, with greater pedal travel. An inspection of the discs with the road wheels off the car may also reveal severely corroded areas around the edge of the discs (which might be eating into the face), bad pitting on the face, and severe uneven-wear ridges, all of which dictate that the discs need changing. They should always be changed in pairs.

They are not difficult or time-consuming to change by removing the calliper body. With the old disc removed, it is important to clean up the hub so that the new disc will mate true with it when reassembled. The callipers should also be thoroughly cleaned, and always fit new pads when the discs are changed. The callipers' securing bolts should be thread-locked to ensure they don't come loose.

The handbrake cable mechanism is very much based on the XJS, and it is quite common to find them incorrectly adjusted, in the worst case leading to the

It is vital that the rear spring seats correctly with the wishbone forging. (Nigel Thorley)

cable snapping. Cheap and relatively easy to replace, this also brings up a common fault with XK8s – that the cables rattle on the road.

Only three bolts (two with important spacers you must not lose) secure the handbrake mechanism to the interior floor. To remove the old cable you also have to lift the one-piece carpeting which, for ease, necessitates undoing the seat slide on the driver's side. Good access is also required underneath the car, necessitating either a ramp, pit or heavy-duty axle stands on which to support the rear. The new cable should be fitted at the handbrake lever end first to optimise the free play inside the car, not forgetting to secure it with the retaining clip provided.

On the underside of the floorpan a large rubber grommet provides access to the location hole through which the handbrake passes into the car. Afterwards this grommet must be replaced properly to prevent ingress of water into the car.

Regular servicing

Service intervals are 10,000 miles for all engines, although the work required will vary according to which 10,000 service it is and whether it is a normally-aspirated or supercharged engine. A full schedule of servicing work is shown in Appendix D.

Most aspects of general servicing can be addressed by the average, competent DIY home mechanic, and you can buy service kits from a Jaguar dealer which provide all the items you require, including a disposable seat cover! The cost of many service components is certainly not expensive, although when it comes to items like the sparkplugs, these don't come cheap. It is more cost effective to buy a kit rather than the individual items, though you will, of course, have to buy all the fluids required as well.

A standard 10,000-mile service involves little more than oil, filter and wiper blade changes and a visual check of other things. At 30,000 miles it gets a little more costly with supercharged and early normally-aspirated engines, as they will need the sparkplugs changing later. This applies to later normally-aspirated engines at 60,000 miles. At this point other items, such as the fuel filter, need changing too, so it becomes more expensive overall.

You can tackle the order of service work in many ways so this is merely a guide. Firstly, the normal principle of jacking up the front end of the car to gain access to and drain the engine sump doesn't apply here. The 13mm sump plug is positioned right at the front of the engine facing down. Draining with the car jacked up at the front will mean that not all the oil will be removed. So you jack up the back of the car instead. Ensure that the front wheels are chocked before jacking. The rear of the car must be supported on axle stands before any work is carried out underneath.

The oil filter on the AJ-V8 engine is somewhat obscured by an alternator cooling duct, force-feeding air to keep it cool. If the car has been well maintained this duct will still be there and will need removing by undoing the bolt, to gain easy access to the filter.

While the oil is left to thoroughly drain, your attention can be switched to the rear of the car, still supported on axle stands. The A-frame supporting the rear suspension and axle is of a similar design to that used on Jaguar saloons. Check its bushes to ensure they have not degraded or collapsed. Although much longer-lived than those used on other models, they will still deteriorate over time and should be inspected at every service.

Then there is the rotoflex coupling, a rayon-reinforced rubber mounting at the gearbox end of the propshaft that reduces harmonics inside the car. This needs to be checked for distortion or cracking, as it will induce vibration or, at worst, come loose, damaging the companion flange or even the propshaft itself. If this has been changed or needs to be changed, it is vital it is fitted the correct way round, identified by an arrow cast into the rubber. This arrow dictates the direction in which the bolts should pass (back to front), and therefore the direction of fit.

The rear suspension bump stops should always be

A visual check can be carried out to ensure that the springs have not become dislodged from their seats, and by exerting pressure on the rear wings (when the car is back on the ground) you can determine the condition of the shock absorbers.

On to the rear brakes. The handbrake cross brace area is essentially the same as that used on previous saloons. The fulcrum pin is prone to seizing, but the regular and liberal use of a release agent should help. Using an impact gun to revolve it, you can check it is completely free. If it isn't or hasn't been free the handbrake shoes will remain against the drum part of the disc/drum assembly, causing overheating and,

All that is required for a standard 10,000-mile service of the Jaguar V8 engine, supplied as a 'kit' from a Jaguar dealership. (Nigel Thorley)

checked to ensure that they are firmly secured. The metal backing never comes away but the rubber will de-bond. Pull any de-bonding off if loose, or it could fly out and cause problems for other road-users. There are different types of bump stop for different models, so ensure you get the right one for your car.

The alternator cooling duct being removed to reveal the oil filter (white) above. The front of the sump-mounted oil drain plug is arrowed. (Nigel Thorley)

DISCONNECTING THE BATTERY

The battery should be disconnected before carrying out any electrical work. The battery is sited under the boot floor, access being gained by removal of the right-hand panel. The battery can be disconnected via the 10mm bolt negative earth connection. Ensure you fold the terminal firmly underneath or away from the battery so that it won't spring back at some point later on and form a connection and spark that could prove disastrous.

You also need to be aware that it is not unknown for the car doors to self-lock once the battery is reconnected, so always remove the ignition keys from the car when working on it. The boot lid also has an electronic release, from the dashboard on all models and from the boot lid plinth on later cars. So if the car does self-lock when the battery is reconnected, and then you close the boot lid, how are you going to get in if you did leave the keys in the ignition? There is a conventional keyhole within the 'XK' badge on the boot lid, but few people ever use it so the lock often corrodes inside or gets filled with debris from the road and seizes up.

As well as removing the keys from the ignition, another way to avoid locking yourself out is to 'throw' the boot latch with the aid of a screwdriver or similar so that the boot lid can't close at all until you release the lock when you have finished. Otherwise you could end up having to remove the number plate and drill the boot lid to gain access to the release mechanism!

A final point on batteries: if a battery goes flat on an XK, don't jumpstart the car from another battery on a vehicle with its engine running. This could lead to a spike in the electrical circuits that could have disastrous and expensive results somewhere. Always remove the offending battery, charge it off the car and then refit it, or just disconnect both terminal leads so it is isolated from the car while charging.

The A-frame bushes at the rear can easily be visually checked for condition. (Nigel Thorley)

The rotoflex coupling on the propshaft should always be checked when servicing these cars. (Nigel Thorley)

perhaps, de-bonding of the shoe material, which can drop into the drum. Shoes are expensive to replace.

Conventional vented discs are fitted to all XKs (unless they have had R-Performance Brembos fitted) using conventional Teves sliding callipers. Life expectancy of discs varies dramatically with driver and type of driving, but they will inevitably have been changed on even very late examples by now (see earlier comments on visual checks of discs and callipers). The subject of changed discs at the rear brings up another issue regarding effective maintenance.

There is a small access port in the drum to allow for handbrake adjustment. Time and again discs have been changed and the access hole not lined up with the adjuster, because the discs will fit in any position over the studs. As you have to slacken off the handbrake shoes to remove a disc, you need to retighten them again when the new disc is fitted, but you can't if the holes don't line up – an excellent example of possible poor maintenance.

Adjusting the handbrake from underneath the car provides an improvement over XJSs via a self-locking nut at the end of a threaded rod passing through the compensator assembly. It is important not to over-adjust as the shoes will remain on and will grab.

Another visual check at the rear should involve the exhaust system. Whilst generally long-lasting, the rear silencers are prone to corrosion on all models.

For safety, the fuel filter is these days tucked away under the floor towards the rear on the left hand side.

Inaccessible due to exhaust heat shields, it can be awkward to remove.

You can depressurise the system by running the car and pulling fuse No 7 from the boot-mounted fuse box. This de-energises the pump and the pressure will fall off. When replacing the fuel filter, it only goes on one way, shown by the arrows on the casing.

The rubbers on the rear anti-roll bar can fail, causing a 'chatter' from the back of the car. The drop links don't fail in service but the nuts and locking compounds attaching them are prone to seizure over time, and the studs can break. If you need to replace a drop link, bear in mind that they're easy to break, so it is advisable to do such a job when you can get access to new parts.

Checking the condition of the rear bump stops. (Nigel Thorley)

With the wheel removed, the rear brakes and suspension assembly can be seen. A visual check of the disc should determine its condition. The suspension bump stop and the A-frame bushes can also be easily seen and checked at this point. (Nigel Thorley)

The access port in the drum for handbrake adjustment. (Nigel Thorley)

There is no drain plug on the differential casing and even getting at the filler plug is difficult because of the anti-roll bar and strengthening bar across the axle. Ideally use a socket with a small extension bar, and the car must be level but far enough off the ground to do it. All the differentials take a new synthetic 65/90 grade oil or similar, but for top-up purposes a conventional 90 grade is alright to use.

Despite the modernity of the XK there are still four grease nipples to look after, two on each halfshaft, one on each universal joint. Often neglected (another sign of poor maintenance), access is easy and normal grease can be used. At service intervals they should be checked for play, although you should first carry out any greasing required. Also check the outer fulcrum and rear wheel bearings. It isn't possible to grease either the wheel bearings or the outer fulcrums. Life expectancy for these is quite long, usually in excess of 100,000 miles.

Checking for play should not only be done in the six o'clock and twelve o'clock positions, but also at three and nine o'clock as well. Changing the outer fulcrum is difficult as the races are awkward to get out if seriously corroded, in some cases necessitating cutting them out.

Still underneath the car, working methodically towards the front, you should also regularly check the fuel and brake lines, thoroughly wax-protecting them against corrosion. Unfortunately the modern materials used for these lines are not as long-lived as on many older vehicles, and although it is not within the normal Jaguar service schedule to carry out any waxing, it is a worthwhile task which improves longevity. The waxing should also be done in and around the brackets securing the pipes, as the lines will still corrode in such places if not protected.

All XK8 models were designed around the use of Pirelli tyres of the appropriate size, although these may have been replaced at some time by previous owners. All tyres should be checked for uneven wear, which will provide valuable information on current or previous problems with steering, ball joints or suspension issues.

As all XKs were equipped with alloy wheels the inner face mating to the hub should always be greased before fitting. The alloy wheel nuts should always be tightened with a torque wrench to 75lb ft. If the wheels are fitted too tightly, damage to the wheel nuts, the wheels, or even the locking nut (one per wheel) can occur. Whilst on the subject of wheels, these should always be checked for damage.

This is the fuel filter position underneath the XK8.
(Nigel Thorley)

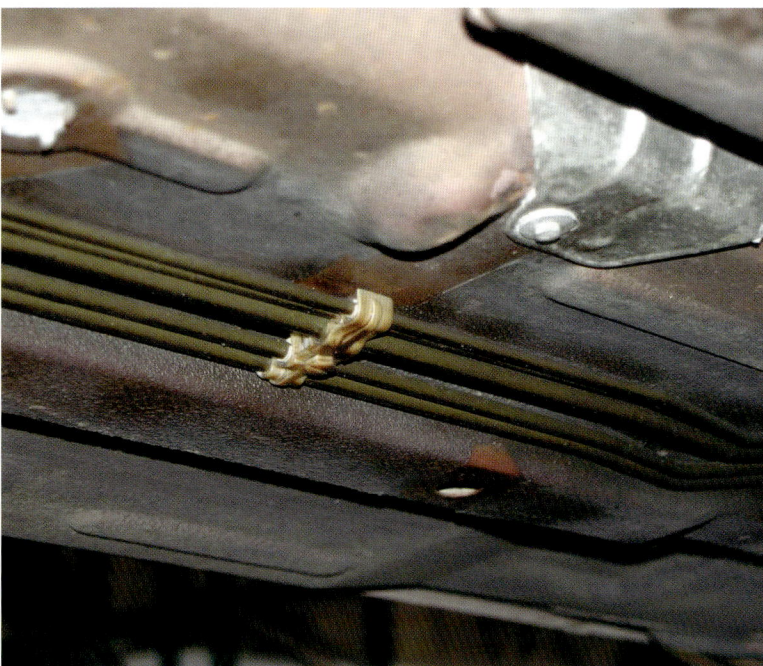

Regular checking of brake and fuel lines is important with so much salt on the roads during the winter, particularly in the UK. (Nigel Thorley)

Tyre pressures vary according to type of driving and the tyres. With Pirelli, about 32psi will normally provide a good comfortable ride. Space saver spares, where fitted, should always be maintained at a pressure of 60psi. When using a space saver a car cannot be driven at more than 50mph.

Returning to the front end, now that the oil has completely drained it is useful, in some circumstances, to consider removing the sump pan to clean out the internals. This is recommended if the oil is particularly dirty or there are indications of deposits built up inside the engine. Unlike some other Jaguar models, sump removal is not hindered by cross members or other items. You should remember to use a new gasket if doing this job, to ensure a good seal afterwards. When replacing the sump plug, before refilling the engine with oil, a new washer should always be fitted (supplied with the Jaguar service kit). The same applies to the oil filter.

When filling engines with oil use a funnel because the neck of the filler is low down and it is easy to spill oil onto one of the coil housings or a catalyst and exhaust manifold. The type of oil for a normally-aspirated V8 is a semi-synthetic 10/40 grade, and for a supercharged engine Castrol Magnatec 5/30 is recommended.

Now the rear of the car can be lowered, and the front end raised to carry out other inspections, such as the ball joints. A visual sign of their failure can be identified

Not only is it important to regularly check the condition and wear of tyres, but when replacing the alloy wheels it is important to grease the faces where they come into contact with the hubs, to prevent them 'sticking' metal to metal. (Nigel Thorley)

The correct way to check for play in the lower ball joints: with the car supported on axle stands, jack the lower wishbone until a crowbar can be used between the tyre and the ground to check for play in the ball joint. (Nigel Thorley)

by extreme inner-edge tyre wear. An important point here is to jack up the car the correct way.

Jack up the front of the car so that the wheels are just touching the ground and support it on axle stands. Place a jack under the lower suspension wishbone, as close to the wheel as possible, and jack the suspension until a crowbar or large flat screwdriver can be inserted between the ground and the tyre. Gently lever the wheel upwards and watch for any play in the ball joint between the wheel hub carrier and the lower wishbone. Any play indicates that the ball joint is worn.

Front wheel bearings are a regular area of concern with these cars and most of the time don't last beyond 30,000 miles. As mentioned earlier, special procedures are required for this work.

As with the rear, check the brake callipers for smooth operation and the discs for damage or wear. If you need to remove any callipers, they are held in place by two Allen-headed screws at the back. Undoing these and removing the spring clip at the front allows the calliper

to be withdrawn. Check the disc faces front and back for corrosion: they start to corrode on the inner edge outwards and outer edge inwards and are always worst on the inside face. These brake discs should not be skimmed and are expensive to replace.

Check the power-steering reservoir, which should always remain full. Leaks here are not common. Also check the windscreen washer reservoir, but do not spill any fluid when replenishing as it can enter wiring around this area.

These engines don't take (or use) a lot of coolant compared to older cars – about 8 litres maximum – which should always be maintained at a 50/50 mix of water to antifreeze. Replenishment is carried out via the expansion tank filler in the engine bay. Note that there are bleed plugs within the centre of the engine which must be undone to purge air from the system. Beware that around 2001 Jaguar introduced a long-life antifreeze solution, and if your car is so provided you should not mix it with other types of antifreeze, which can cause gelling of the coolant.

Radiators should be periodically drained and flushed out to remove debris, not just from the internal area but also from the core using a high-pressure water jet. It is just possible to reach the drain tap, on the right at the base of the radiator, from the top of the engine bay but access is very fiddly. Once undone, the coolant will release everywhere, causing some mess around the front valance, which will need cleaning off afterwards. It may be that the radiator will need removing from the car for closer inspection and to remove ingrained debris from the core. Whilst relatively simple on a normally-aspirated car, it is an awkward job on supercharged versions.

On to other engine components. To start with, pay particular attention to the condition of the main drivebelt at the front. The Jaguar service schedule dictates that this should be changed at 60,000-mile intervals, but for safety always check it at 40,000 miles. If it has started to crack, it must be changed immediately. A strange noise from the front of the engine can often be attributed to this belt breaking up – as the pulleys rotate, the 'missing' part of the belt creates the noise.

The belt is of a serpentine design with an extensive run, driving many different components of the engine. It takes its maximum grip over the crankshaft pulley and the highest load over the alternator. There is an additional belt on the supercharged models around the crankshaft pulley to the supercharger. This makes it more difficult to change because it passes through a narrow gap around the tensioner, so it can prove easier to remove the tensioner first.

Removing the belt involves rotating a left-hand threaded 15mm bolt towards the centre of the engine. This is done using a suitably long combination spanner, bringing the pulley into the centreline of the engine to allow the belt to be removed. There is no tension adjustment on items like the compressor or alternator, all tension being via just one tensioner.

There is no conventional distributor and coil on these engines. Instead individual coils sit underneath plastic covers, all of which need to be removed to change the sparkplugs. The covers are secured to the engine by six 7mm headed bolts. Four of these are easy to access, but two are fiddly and are sometimes missing on poorly serviced cars. You will need a good-quality ¼in drive socket set, also useful for other areas of maintenance on these cars. There are small inserts on the covers which tend to pull out with the bolts. Using a pair of mole grips, take them off the bolts and replace them in the covers to avoid losing them.

Removing the covers provides access to the four coils per bank. Disconnect the wires (quite idiot-proof as the wiring loom is a tailored fit). The coils are held

This main drivebelt is breaking up badly with part of the inside core now disappearing. (Nigel Thorley)

The main drivebelt is easily removable by rotating this tensioner counter-clockwise via this 15mm bolt. (Nigel Thorley)

The inserts in the engine covers tend to come away and get lost. (Nigel Thorley)

The coils have to be removed to gain access to the sparkplugs. Sometimes small amounts of oil will be found inside the sparkplug area, mostly on the left-hand side because of spillage when topping up the oil level. A tip: if oil is found here yet the surrounding area is very dry, this could mean that the sparkplug boss seals have been weeping slightly and need changing.

Sparkplugs for these engines are conventional but expensive, and can be removed with a normal sparkplug socket. The gap should be around 1.2mm, but there have been many changes over the years, so check with your particular handbook.

Moving on we come to the air filter, which sits in a box at the front of the engine bay. Undoing a quite fragile breather pipe and five clips (one of which is difficult to access and requires removal of a duct), the box can be opened and the disposable filter removed.

While in the engine bay, carry out a visual check of all areas for leaks, seepages, or anything that looks untoward. It is also a good idea to clean off any loose debris and dust. It is all too common for owners not to visually check the engine oil level between the 10,000-mile service intervals, thereby. missing unseen oil leaks that need to be rectified. For example, take the style of cam cover gaskets used today. Although quite heavy-duty, and sitting in ridges within the cam covers, as they get older the ridges can begin to crack so the gaskets don't seat correctly and oil can leak out.

in place by 7mm bolts. You will need to disconnect the electrical connectors first. The coils lift out, being directly above the sparkplugs. Once removed for the first time or changed, interference on FM reception can often be encountered. Removing the coil, pulling off the rubber boots to clean the metal at the base of the coil, and stretching the spring will make contact better and relieve the interference.

Underneath the covers of the V8 engine, the coils with their neat wiring are revealed. (Nigel Thorley)

Finally, on internal servicing issues, move back to the rear of the vehicle. The battery in the boot is not normally of the 'sealed for life' type so care should

be taken when topping up to avoid spillage. Acid could soon damage the boot floor or surrounding wiring.

Now the external checks. Radio aerial masts tend to stick. Unlike many modern cars, XKs still use a mast on the rear wing that raises and retracts as the audio system is turned on and off. The mast should be raised and regularly cleaned with WD40; do not use oils or grease, because these will attract dirt and eventually stop the mast from moving. Even using WD40 the mast should be wiped clean afterwards.

A visual check of all lights should be carried out, replacing the bulbs as necessary, none of which present any major problems (relevant information is provided in the handbooks).

It has, in the past, been normal practice to replace the windscreen wiper blades at 10,000-mile service intervals. Although Jaguar's policy on this has changed now, they should still be checked, and for the sake of the minimal cost involved the blades should be replaced both for safety reasons and to avoid unnecessary damage to the screen.

Last but not least, and again not identified in the normal Jaguar schedule, all door locks, hinges, etc. should be cleaned and oiled.

Variable valve timing

The normally-aspirated AJ-V8 engines fitted to the XK range are equipped with variable valve timing, which produces the best idle quality of any Jaguar engine, the timing altering throughout the rev range. The solenoids to control this fit on the outside of the engine, fed from the ECU via a relay. You can occasionally get rattling noises from a build-up of coked oil. By disconnecting a multi-pin connector, you can apply 12 volts to ensure they move properly. Do not confuse this noise with a rattling timing chain tensioner or chain.

Throttle bodies

Common running problems can often be attributed to the electronic throttle body on these engines, which is to some extent overly complex. Numerous sensors and overrides are built in to prevent problems such as over-revving. Cumbersome, and not the most reliable piece of equipment, there have been cases where an engine has stalled for no apparent reason, particularly when at speed. There has been an unofficial recall because of this, in which modifications have been made.

Throttle plates can gum up with carbon, causing them to stick. This also applies to the gears, causing erratic control of the throttle. If changing throttle

Access for the air cleaner element – a disposable item. (Nigel Thorley)

bodies, it is vital to first disconnect the battery because of the new 'learning process' the system goes through when it is reconnected.

Emissions

XK engines are not prone to problems in this area. Normally, if substantial problems arise at MoT time, this can be put down to using the wrong petrol or damage to a catalytic converter.

The throttle body of a V8 engine removed, showing the butterfly-style plates (arrowed) which will gum up and cause problems. (Nigel Thorley)

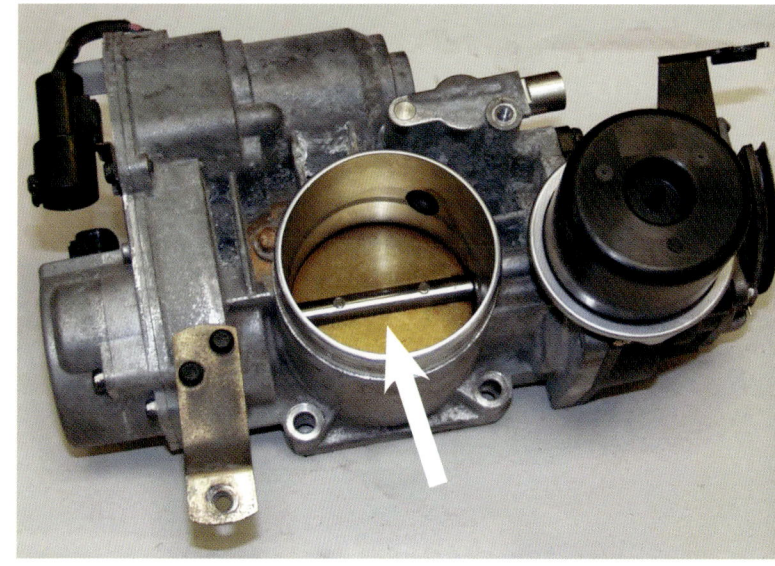

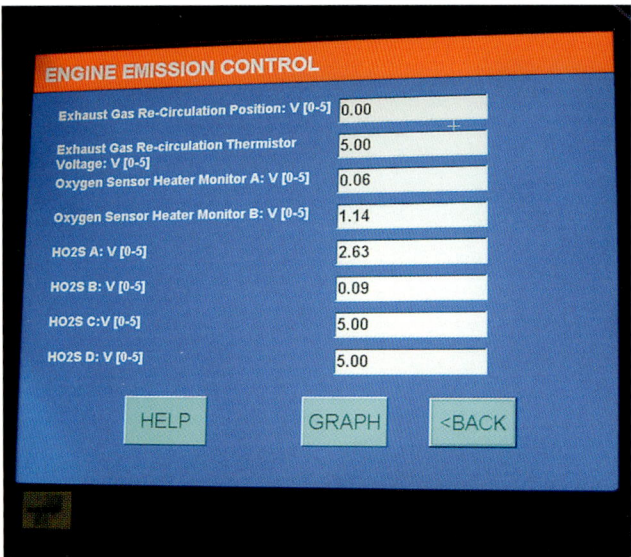

ENGINE EMISSION CONTROL

Exhaust Gas Re-Circulation Position: V [0-5]	0.00
Exhaust Gas Re-circulation Thermistor Voltage: V [0-5]	5.00
Oxygen Sensor Heater Monitor A: V [0-5]	0.06
Oxygen Sensor Heater Monitor B: V [0-5]	1.14
HO2S A: V [0-5]	2.63
HO2S B: V [0-5]	0.09
HO2S C:V [0-5]	5.00
HO2S D: V [0-5]	5.00

HELP   GRAPH   <BACK

The Autologic system from Diagnos.co.uk Limited is extremely useful (in some cases vital), if very expensive for the home mechanic. (Nigel Thorley)

Electrics

These are without doubt the most complex part of an XK and a totally different concept to the wiring in older cars. Some circuits transfer data along multiplexing lines, passing through several components that appear unconnected in their use or purpose, down the same wire but at different frequencies. As such the electrical system on XKs cannot always be measured in the conventional way by use of voltage meters.

In some cases these data circuits have series connections, which means if one wire or connection breaks then everything on that network could fail to communicate. This will lead to erroneous messages on the dashboard, which may result in error messages in the diagnostics that bear little resemblance to what has actually gone wrong. The gearbox selector switch is a common source of problems, as by misuse or rough handling these switches can become dislodged or break. If a break is determined via messages on the dashboard, this is a good place to start looking, being a common area of concern.

Engine fail-safe modes, 'limp-home', etc. can all often be attributed to a simple breakage in the system like this, and you can't pick up the fault by the use of fault codes as you could with cars like the XJ40 and XJ-S. Instead you need diagnosis from a computerised link using a system like Autologic, which can not only 'read' the car's electrics but can transform the data into lists of faults, identify areas to inspect, and provide solutions – all at a price which is normally too high for the home DIY mechanic to consider. Similar in basic format to the sophisticated systems used by Jaguar dealerships, more and more independent Jaguar specialists are now going down this route, so it is important to entrust such work to one of these in order to determine the true problems with a car.

Unfortunately, different mechanics having attempted to rectify problems over the years will, in itself, result in several pages of erroneous faults showing up on diagnosis. The only real answer, if the car is still drivable, is to cancel out all the faults on the readout, continue to use the car, and then download the latest information a few days later to give you a more viable starting point for repairs.

On a simpler note, the condition of the main battery is crucial to good running. If it is in a poor state or is not of the correct size and power for the car, all sorts of faults can occur which can even affect engine running.

It is worth pointing out here, for the benefit of owners who don't read or remember items from their handbook, that the XK8 models are currently unique in Jaguar terms in having side windows that move up and down as the doors are opened and closed. This is done to ensure an efficient seal of the window glass edge with the rubber seal to reduce wind noise in both Convertible and Coupé models, as the side windows are frameless.

Whenever the battery is disconnected or goes flat, the system memory on the windows will fail and has to be reset. This is done by turning on the ignition and lowering each window fully, keeping the appropriate button pressed all the time until a 'click' is heard, then repeating the same operation with the window going up until they 'click'.

If indicators or other lights don't work, this can often be down to broken wires. The wiring looms are tightly attached to the steering column and can come apart at multi-pin connectors. To get to this area you may have to remove the steering wheel and airbag assembly. The airbag should never be tampered with – there are adequate warnings on the reverse, and if the bag inadvertently went off it could cause severe damage.

All the electrical signals affecting the steering wheel controls and the airbag pass through a cassette at the top of the column. If a fault occurs, the cassette will need changing. Incidentally, an airbag fault warning may also be down to high resistance caused by this cassette.

Air-conditioning

All XKs were equipped with air-conditioning as standard, essentially the Nippon Denso system also fitted to corresponding XJ saloons. This is generally reliable, but will only work as efficiently as the cooling system as a whole, for which see the appropriate section above. The vulnerable part is the condenser situated at the front of the car, which is manufactured from light alloy, and gets covered in debris as a result of its location. It also deteriorates naturally with age.

Interior temperature sensors can also give trouble. The ambient temperature is measured from outside, underneath the front bumper. Inside the car, a sensor sits adjacent to the boot-lock opening button in the dash liner. Over time, dust and dirt gather inside this, insulating it from temperature changes and thereby compromising the efficiency of the whole air-conditioning system. It can be easily cleaned and reused. Simply pull down the dash liner from its clips to get at it.

Other problems can occur with the heater electric scavenge pump and electric control valve. This pump is especially for the cooling and heating system, and is designed to ensure that coolant passes through the matrix at a controlled rate. Both components can fail.

If the valve fails, this normally shows up in the form of cold air and no heating. If the pump fails, when engine speed is above 2500rpm one tends to get a degree of air inside the car due to high water pump speeds forcing coolant through the matrix. Changing these components is not easy. The pump, for example, is situated above the gearbox, and a catalyst on the left-hand side has to be removed for best access.

A lot of common problems associated with air-conditioning really relate to lack of proper use. It is advisable to thoroughly read the instruction manual supplied with the car to familiarise oneself with how the system operates.

Trim

Generally speaking, the trim is much more durable on these cars than on Jaguar models from the 1970s and 1980s. However, with the greater use of plastics and other lightweight materials, they only appear fine until disturbed, so great care should always be taken when prising off trim panels and removing clips, fasteners and cables, etc.

As already mentioned several times, take extreme

A diagrammatic view of the air-conditioning layout. (Nigel Thorley)

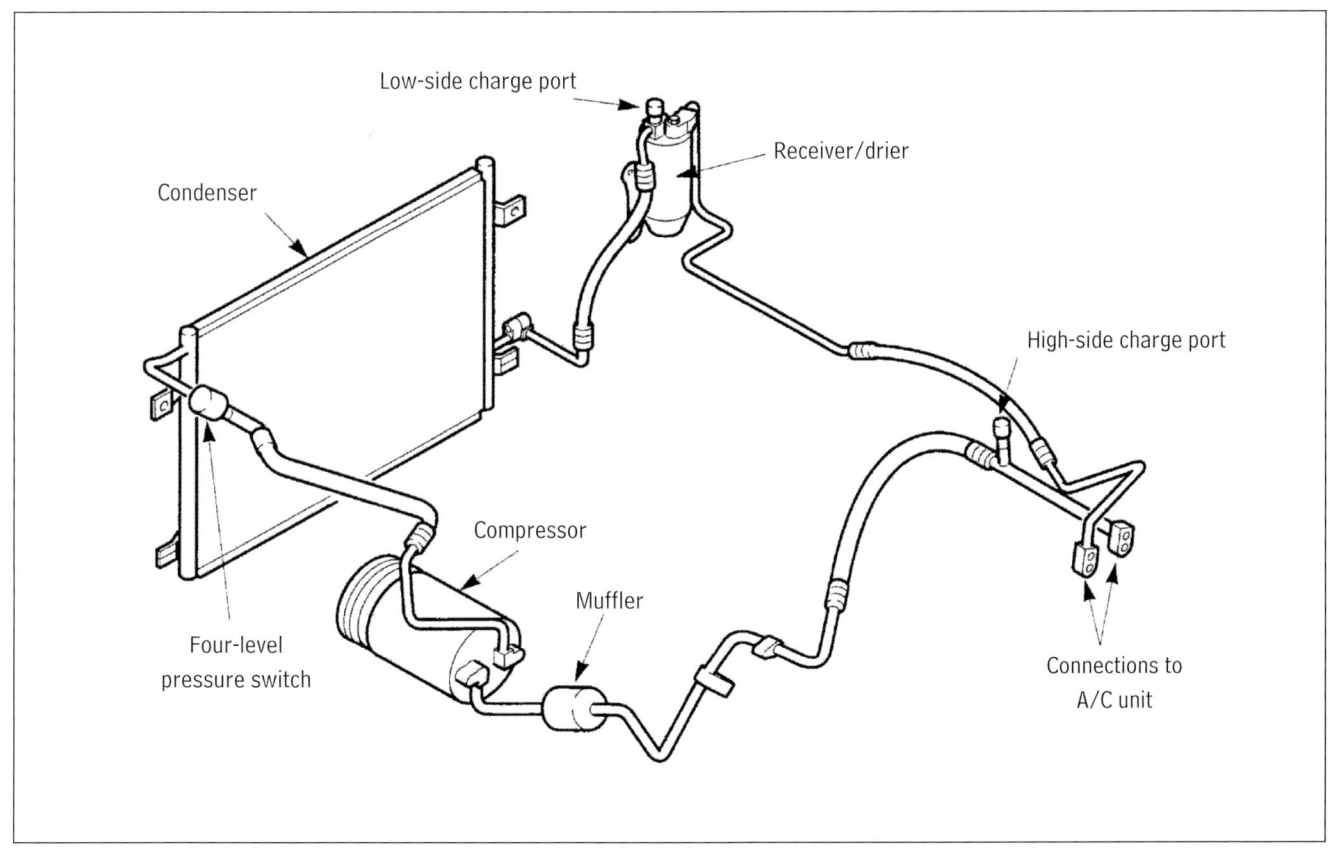

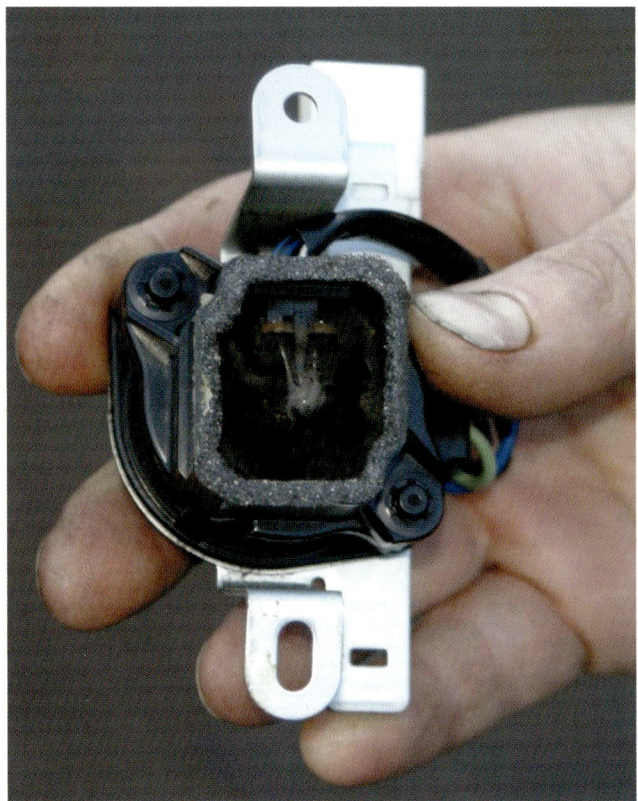

care with wiring. Some wires are gathered together in clusters or intertwined, and can easily get dislodged from their connections or damaged. Wires can also corrode easily with the advent of any damp, even inside their insulation.

Accessing equipment like the radio control unit involves the removal of the whole centre console. The retaining clips around the gear select often break, and then a replacement panel will be required.

Instrument illumination bulbs can be problematic. Although not over-complicated to deal with, a considerable number of different bulbs (over 30) are used in the dashboard and centre console area. They may look the same, but they are all very different wattages, and replacing them with the wrong bulbs can either cause overheating or can have a negative effect on other illuminations. Replacing bulbs in the dashboard area requires the removal of the wood-veneered panels. These are merely veneered onto aluminium substrates, some of which are clipped onto the dash area. The central small gauge unit will just prise off, but the main instrument surround is secured by two screws at its base. Various fasteners and screws allow the main instrument pack to be removed, the same applying to the central auxiliary gauges (non satnav-equipped cars), which are removed as one complete unit.

A 'before and after cleaning' comparison of typical air-conditioning components, which gather debris over a period of time.
(Nigel Thorley)

Hood problems

Back in 1987, the then new XJ-S Convertible used a type of hydraulic fluid in the rams to pull the hood up and down electrically without problem, but with the introduction of the XK8 model in 1996 Jaguar opted to change the type of fluid. However, the new type was later found to gel, which caused the hood to open and close either very slowly or, at worst, stopped it entirely, obliging the electrical system to shut down to avoid unnecessary damage.

Although initially put down to insufficient hood use in certain countries (such as the UK) or to cold temperatures, it eventually became clear that this fluid was just not suitable for sustained use. Jaguar now uses Pentosin CHF 11S fluid in all Convertibles, and this is what you should use to replace the fluid in earlier cars.

To do this, the old fluid has to be completely purged from the system, to avoid contaminating the new fluid. This requires accessing all the areas of concern, and you must begin with the hood in the retracted position. If this can't be done via the hydraulics, it can be manually unlatched by means of the Allen key found in the boot area. Access is also required to the

top screen rail inside the car, which requires removing the sun visors, trimmed panel, roof lighting panel, and top and side upholstered panels, and disconnecting the electrics. A substantial strengthening frame has to be undone, which gives access to the hood latching mechanism. Eventually the top rail can be withdrawn from its position revealing, on its left side, the pipes that run the fluid from the pump at the back of the car to the latching mechanism.

The pipes need to be carefully prised from the rail and disconnected so that the rail can be removed completely. The old fluid is then purged by a combination of bleeding the pipes to the latch-box inside the car and bleeding the hood hydraulics. This is done by electrically operating the hood several times and continually draining off the fluid, and manually operating the latch-box several times to extract the old fluid from it and its adjoining connections. The pump then has to be removed from its mounting in the boot and, with its filler plug removed, inverted to allow all

To carry out the fluid change in an XK Convertible the top screen rail and trim must be removed to access the pipes and latch-box. (Nigel Thorley)

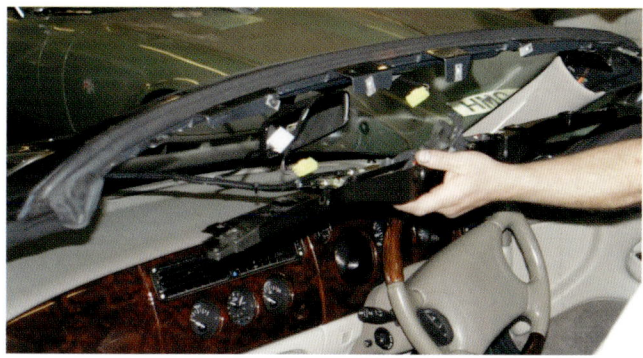

The jelly-like substance formed by the old fluid, which has to be purged from the system. (Nigel Thorley)

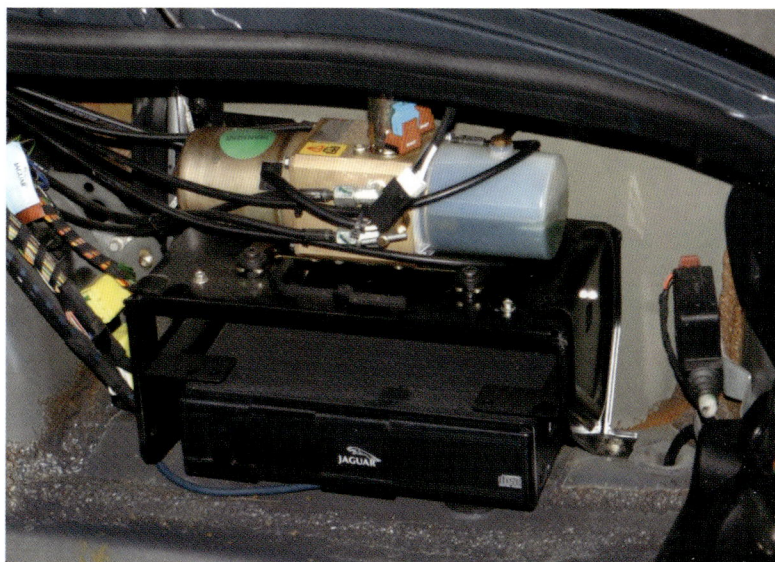

The boot-mounted pump which also has to be disconnected from its mounting to purge the old fluid. (Nigel Thorley)

the fluid in the reservoir to drain out (being careful not to let any run into the boot or onto the surrounding trim).

Refilling with new fluid and temporarily remounting the pump, the hood mechanism is powered up whilst containers collect the fluid as it is expelled from the disconnected pipework inside the car. This can take some time, as the old gelled fluid creates quite a resistance. Often compressed air is required to clear the pipes out individually. Once the pipes to the latch-box are clear, they can be reattached to the flushed latch-box and reassembled. Now the hood must be operated at least two or three times, draining off the fluid after each operation.

It goes without saying that the utmost care and cleanliness should surround these operations to avoid contamination of trim and, of course, the pump mechanism and piping.

Rear bumper mountings

It is quite common for the mountings of the rear bumper bar on XK models to corrode badly, eventually leading to departure of the bumper bar! This is down to the mounting bracket, which is made from a form of glass-reinforced fibre composite plus an alloy stud with steel insert, which corrodes. The only answer is to change the mounting brackets, which are not costly, and then protect the components by the liberal use of copper grease to prevent similar problems in the future.

On the assumption that the bumper hasn't dropped

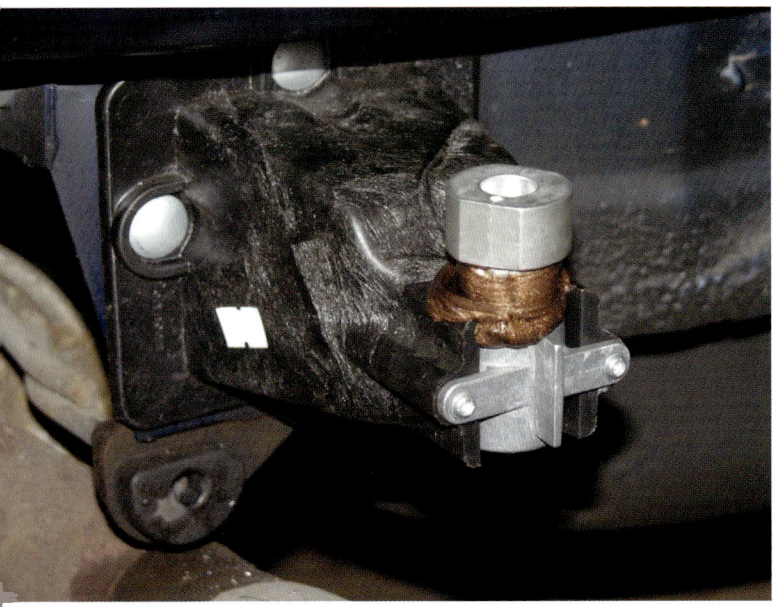

A new bumper-bar mounting fitted to a car and well greased to guard against future corrosion. (Nigel Thorley)

off there are under-rear-wing closing panels to be removed to gain access to the bolts. These will probably be seized in position anyway, and it is probably best to prise away the bumper as by this time little is holding it in place. In many cases a brass ferrule in the bumper will seize and eventually become dislodged, which will need re-gluing in position and even tapping out to reclaim the thread.

Window trim strip corrosion

Now the cars are getting older, the aluminium/rubber Dorchester Grey coloured finishing strips at the top of the doors corrode badly. After some time, replacements are now available again from Jaguar, but they are very expensive. The trims are held on by push clips, but these may be difficult to remove, so care should be taken if you intend to 'repair,' rather than replace the trims.

Depending on the condition when removed, refurbishment may be possible by pulling back the rubber to reveal the extent of the corrosion in the aluminium. A pointed knife may help to remove the debris, and if sufficient aluminium is still there, glue the rubber back onto the metal. The outer surface of the trims will have to be sanded down to remove any other marks, and repainted before refitting to the doors.

The success of any repairs is down to how good the metal still is, but this is worthy of an attempt to avoid the very high cost of replacement with new trims.

The finishing trims — which corrode badly — simply held on by spring clips.

The degree of aluminium corrosion that can be found in these trims.

Spare wheels

If a car is equipped with some of the larger alloy wheels, it is not possible to carry a full-sized spare. Both from new and as the cars have got older, they were fitted with a space-saver spare made of steel. However,

for these to be of practical use, they must be the right type for the car. Given also that some cars have larger Brembo brakes, clearance for the wheel is also vital. For these reasons, X-100 models should be fitted with the 18in *red* space-saver wheel.

Parts availability

Unsurprisingly, there are now parts availability issues for these older models. In particular, some electronic control units (of which there are many) are no longer available, and second-hand units have become difficult to find.

The security and locking module is a prime example. It uses old technology electronics that have fallen out of use and for which, to date, no-one manufactures suitable replacements. Similarly, ABS control unit failures are not uncommon, but, in many cases, with care these have been shown to be repairable.

Jaguar Classic Parts has been given a brief to investigate continuing parts availability for its more recent models, which should mean that in time some critical parts will be returned once more to stock, with availability from Jaguar dealers. One example is door latch assemblies complete with micro-switches controlling the window drop on opening and closing

It is important that X-100 models fitted with a space-saver wheel have the red 18in version.

doors. At the time of writing, work on reintroducing the assemblies is well advanced

Keeping your XK clean and presentable

Following most of the prior information will give you a good grounding in what to watch for, and how to look after these cars. After this it is down to you, the owner, to fettle the car to ensure it stays in shape.

Cleaning the exterior is something many leave to the power-wash at their local garage, but there is a lot more you can do to keep your XK in top condition. The first thing to remember – and I keep plugging this point – is that the XK8 is very much based on XJS technology as far as the body and floorpan are concerned, and this spells the word 'care.' If you regularly and personally wash your car, look out for the telltale signs of corrosion starting, and stone chips that will allow damp to corrode the metal underneath.

Modern paintwork is more robust than in the past but it still benefits from care and attention, so polish the exterior once a year with a good quality wax. Every two to three years, for a regularly used example, the paintwork will benefit from 'cutting back' to remove road grime and minor scratches, followed by a good polish to bring the shine and brightness back.

Tips on doing this work start with good preparation.

That means wear clothing without exposed buttons, and not wearing jewellery or having anything else on you that is likely to scratch the paintwork accidentally. Thoroughly wash and dry the paintwork to remove any loose dirt and grime before the main work begins. It is always worth taking care of other parts of the car (just in case); for example, if it is a Convertible, cover the hood and even the glass areas for protection, and always remove the wiper blades, because if cutting or buffing paste gets into the blades they could seriously scratch your windscreen afterwards. The use of cutting paste should be minimal, one panel at a time, in a rotational action and without being heavy-handed. A non-orbital electrical polisher can be used, but they need to be handled carefully and lightly so as not to buff too far into the paint. Also be aware that trailing electrical cables can scratch your car.

Using clean cloths and operating in a circular motion, polish each panel, removing the remains of the cutting compound. Then polish the car using a good quality wax, again working on small areas at a time and moving in a circular motion so as not to leave streaks in the paintwork.

The final result is gratifying, and it is satisfying to the eye to keep your XK as good, if not better, than when it left the factory.

Chapter Ten

The shape of things to come

On 10th January 2005, at the NAIS Motor Show in Detroit, Jaguar announced a stunning new sports car concept, the Advanced Lightweight Coupé (ALC). It personified the direction in which Jaguar was moving and was a physical expression of Jaguar's Design Director, Ian Callum's new styling philosophy at the company for the next generation of models. As Callum put it, "I firmly believe that Jaguars should appear powerful as well as elegant. Look back at the great cars from our past, and you will see that they were as muscular and taut as they were subtle and curvaceous. That's what confident Jaguar design is all about."

Jaguar's Aluminium Lightweight Coupé (ALC) concept car. Significant styling features of the ALC found their way into the New XK. Compare these pictures with the new car in the next chapter. (Jaguar Cars/Nigel Thorley)

Exterior design features

The ALC introduced a distinctive tapering shape both front and rear, eliminating much of the conventional overhang of previous designs. In Jaguar's words, this gave the car an exciting presence and a real sense of power and potency. At the front, the ALC looked similar to the then still-current X-100 (XK8/XKR) models, and presented more than a nod towards the timeless E-type sports car of the 1960s. At the rear, it offered a very different approach – something similar to a previous Jaguar concept vehicle, the RD-6. Every curve of bodywork, and the rise and fall of each surface had its purpose. Callum stated that nothing was included for aesthetic reasons only, with no unnecessary surfacing.

The car rode on unique 21in alloy wheels with specially-produced Pirelli tyres, sitting below wide, flowing haunches. The rear haunch was of particular note, its prominent shoulder helping to emphasise the size of the wheels relative to the bodywork. The visual

"A RALLYING CALL FOR JAGUAR LOVERS THE WORLD OVER"

"This show car is a rallying call for Jaguar lovers the world over who appreciate sporting luxury. We want them to know that we are committed to a product-led transformation of this company that will see us making Jaguars with great design and wonderful interiors, that are fast, glamorous and evocative. A new Jaguar sports car is always an important event, and we absolutely believe that the Advanced Lightweight Coupé demonstrates that the direction we are taking is the right one."

– Bibiana Boerio,
the then Managing Director of Jaguar

Excellent luggage facilities for a sports car made the ALC look like the ideal grand tourer. (Jaguar Cars/Nigel Thorley)

drawing the eye around the corner of the car. The addition of the chrome 'gills' as they were called at the time (later known as power vents) in the front wings, had the practical purpose of aiding aerodynamics and engine cooling.

Interior designing

The task for the interior design team was to create a cabin that wasn't overpowering or fussy – so it needed to be clean, simple and straightforward – yet retaining the virtues of quality and finish that Jaguar had long been associated with, a move away from tradition, but at the same time retaining that Jaguar ambience so important to the brand.

Using the classic 2+2 sports car format of previous models, the ALC cabin was more spacious and better packaged than before, with impressive headroom, multi-directional sports front seats, and individual rear seating. The interior was trimmed throughout in tan leather, with visible stitching on the hides that lined the doors and the dashboard. Aluminium inserts were spread throughout the car to act as 'jewellery', accentuating the contemporary feel of the whole car.

The focal point of the interior was the central dashboard console, housing an advanced Alpine telematics screen to give user feedback in the form of a 'pulse' when the onscreen buttons were touched. The instrument binnacle was designed to relate to the shape of the steering wheel, housing a high-resolution screen between its dials, providing the driver with secondary information. Behind the steering wheel were gearshift levers to operate an automatic paddle shift

mass of the cabin area was drawn back towards the rear haunch, giving an impression of forward movement even when the car was standing still.

The front mouth was another indication of Jaguar design to come, drawing inspiration from the classic Jaguars such as the E-type and D-type, but with a polished aluminium grille to reinforce the engineering integrity of the car's design.

The bonnet incorporated a more pronounced power bulge than the old XK design. The cabin area flowed back in a clean spontaneous line to the car's rear end, which tapered sharply to a focal point of two, centrally-mounted tailpipes – another throw-back to the E-type era.

Returning to the front, the headlights were a complete departure from the simple elliptical lenses of then current models, with a more contemporary angular design creating an 'edgy' look, and

An entirely new approach to a Jaguar production car interior for the ALC. (Jaguar Cars/Nigel Thorley)

transmission, a system seen for the very first time in any Jaguar. The paddles were mounted on the wheel, rather than the steering column, so that they could be operated with the wheel in any position.

Engineering

Jaguar called the ALC the most performance-potent car it had ever produced, thanks to its technologically advanced aluminium construction. This was around 40% lighter, and 60% stiffer, than a standard steel body. With its contemporary 4.2-litre V8 engine, the car offered class-leading performance, accelerating from 0 to 60mph in under 5 seconds and with a top speed of 180mph.

The aluminium chassis was similar to that introduced in the new XJ (X-350) saloon model, in 2003, and used

The ALC was a 'real' car as seen here on display, and now in the Jaguar Heritage Trust collection of vehicles. (Nigel Thorley)

many of the same technologically-advanced features. The benefits of this included not just a lighter and stiffer shell, but also improved performance, fuel economy and emissions.

The ALC also featured Computer Active Suspension (CATS), Adaptive Cruise Control, and Active Restraint Technology – all modified from similar systems used on the existing production models.

And where from here?

Although unstated at the time, the ALC was obviously the precursor for the next generation XK sports car, due to be launched in 2006.

The XK8 is dead, long live the XK

The XK competed in what the motor industry categorises as the 'Large Premium Sports Car' sector, an area of the market that was growing in importance and competitiveness. It consisted of two key groups – Grand Tourers (with a high degree of luxury and refined comfort), and unequivocal Sports Cars (with high-performance and great handling). The total worldwide market for this type of car had more than doubled from 48,000 to 99,000 since 1996, and the number of competitors increased over that period from four to seven, with more to follow.

The New XK (code named X-150) had to be targeted not only at existing XK8/XKR customers, but also to a select group of affluent potential purchasers who were looking for a grand tourer as well as a car with pure sporting credentials – a car that was exhilarating and provided escapism combined with status and exclusivity – luxury in a sports skin.

The XK8/XKR (X-100) models ceased production in June 2005. Jaguar's intention was to build on the success of those models with a totally new XK design. Jaguar launched their New XK, earlier than anticipated, in late 2005. It was no surprise that the design echoed that of the Advanced Lightweight Coupé, showcased the previous January.

The New XK showed its pedigree, with the best of the XK8 design, while incorporating many new and intriguing features developed from the ALC concept. As Jaguar Design Director Ian Callum said, "The fundamental values of Jaguar design do not decline, not even since Sir William Lyons created the first

Evolution of a design. (Jaguar Cars/Nigel Thorley)

Initial drawings taking inspiration from the 1960s E-type.
(Jaguar Cars/Nigel Thorley)

A modern interior was called for. (Jaguar Cars/Nigel Thorley)

Jaguar all those years ago … We took influences from our heritage and evolved them to produce a car that is beautiful, visually fast, yet undeniably modern, just as Sir William's own designs were in their day."

What car to build?

While some manufacturers were opting for a hybrid car design, Jaguar's first important decision was to launch the new Jaguar model with two variants, Coupé and Convertible. The Coupé offered superbly elegant 'fastback' styling, a well-known feature of previous Jaguar sporting cars (the E-type being the prime example), plus better luggage accommodation.

The all-alloy construction of the New XK resulted in a light but exceptionally strong structure. (Jaguar Cars/Nigel Thorley)

The Convertible promised classic open-top motoring. Other manufacturers were choosing to design cars that combined the two, with a metal folding roof – the idea being that one vehicle could combine the benefits of open-top motoring with the security of a hard top, but Jaguar had good reasons for keeping to their existing format. By opting for a conventional 'soft top', Jaguar felt there would be less compromise over styling, and fewer issues over space. Furthermore, with this class of car, the majority of owners would be expected to have at least one other car to fulfil the requirements of a hard top vehicle – reasoning shared by other prestige brands such as Bentley.

Jaguar convertibles had tended to be a compromise, both in terms of build, and, most importantly, in rigidity of structure. With the previous two generations of Jaguar sporting cars for example, the X-100 was designed as a coupé but adapted as a convertible, and the XJ-S was initially not launched as a convertible at all, and it was several years before the car could be re-engineered into one. In the case of the X-150, from the start Jaguar took a different approach. It was designed as a convertible first. In so doing, Jaguar would ensure greater rigidity and no compromises in the car.

The next most important decision was how to build the X-150. To use aluminium was a natural progression for Jaguar, as it had been successfully employed for the X-350 XJ saloon, introduced in 2003. Although much more expensive than steel, aluminium had significant benefits: it was much lighter, improving efficiency and overall dynamics, and was less corrosive. Although the

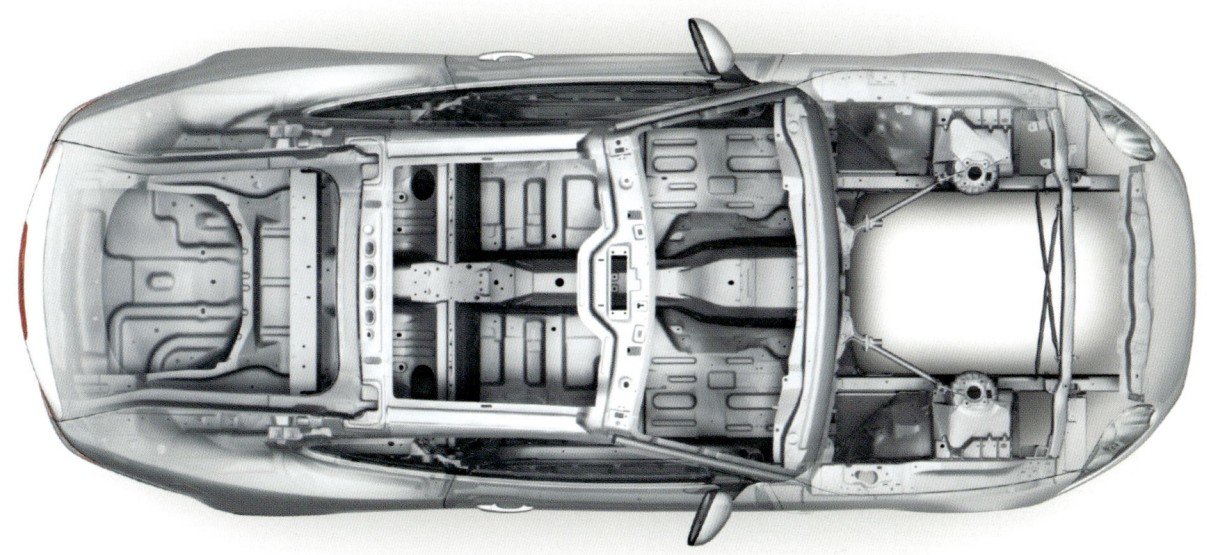

Various aspects of the New XK style.
(Jaguar Cars/Nigel Thorley)

X-150 would be well publicised as the first production Jaguar sports car to be built in all aluminium, this material had been used before in the production of the first XK120 sports cars in 1949/1950.

The major difference now was that the whole body would be a true aluminium monocoque, with much of the structure actually load-bearing. With the ever-increasing demands on car manufacturers to produce more sophisticated vehicles, with high-tech equipment levels, and the need for those cars to be more efficient, aluminium was the natural choice in keeping down weight, and with modern production processes, cars can also be stronger and safer. Other advantages were that there would be a common structure between convertible and coupé, which would keep down production costs.

Computer Aided Design

As explained in Chapter One, the earlier X-100 had gone through a whole range of designs and prototypes constructed 'in the flesh' for evaluation and testing. With the advent of Computer Aided Design (CAD), the development process had changed dramatically. The majority of work was now carried out on computer without actually producing anything! Russ Varney was the Chief Project Engineer for the new car and, in an interview with Paul Skilleter at the time, he commented: "In the past we used to design cars and then test them, then redesign them, put the parts on and see what happened, what broke. It's nothing like that now. We go through the virtual process where we design the product and facilities at the same time."

This made the whole process of designing the new car quicker, more efficient and less costly. Because of this, apparently the first prototype X-150s were almost indistinguishable from the production model.

The detail on the style of the New XK is covered in more depth in the next chapter – suffice to say that it bore an uncanny resemblance to the ALC show car shown only a few months earlier, one of the first times that a concept vehicle would turn out to be so similar to a final production design.

Power train

It was always intended that the New XK would carry the existing and highly successful AJ-V8 4.2-litre engine, which would satisfy the then Euro 4 emissions requirements and stringent US emissions regulations. The engine delivered more than 85% of torque all the way from 2000 to 6000rpm, yet it still offered good fuel economy and low emissions figures, with a drop in CO_2 emissions of 6%.

The gearbox was a new version of the ZF 6-speed automatic transmission previously used in the X-100 but now brought up to date with Jaguar's own Sequential Shift transmission, introducing a new shift system and steering wheel mounted paddles, replacing the previous J-gate operation.

The braking system was also upgraded with larger discs, hydraulic brake assist and the fitment of the still relatively new Electronic Park Brake function, first seen on the Jaguar saloons.

Another adaptation from the X-350 saloon was the Sevotronic 2 steering system, providing easy low-speed manoeuvring with optimum high-speed feedback under all conditions. The suspension also came in for revision – in many ways more akin to the current crop of Jaguar salons than the X-100 and previous models.

Judicious use of new materials and technology resulted in class leading build quality. (Jaguar Cars/Nigel Thorley)

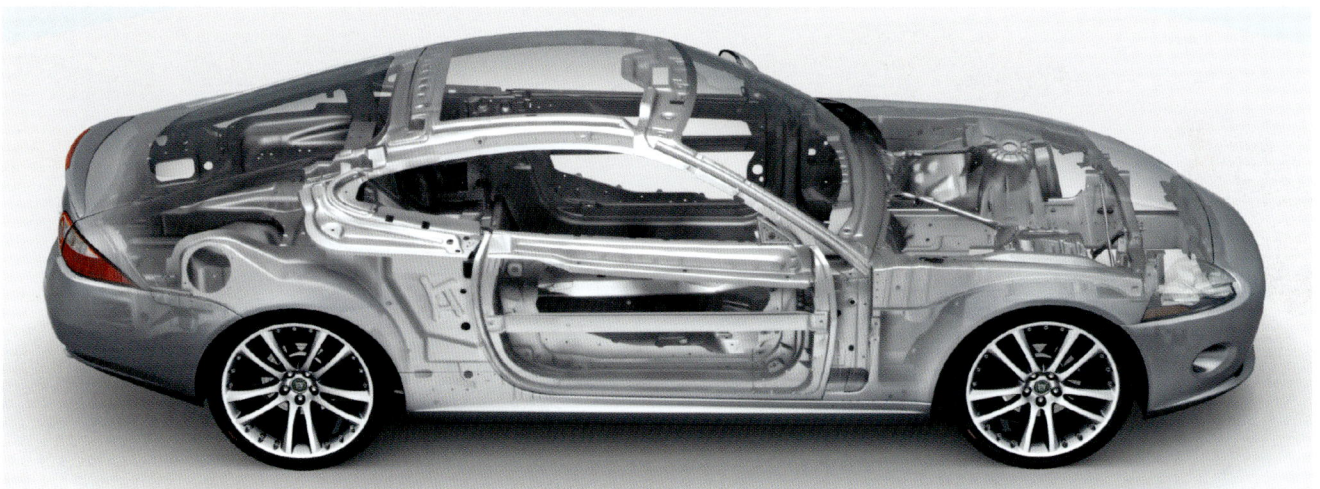

Many aspects of the drivetrain were adapted from the previous model. (Nigel Thorley)

In-built safety

Safety was a major benefit of this type of construction – aluminium absorbs significantly more energy per kilogramme of material weight than steel when it is deformed. That strength advantage doesn't only apply to high speed impacts but it also means lower speed accident repair costs are kept to a minimum.

Over and above this, there were other important safety features unique to the model at the time. These included the shape and construction of the bumpers and bonnet, and, most importantly, the completely new Pedestrian Deployment system – unique to Jaguar. Jaguar became one of the first manufacturers to meet Phase One of new European safety legislation by using this system. Upon impact with a pedestrian, in milliseconds the bonnet is deployed upwards away from its rear edge. Those few inches create a cushioning effect between the engine and the bonnet, forming a safety zone and reducing significantly the potential for injury. This all happens in less than a tenth of the time it takes to blink an eye!

Returning to the bumpers, their design had to reduce the risk of leg injury through the use of crushable foam and plastic coverings. To do this, an advanced sensing system is mounted in the front bumper to help

Suspension and steering aspects were modified from then current models. (Jaguar Cars/Nigel Thorley)

The new Pedestrian Safety Deploying system used pyrotechnics under the bonnet. (Nigel Thorley)

discriminate between a pedestrian collision and any other possible front-end contacts to ensure the correct degree of absortion.

Building the new car

These features made the New XK the most technically and technologically advanced car the company had ever produced, so it is worth covering this in some detail.

It was an obvious move for Jaguar to continue to develop the lightweight aluminium construction method pioneered by the company with the X-350 XJ saloon. This resulted in the New XK Coupé being significantly lighter than its predecessor or any of its key rivals in the marketplace at just 1595kg, and 30% stiffer. A good example of the weight-saving was in the car's doors, each 6kg lighter than steel equivalents and with stiffer mountings, it meant door gaps were better maintained to improved levels. Better sealing was achieved with the frameless window glasses through mounting their rails directly to the aluminium castings front and rear.

The New XK took the technology a stage further, with extended use of lightweight aluminium castings and extrusions, as well as the pressed alloy panels. There was, for example, only a single welded joint in the body, the cosmetic join on the roof. All the other joints in the body are formed using Jaguar's unique combination of riveting and bonding. Most joints were produced using self-piercing rivets applied by hydraulic pressure against a fixed tool. Where access was difficult a new riveting process was developed, and, where particularly strong stiffness was required, a combination of rivet and bonding was carried out. All visible exterior panels were bonded to the underlying structure and a new

Massive box section sills ensured that both Convertible and Coupé models were rigid structures. (Nigel Thorley)

automated seam-sealing process sealed everything off before painting.

The New XK had a secondary front bulkhead of aluminium and composite materials helping to reduce noise transmission from the engine compartment, and providing a dry area under the bonnet for accommodating electrical components.

The new structure also had benefits in refinement – castings used for the mounting points for the engine, transmission, and suspension are much stronger and stiffer, reducing transmitted noise, and improving suspension dynamics. Yet another advantage of the new technology was that all the necessary stiffness was in the bodyshell, with very large rectangular section side sills.

The principles of X-150 production started with the bringing together of parts to form three specific modules, the front, main floor and rear structures, to

A new assembly line was set up at Castle Bromwich to build the New XKs. (Nigel Thorley)

Robotics improved efficiency and build quality but highly skilled operatives still carried out significant areas of the build. (Nigel Thorley)

complete the full under-body area of the car (common to both Coupé and Convertible models). The majority of that work was carried out by over 30 robots. A considerable amount of the work, however, was still not automated, by the very nature of low-volume sports car production compared to saloon models like the XF.

After this, the under-body structure received the body sides (different panels for Coupé and Convertible). Doors, bonnet, tailgate/bootlid and front wings, all again of aluminium, were fitted manually, attached by self-piercing rivets and special adhesives. The final panel was the roof for the Coupé – the one external panel finished with MIG welds, completed by hand.

The finished bodies then went through dimensional checks, before progressing to the next stage – painting, under strictly-controlled conditions, with much of the work being done in sealed areas by robots.

With the bodyshells painted, they were moved onto specially-designed skillets for the conveyor-style assembly process. Such operations as the fitment of wiring looms, dashboard, sound-deadening and interior were carried out by operatives as the skillets progressed along the track. At later stages, the engine, gearbox, axle, suspension and brakes were similarly installed.

At the very start of production, a number of Field Evaluation Units (FEU) were produced to verify the production process. These were later used for a range of purposes, from engineering assessment to press and publicity cars. According to Paul Skilleter, some of these were so good that they were eventually sold off as secondhand units, something that would have been unheard of before, in previous manufacturing days.

The whole production process was certainly more automated and efficient than with the previous model, and, of course, all assembly was carried out at Jaguar's central Castle Bromwich facility, and not, like the X-100s, at the old Browns Lane Plant in Coventry.

First off the line

Christmas came early at the Jaguar Castle Bromwich assembly plant in Birmingham in 2005, when the very first production New XK came off the line on Monday 19th December. A Liquid Silver Coupé model, with Charcoal interior and Burr Walnut veneer, the car was handed over to the Jaguar Heritage Trust by John Naughton, Plant Director, a car still in the hands of the Trust to this day.

The structure passed very stringent crash tests. (Nigel Thorley)

IAN CALLUM

Born in Scotland in 1954, Callum studied at the Glasgow School of Art, Aberdeen Art College, Coventry University and the Royal College of Art in London. At the age of 14, he submitted a car design to Jaguar Cars in the hope of getting a job!

From 1979 to 1990, he worked for Ford globally on various design projects. From 1990 until 1999 he worked for TWR (Tom Walkinshow, well known for Jaguar racing and other projects). There he was instrumental in the design of the Aston Martin DB7 and later designed the Vanquish.

In 1999, Ian joined the Ford Motor Company, to succeed the late Geoff Lawson as Design Director at Jaguar Cars. Working on several products with Jaguar (and Aston Martin as it was owned by Ford at the time), his first concepts for Jaguar were the R-Coupé and RD-6.

The New XK was Ian Callum's design and from which he has steered Jaguar's styling into the XF, New XJ, F-TYPE and future models.

Ian Callum. (Nigel Thorley)

Chapter Twelve

The new XK in detail

(Jaguar Cars/Nigel Thorley)

"The new XK delivers the unique blend of performance, luxury and style that only a Jaguar can. And its beauty is more than skin-deep – this is a sports car with the heart and soul of every great Jaguar." Bibiana Boerio, Managing Director, Jaguar Cars at the time of launch of the New XK in 2005.

The powertrain

As with any Jaguar sports car, the heart is the engine. The New XK was powered by the existing 4.2-litre V8 engine, a development from the XJ8 saloon, and much modified from the outgoing X-100 variant. It produced 300bhp, with maximum torque of 303lbs ft at 4100rpm with 85% of torque all the way from 2000rpm to 6000rpm, yet it still offered good fuel economy and low emissions figures, with a drop in CO2 emissions of 6%

– satisfying the then Euro 4 emissions requirements regulations. Compared to the Euro 3 requirements, that meant a 50% reduction in hydrocarbons (HC) and oxides of nitrogen (NOx), and a 60% reduction in carbon monoxide (CO) emissions. The new engine also satisfied more stringent American regulations requiring a 50% reduction in HC emissions. It featured Exhaust Gas Recirculation, and the latest generation of catalyst cores with thinner coatings of higher density catalysing material – which reduced exhaust gas restriction, and was more efficient.

The major difference between this engine and the previous generation 4.2-litre X-100 engine was in the fuel-injection technology. This V8 used multi-hole injectors, which improved the fuel spray pattern in the combustion chambers, improving both power and fuel efficiency. Optimum throttle response (a crucial ingredient in confirming the New XK's sports car character) was delivered by full 'drive-by-wire' electronic throttle control, with no mechanical connection between the accelerator pedal and the throttle body. The response was based on the torque demand for every instantaneous driving situation. That was calculated by the electronic engine management control, based on parameters including the driver's accelerator input, and other vehicle

Although using an existing 4.2-litre V8 engine, it was significantly modified for the demands of the new car. (Nigel Thorley)

factors, such as road speed, engine speed and gear selection. The electronic controls then call up the required torque at any instant, by adjusting throttle position, variable cam phasing, fuel flow, and exhaust gas recirculation settings.

Equally important for its role in the New XK, the 4.2-litre engine was engineered to give the sound expected from a real sports car engine – especially under acceleration – but without being undesirably noisy. The new XK's Semi-Active Exhaust system varied the flow of exhaust gases through the main, large silencer box, depending on the pressure in the system, and featured acoustically-tuned tailpipes that eliminated low-speed boom. There was also an underfloor resonator with two chambers (one for each cylinder bank) which balanced the sound from the two banks. By tuning the sounds from the air-induction system and the exhaust system, Jaguar concentrated on both the solid, powerful low-frequency sounds, and more technically 'sophisticated' higher-frequency sounds, to give a feeling of power and performance.

The engine had an electronically limited maximum speed of 155mph, supplying a 0 to 60mph acceleration time of 5.9 seconds, plus instant throttle response, and broad flexibility for punchy performance across the range. With the weight savings offered by the aluminium construction of the body, the standing quarter mile time of 14.4 seconds was less than half a second off the pace of the X-100 4.2-litre XKR supercharged model.

The New XK's ZF 6-speed transmission was another carryover from the previous model, but was substantially improved with the Bosch Mechatronic shift – an electro-hydraulic shift mechanism whose adaptive shift strategy responds to both road conditions and driving style, to give the smoothest shifts with optimum performance. There was a new automatic gearshift replacing the familiar J-gate. The new system incorporated the Jaguar Sequential Shift system with Park, Reverse, Neutral, Drive and Sport modes. The fully automatic Drive mode adapted to individual driving styles, while the Sport mode could also be selected, offering more responsive fully automatic blip of the throttle gearshift changes.

Steering wheel mounted paddles were fitted to change gear with the Jaguar Sequential Shift transmission. In either Drive or Sport modes, very fast gear shifts were achieved by combining the use of the one-touch paddles with an automatic blip of the accelerator pedal, from the drive-by-wire engine management system during downshifts. Because of this

positive torque enhancement control, the shifts were faster and more responsive than before, regardless of the mode the driver had selected.

The epicyclic geartrain utilised clutch-to-clutch synchronous shifting to ensure that a controlled amount of torque was always being transferred during power on upshifts. This made the shift much smoother than in the automated manual gearboxes adopted by some of the New XK's competitors, where the use of an automated clutch completely interrupted the flow of torque during shifts. The extremely rapid shift times often quoted for automated manual transmissions related solely to the duration of this torque interrupt; the true shift time being significantly longer since the clutch must be disengaged prior to the ratio change, and re-engaged after. In contrast, the Jaguar Sequential Shift suffered no torque interrupt, resulting in a smoother, more powerful shift feel, and a very short

An uprated 6-speed transmission with paddle shift controls.
(Nigel Thorley)

total shift time of approximately 600 milliseconds from the driver touching the shift paddle to the completion of the shift event. In fact, during development, comparison tests between Jaguar Sequential Shift and rival automatic transmissions in the class showed the new XK's transmission to be the fastest system of all, changing gear at least 400 milliseconds faster than a standard automatic and 100 milliseconds faster than the best automated manual system.

Suspension, steering & brakes

The light, ultra-stiff all-aluminium monocoque body structure of the New XK formed a solid basis for the suspension components. The reduced body weight also

The suspension system took much from the technology gained from the S-type and XJ saloons of the period. (Nigel Thorley)

allowed other components to be located as required, to deliver optimum weight distribution and avoid any compromises with the suspension layout. The car used Jaguar's well-proven and classically-sporty combination of unequal length wishbones at the front, and unequal length wishbones using the driveshafts as upper links at the rear. Jaguar used a conventional, mechanically-sprung suspension layout, with coil springs and telescopic dampers all round, that provided more natural, more positive feedback to the driver.

There was a new version of Jaguar's Computer Active Technology Suspension (CATS), a two-stage adaptive damping system that ensured the optimum balance between ride and handling, whatever the road conditions or style of driving. The car's pitch and yaw rates are measured using accelerometer sensors. That data, plus information on steering wheel angle and brake demand, is processed, and electronically-controlled hydraulic valves continuously vary the damper settings accordingly. In the previous XK, the CATS system adjusted front and rear dampers in pairs, limiting the control variation to pitch only. The New XK's version controlled all four dampers separately, which allowed control of roll as well as pitch, for even better ride and handling balance, with a very sporty feel.

Jaguar's Servotronic 2 steering was fitted to the New XK, as used on the XJ saloon but re-engineered to suit a high-performance sports car with a faster-ratio steering rack, a mechanically assisted system (hydraulically powered by an engine-driven pump) with electronic control. The control module used data about vehicle speed and steering input to regulate the degree of steering assistance. It provided higher assistance at low speeds for easy manoeuvring, and less assistance at higher speeds for increased feedback to the driver – resulting in class-leading steering characteristics.

The braking system came in for major revision over the previous model. Larger, ventilated discs contributed to better pedal feel, optimum stopping distances, and were resistant to brake fade. Four channel, ABS, electronic brake force distribution, and hydraulic brake assist improved brake pressure during an emergency stop.

Unlike conventional digital ABS systems used on many cars at the time, the XK's system could vary the brake pressure at each wheel using analogue valves in the hydraulic control unit. This gave more refinement to the hydraulic pressure control, and allowed drivers to benefit from increased steering input during heavy

braking. Jaguar's Electronic Park Brake function, first seen on the saloons, was also fitted to the New XK.

Exterior styling

The New XK was certainly more visually assertive and sporting than the model it replaced, yet it was also elegant and somewhat understated. It incorporated classic, ground-hugging proportions with a long bonnet, steeply raked windscreen and rear window, fashionable arch-filling wheels, and minimal body overhangs.

The new car sat on a longer wheelbase than the previous model, but with substantially fewer overhangs

The refined suspension and drivetrain ensured excellent agility and quality of ride. (Nigel Thorley)

front and rear of the wheelbase. Its width, strong, high waistline and short, powerful haunches gave an impression of a car crouched ready for action. It certainly looked more contemporary, extremely muscular and athletic – suggesting movement, power and agility, even when stationary.

The rear haunches accentuate the style of the New XK Coupé. (Jaguar Cars/Nigel Thorley)

The light units are more striking, the 'mouth' is larger and the bonnet bulge is more prominent than on the X-100. (Jaguar Cars/Nigel Thorley)

The beautifully-executed tailgate of the Coupé with large fixed screen. (Jaguar Cars/Nigel Thorley)

The general frontal aspect of the car was all very much as the ALC show car had been, but with more subtle treatment of the lower area, with inset auxiliary lighting. It was also not dissimilar to the X-100, but visually more assertive, with a larger mouth area, retaining the central splitter bar, but with a stylized growler badge and a mesh grille (normally only associated with supercharged models). The new high-tech lighting provided a more modern approach to the styling, but the inset fog lights were a throw-back to the early X-100s.

The design of the bumper had to mitigate leg injury through the use of crushable foam and plastic coverings. To this aim the advanced sensing system was mounted in the front bumper to help discriminate between a pedestrian collision and any other possible front-end contacts, as mentioned previously.

The bonnet now had a more pronounced power bulge, and the windscreen was more steeply inclined into the flowing roofline.

The front wing 'gills' of the ALC featured, but were now called 'power vents' and finished in body colour,

the first seen on a production Jaguar – a feature that would be adopted for all subsequent models.

The side view of the New XK was nothing less than impressive. The short overhangs, large wheels, and the flowing lines of the Coupé made for great impact. The pronounced rear haunches really gave an impression of performance and striking stance to the car.

At the rear of the Coupé, gone was the separate boot lid with a fixed solid rear screen from the X-100. Instead, a large one-piece top-hinged aluminium tailgate (or 'liftback door', as Jaguar called it) now allowed easy access to a quite large boot area. The tailgate was immensely strong, lightweight and easy to operate. The liftback pivoted on two hinges, which ensured the edge moved away from the operator's head as the lid was raised. Such a large 'door' gave unprecedented access to the luggage-carrying area.

The rear end styling was much more imposing than the X-100 model it replaced, with modern light units, a spoiler incorporating the high level brakelight, and a Jaguar 'signature' panel.

The finished article interior with much more prominent centre console, and in this case Poplar wood veneer. (Jaguar Cars/Nigel Thorley)

Rear seat accommodation was, as with the previous model, more a token than very practical. (Nigel Thorley)

Interior design

There were no shocks here, as the design incorporated many of the features from the ALC show car. An abundance of high tech trim surfaces were cleverly fused with traditional quality materials like leather and wood, and Jaguar went to great pains to emphasise the quality and ambience –more forward thinking, with a wider range of trim and equipment choices, was the order of the day.

Internal space had never been the strong point of the X-100 model and the X-150 was much improved here. There was now 59mm more seat travel, 54mm more front legroom, 31mm more front headroom, 32mm greater shoulder room, and better foot space in the New XK. All this was achieved due to the longer wheelbase, wider track and taller roofline. The car was claimed to be the class leader in terms of driver/ passenger front and shoulder room. Jaguar's electronic parking brake liberated the space normally used for a manual handbrake lever. Jaguar also asserted that there was improved interior stowage space, but in reality this was marginal, as were any gains in rear seating accommodation,

The intuitive touch-screen display. (Nigel Thorley)

the 2+2 arrangement being more suited for children than adults.

The dashboard lines flowed from the A pillars to the centre console, where a new touch-screen carried controls for several in-car features. A relatively small instrument cluster housed the two prominent analogue dials for speedometer and rev counter, backlit in green, with pointers, highlighted in white, either side of a Driver Information Centre high-resolution colour display based on thin-film transistor technology. This display was split into several zones, showing vital information such as gear selection, cruise control information, low tyre pressure warnings, and satellite navigational instructions, all dependent on specification and market sector model. The border of this Driver Information Centre changed colour through white to yellow to red to illustrate the urgency of any problem. Jaguar considered there was no longer a need for auxiliary gauges except for a fuel bar gauge. Basic controls were kept to a minimum, and laid out for quick, easy and logical operation.

Returning to the centre

dashboard area, the 7in touch-screen allowed intuitive selection of climate control, audio, navigation and telephone settings, with minimal distraction and complexity – an entirely new design for Jaguar saloons at the time, and a major departure from anything fitted to later X-100 models. The system was designed so that in each menu, there was a maximum of five items to select. For even easier selection, in some modes, just approaching a selection with a finger would make the icon 'grow' and sound off, ensuring the operator touched the correct selection. The touch-screen also incorporated the standard DVD based satellite navigational system controls. Now fully operational with the postcode system, audible messages, a wider range of on-screen information and display options. Furthermore, in Europe, the system was supplemented by Traffic Messaging Channel information, received from local stations via the radio antenna.

The climate control system had been totally revised as well. The New XK had was fitted with a dual zone system that could be regulated via the touch-screen, as well as by conventional control buttons. Humidity control sensed the risk of misting, and was switchable for dehumidified airflow to the windscreen and automatic demisting after cold starts. The defrost system incorporated heated front and rear screens and door mirrors. Heated front seats and the option of a heated steering wheel rim were also controlled by the climate control system, via the touch-screen.

There was an initial choice of standard or Premium sound audio systems for the New XK. The standard system incorporated six speakers, supporting analogue audio and CDs, as well as disks containing WMA and MP3 digital files. The Premium Sound system, produced by Alpine for Jaguar, incorporated eight speakers, a remote 6-channel amplifier with 520watts output, and Dolby Pro-logic II Surround Sound.

The built-in communications interface was Bluetooth™ based, which could communicate wirelessly with compatible mobile phones (which only had to be in the passenger compartment or in a briefcase or pocket, to operate). The completely hands-free system had volume and answer controls on the steering wheel, and even a 'Do not disturb' mode, if required. The telephone dialling keypad was also part of the touch-screen display.

Furthermore, the New XK was the first production Jaguar to feature a Smart Key system, providing keyless starting of the engine via a prominent red push button on the centre console. Also available was keyless entry

The return of the starter button, once usual practice on Jaguars of the 1950s and 1960s. (Nigel Thorley)

to the car, made possible by just carrying the Jaguar Smart Key Fob in your pocket or bag, when approaching the car.

There was an initial choice of two leather trims, including soft grain – which could be extended, as an option, to cover the instrument panel top, door cappings and seats. In each type of interior, there was a choice of four overall colour schemes, two of them two-tone, with contrasting and complementing colours: Ivory and Charcoal; Ivory and Slate Blue; Charcoal and

Three examples of the trim finishes on the early New XKs: top to bottom Aluminium, Poplar and Burr Walnut.
(Jaguar Cars/Nigel Thorley)

Boot space in the Coupé was excellent for a grand tourer, and, with the tailgate closed, nothing was visible to the outside world. (Nigel Thorley)

Charcoal. To accompany them, there were also three veneer options: Aluminium; Burr Walnut; Poplar Wood.

Luggage space was certainly not compromised in the Coupé, being specifically designed to carry the obligatory two sets of golf clubs, or a full sized Samsonite suitcase. Although the rear overhang beyond the wheels was reduced by 122mm compared to the previous model, rear luggage volume was actually only 8 litres less – or indeed 22 litres more when the optional run-flat tyre was specified. Convertibles did suffer, however, as more space was required for the retracting hood and mechanism than before.

Safety features

Along with the items mentioned in the last chapter, there were other safety features, such as Jaguar's Protect dynamic headrest system to guard against whiplash injuries by automatically pushing the headrest forward to support the head and reduce the risk of injuries to the neck. The car was also equipped with ISOfix child-seat fixings in both rear seats. Some features were optional, for example the Tyre Pressure Monitoring System, or run-flat tyres.

The New XK offered 'intelligent' front seat airbags – the driver's one sensed the seat position of the driver and the severity of any impact, deploying the airbag accordingly. In the case of the front passenger airbag, that also minimised injury, even if the passenger was sitting in an awkward position, or too close to the airbag. The car was equipped with two combined front seat head and thorax side airbags, developed to protect occupants from impacts from larger vehicles

and stationary structures such as poles. A Thatcham category 1 alarm system, with microwave intrusion sensing door protection, and tilt-sensing to detect the vehicle being opened, jacked up or moved, was standard equipment. It featured two-stage unlocking, which unlocked the driver's door with one push of the unlock button, and the passenger's door with another push. The steering wheel lock was automatically engaged when the car was locked.

Jaguar enhanced the driving experience of the New XK by not only offering advances in existing technology used in the previous models like Dynamic Stability Control and Traction Control, but also with the availability of entirely new features.

Cruise control for example, was a standard feature in its conventional form. However, Adaptive Cruise Control was also offered, using microwave radar technology to monitor the road ahead, and automatically reduce speed if traffic conditions made it necessary. This was a development of the system used on the last of the X-100 models.

Other standard features on the New XK included rear parking sensors, rain-sensitive wiper systems, and light-sensitive lighting systems. Also standard was the fitment of bi-xenon headlamps, incorporating power-

Jaguar's then unique Pedestrian Safety System, and how it operated. (Jaguar Cars/Nigel Thorley)

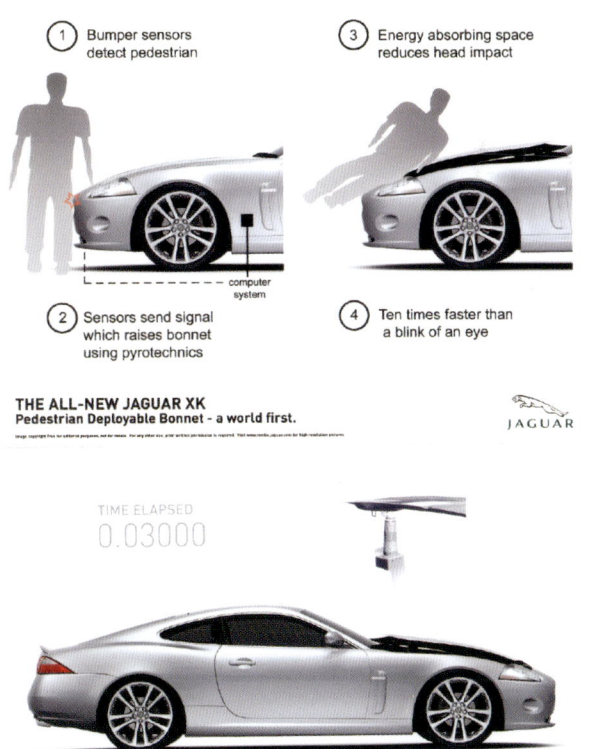

wash and self-levelling. The system operated a separate beam at low speeds, and, when the direction indicator was used, to light up an area to the sides of the car for low speed manoeuvering. An optional Active Front Lighting system provided enhanced night-time visibility by automatically swivelling the dipped beam lenses, depending on road speed and steering angle.

Wheels & tyres

The New XK was initially offered with a choice of aluminium alloy wheel designs in three sizes, with an optional tyre pressure monitoring system and, depending on wheel choice, the option of a run-flat tyre specification.

18in alloy wheels were standard, with the option of 19in or 20in wheels. The 18in and 19in wheels had conventional solid rims, the 20in wheels having a split-rim design. On each model, and whatever the wheel diameter, the rear wheels were wider than the front ones to optimise the steering characteristics, handling, balance and traction.

With 19in wheels, run-flat tyres were also available as optional equipment, designed to allow the driver to drive on following a puncture, and were capable of travelling for 80-120km at speeds of up to 50mph after a total deflation.

The optional Tyre Pressure Monitoring System (TPMS) used a pressure sensor in each wheel, continuously monitoring each tyre. Data from the sensor was transmitted by radio frequency to a receiver in each wheelarch, and in turn to the central control module. In the event of a loss of pressure, the system displayed clear warnings in the instrument cluster to help the driver to take appropriate action. The TPMS system was standard equipment with run-flat tyres, and available as an option with all other tyre types. Where run-flat tyres were fitted, no spare wheel needed to be carried in the luggage compartment, and the unused spare wheel well was fully trimmed and shaped to take a suitcase, increasing the total loadspace by 30 litres.

So, what's in a name?

Jaguar felt confident enough to retain the XK insignia for the new car. However, a subtle change was that the X-150 would be known as just the XK and not XK8.

Enter the Convertible

Announced in Coupé form only, Jaguar stated that, when the car became available early in 2006, there would be a convertible version as well. (No mention was made of a supercharged version, but it was inevitable that such a model would be available, perhaps in a similar time frame to the launch of the original XKR, over twelve months after the XK8.) Only a month after the Coupé, Jaguar announced the Convertible option for the New XK. This was not just a staggering 1635kg lighter than the X-100 Convertible – it was the lightest car in the high-performance 2+2 convertible sector of the market. Jaguar had achieved this without compromising the rigidity of the structure – a common failure previously when manufactures had 'chop-topped' their coupés. The reason for this was that the entire New XK range had been developed around the concept of a convertible first, and those rectangular section sills (mentioned earlier) eliminated the need for extra conventional stiffening panels, and the excess weight usually associated with convertible models.

Jaguar had always been conscious of the important US market for such cars, and the need for luggage accommodation in prestige 2+2 convertibles. It had achieved this in the previous X-100 model, but with the hindrance of having to fit a tonneau cover manually with the hood down. When the X-150 was in development, there was a trend towards metal folding roofs for high-end convertibles, but Jaguar designers decided not to bow to that fashion, instead retaining a conventional but quality fabric 'soft top'. The reasons for this were, first, that an excellent styling 'line' could be more easily achieved with a hood and, second, that it would take up less room in the boot area.

Unhindered lines of the New XK Convertible, now with a fully retractable hood and solid tonneau cover. (Jaguar Cars/Nigel Thorley)

Designed to look good with hood up or down, the New XK was much more stylish than other contemporary convertibles. (Jaguar Cars/Nigel Thorley)

Boot space in the Convertible was more limited than the X-100 model. (Nigel Thorley)

The deployable hoops discussed in the text. (Nigel Thorley)

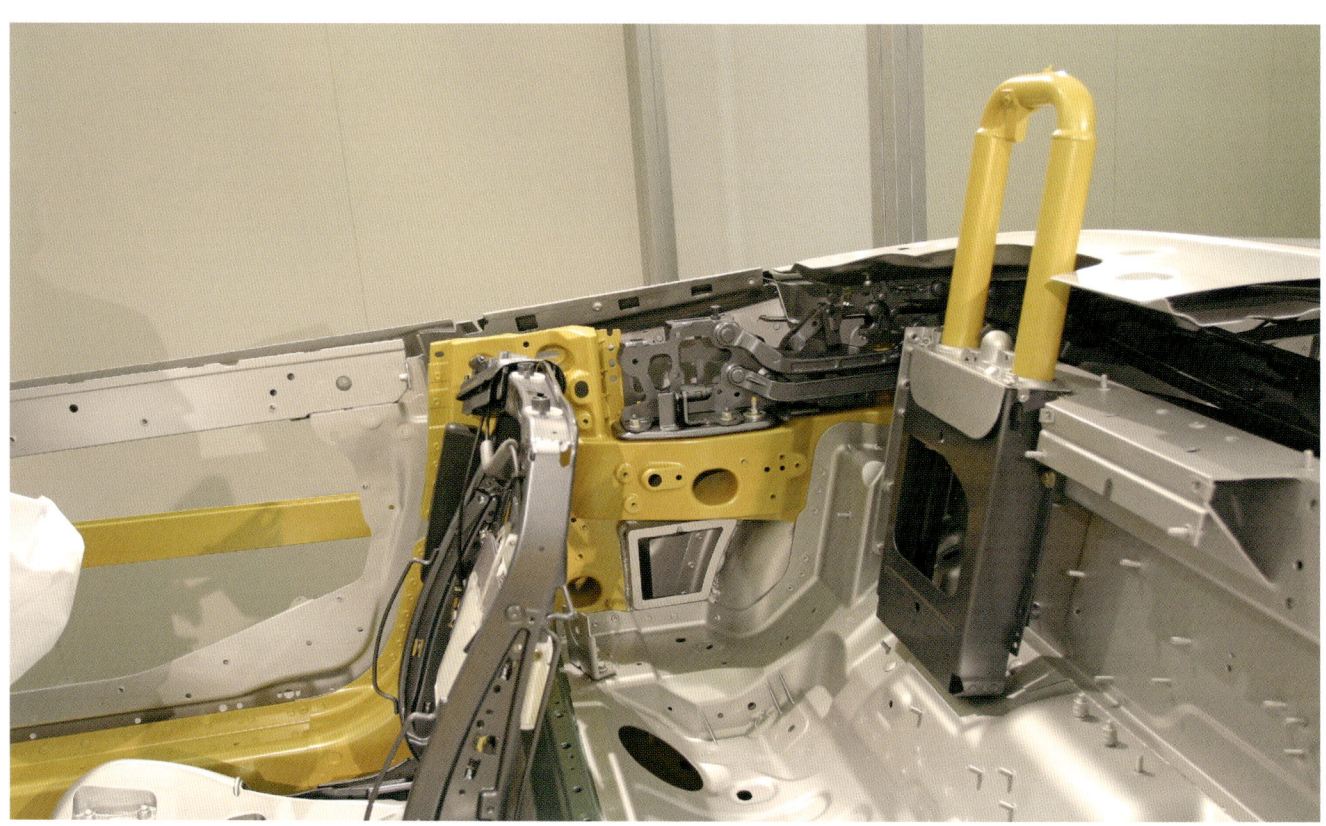

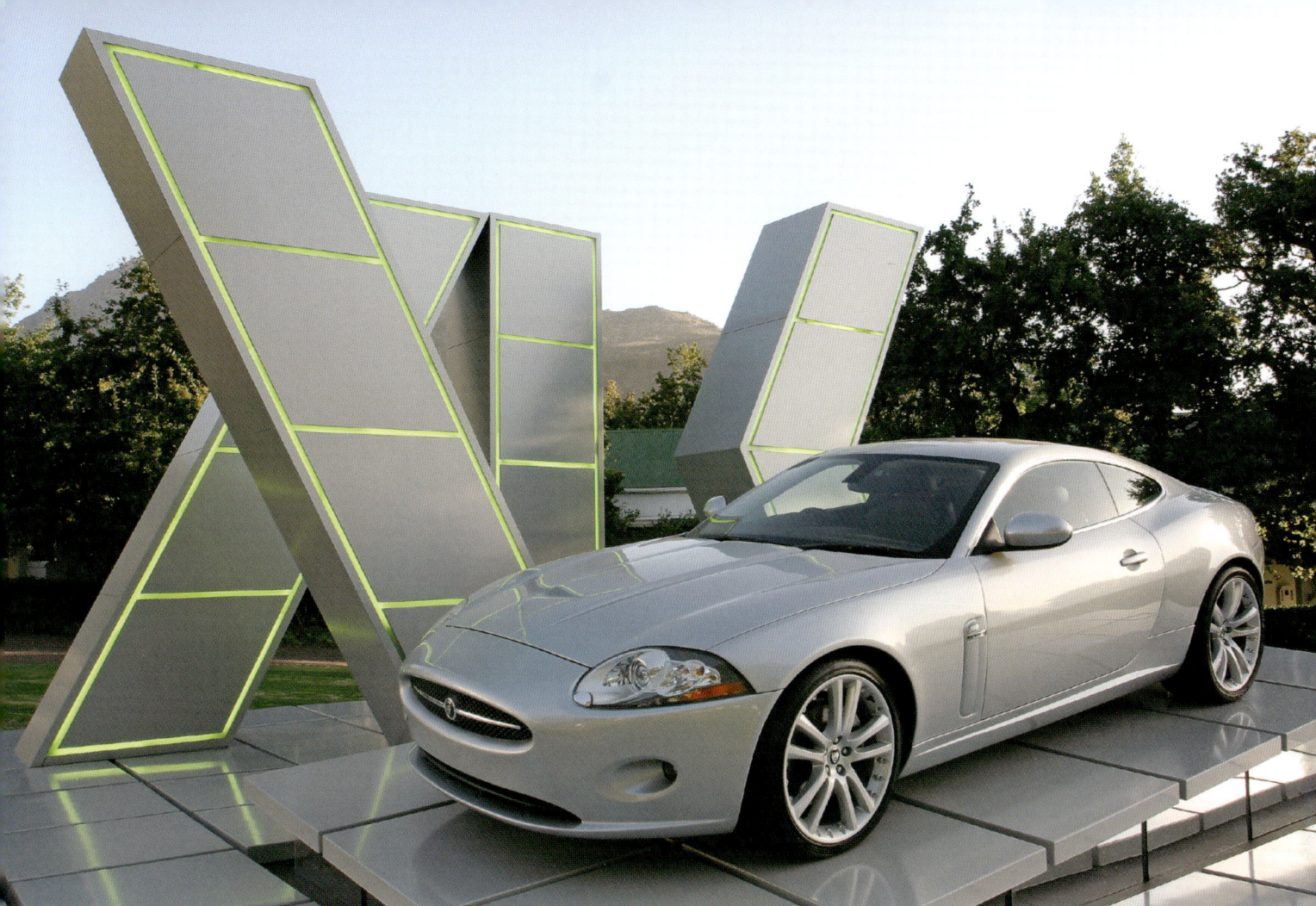

The New XK, launched to the public in 2006. (Nigel Thorley)

The triple-lined hood of the New XK was available in a range of colours. It retained a heated glass rear screen and was, of course, electrically operated. The hood mechanism was now faster to retract and erect, taking a mere 18 seconds including the lowering or raising of the side and rear quarter windows. It could be operated when on the move up to speeds of 10mph. When lowered the hood stowed away neatly in the compartment in the boot, with an aluminium body coloured tonneau automatically covering the area making for a smooth finish across the rear deck of the car.

The boot lid was shallower than the previous model, and space inside the boot was more restricted. However the hood was retained within a retractable loadspace separator, which, when more luggage space was required, could be unclipped and swung out of the way, with the hood in the erect position. This provided an extra 83 litres of load space in the boot.

The hood itself was constructed of three separate layers, the outer a completely waterproof cloth/rubber/cloth laminate, and the inner a luxurious cloth lining, taut and smooth when the hood was in the closed position. The sandwich filling was an insulation layer using 3M Thinsulate material. This combination provided significantly better insulation for less than half the thickness of the previous XK soft top construction. The net result was a quieter, lighter, more compact roof. The roof still retained a toughened glass, heated rear screen bonded into the hood. A new feature was the ability to lower the rear side windows with the hood still erect, to provide better ventilation.

An extra safety feature for the convertible models was the fitting, as standard equipment, of a roll-over protection system. This comprised two hidden aluminium hoops that deployed in the event of an accident. They created a protective area around the restrained occupants, between the deployed hoops and the reinforced windscreen structure. The system was activated via an advanced solid-state gyro sensor system, a patented design which allowed it to deploy through the rear screen if the roof was in the raised position.

The automated climate control system included a dedicated strategy for the Convertible for when the car was being driven with the hood down. This automatically changed the distribution of the airflow (warm or cool), providing greater flow to the face vents.

Public launch

The X-150 Coupé made its global public debut at the Frankfurt Motor Show, in September of 2005, followed by the Convertible at the NAIAS Detroit Motor Show in January 2006. Even before going on sale, the New XK had already been awarded the Engineering and Technology Award at the prestigious Prince Michael International Road Safety Awards.

Soon after, more awards came its way. It was given the Car of the Year award and Luxury Car of the Year, at the UKTV People Awards in 2006. Over 10,000 UK TV viewers voted from a choice of 16 vehicles, choosing the New XK as their favourite car overall. Throughout the week preceding the awards ceremony, viewers watched Formula 1's Louise Goodman test drive all 16 vehicles on the UKTV channel, where she highlighted the various attributes of each car. The New XK had won a total of eight awards by 2006.

LAUNCH PRICES FOR THE NEW XK (X-150)

£58,995 Coupé
£64,955 Convertible

The new 'in' word for promotion of the New XK, 'Gorgeous'.

X-100/X-150 COMPARISONS

	Coupé		Convertible		Improvement
	X-150	X-100	X-150	X-100	
0 to 60mph (seconds)	5.9	6.1	6.0	6.3	0.2secs
Maximum bhp	300	294	300	294	+2%
Power to weight ratio	188	172	183	163	+10/13%
Maximum torque lbs/ft	310	303	310	303	+2%
Torque to weight ratio	263	240	257	228	+10/13%
Torsional stiffness Nm	29600	22590	15300	10317	+31/48%
Head room mm	38.2	37.4	38.3	37.0	
Shoulder room mm	56.5	55.2	56.5	55.2	
Legroom mm	45.1	43.0	45.1	43.0	
Weight kg	1595	1685	1635	1775	+5/8%

Chapter Thirteen

XKR returns

An eager sports-car-buying public had had to wait nearly two years after the launch of the XK8 for the arrival of the first XKR, in 1998 Not so this time around: the New XKR was announced just months after the first New XKs were delivered – and this wasn't just a case of a few trim changes, new badging and the adding of a supercharger to the existing engine, there was much more behind putting this car into a sporting GT class of its own.

Jaguar's Chief Engineer, Mike Cross, said:

"Our aim when engineering the new XKR was to ensure that the car's characteristics remained in balance despite the significant increase in power over the XK. Working with that as our base, our brief was to create 'XK plus 30%' – the ultimate sports GT for the real world.

"We wanted the performance and dynamism you would expect of an XKR, but were careful to retain that exceptional blend of sporting luxury that every Jaguar must have and which is so convincingly demonstrated with the XK. The bottom line is that if you like the XK, you'll absolutely love the new XKR."

The supercharged 4.2-litre engine and powertrain

The supercharged version of the AJ-V8 installed in the XKR produced 420bhp (SAE) at 6250rpm and 560Nm (EEC) of torque at 4000rpm, and was capable of propelling the XKR Coupé to 60mph in 4.9 seconds

The New XKR Coupé with alloy finished power vents and 20in Senta alloy wheels. (Nigel Thorley)

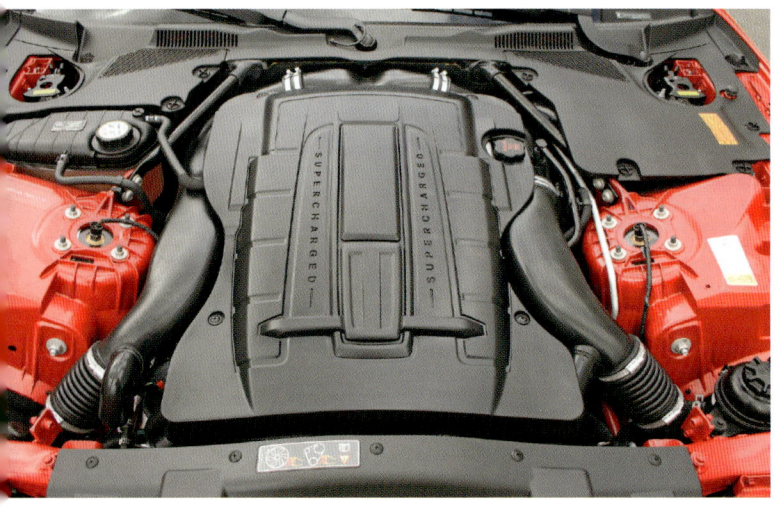

The performance from the supercharged engine surpassed the previous XKR models.(Nigel Thorley)

(5.0 seconds for the Convertible) and on to an electronically-limited top speed of 155mph (250kph).

The addition of a supercharger and twin air intakes meant the new XKR benefited from a 120bhp (SAE) power increase over the normally-aspirated 4.2-litre XK. Torque, essential for instant acceleration at any engine speed, also increased significantly – by 36% over the XK. The overall weight of the XKR was raised by just 70kg, consequently the power-to-weight ratio compared to the normally-aspirated 4.2-litre XK was an impressive 34% higher.

In comparison to the previous generation XKR, the new engine produced more power and more torque. Combined with a significantly stiffer and lighter aluminium monocoque body structure, these performance improvements led to a significant leap in the power-to-weight ratio of 12% and an equally useful jump of 7.7% in the torque-to-weight ratio. To achieve the equivalent improvements in power and torque-to-weight in the outgoing XKR would have required nearly 50 more horsepower.

Among the benefits of the increases in power and torque was a Coupé 0-60mph sprint time reduced by 0.3 seconds compared to the previous XKR, and acceleration from 50mph to 70mph in just 2.5 seconds.

This increase in power and torque was down to two major engine additions: the air intake had been significantly enhanced thanks to the use of twin air inlets; and a Variable Inlet Camshaft Timing (VICT) system was used for the first time on the XKR. By continuously adjusting the timing of the inlet camshaft on both banks of the V8, depending on the engine speed and load, Jaguar's engineers ensured significant improvements in torque, particularly at lower revs.

The VICT system was controlled by the Engine Management System (EMS), which receives engine speed, throttle position and oil temperature data from its sensors. The EMS determines the correct inlet camshaft timing by continuously referring to a digital three-dimensional map, developed to provide optimum performance. The EMS then transmits the appropriate signals to two solenoids that control the degree of hydraulic force provided to the valve actuators.

A separate characteristic that the XK had been praised for was its acoustic quality, remaining unobtrusive and relaxed at modest speeds, but producing an unmistakeable V8 'soundtrack' when worked hard. On the XKR, the presence of supercharger

The exhaust sound was accentuated for the XKR model. (Nigel Thorley)

Unique alloy trim finish, gear knob and uprated gearbox software for the XKR. (Nigel Thorley)

(Nigel Thorley)

whine threatened to dominate the acoustic character and mask the underlying sound quality. However, through enhancements to the vehicle acoustic pack, the supercharger noise was reduced by 5dB compared to the previous XKR, eliminating any potential issue. This approach to acoustics allowed engineers to concentrate on using the exhaust system to deliver the best possible sound quality character. This was accomplished through the use of the XKR's Active Exhaust which varied the flow of exhaust gases through the main silencer box to ensure that the XKR remained quiet at cruising speeds but delivered a substantially more purposeful V8 roar under hard acceleration.

The three modes of the 6-speed XF gearbox were suitably adjusted to provide the New XKR driver with total flexibility to use the transmission to match whatever driving style he or she chose. In Drive mode, the gearbox behaved as a conventional automatic, with the software optimised for everyday driving conditions. In Sport mode, the gearbox's adaptive software became more prevalent, adapting and reacting more dynamically to demanding conditions. This software took account of the prevailing road conditions and the driver's inputs, and adapted accordingly. Hill Recognition enabled the XKR to choose the ratios to optimise the ascent or descent of a hill; the gearbox's software also matched the engine speed precisely to the engine and road speeds, 'blipping' the throttle during rapid downshifts. Manual mode was activated by simply operating one of the steering wheel-mounted paddles, delivering a state-of-the-art manual gearshift feel from the automatic transmission.

Chassis, suspension and brakes

The XKR's springs and dampers were uprated compared to the XK. The front spring rate was increased by 38% and the rear spring rate by 24%. Allied to this, the Servotronic steering system had also been tuned both mechanically and electronically to give the steering more weight and even greater response.

Because of the inherent strength and stiffness of the chassis, and the addition of a rear suspension brace engineered to accommodate the significant increase in rear spring rate, the XKR Coupé and Convertible had the same dynamic settings. The Computer Active Technology Suspension and new switchable Dynamic Stability Control with Traction Control System (Trac DSC) were also recalibrated to complement the additional power of the supercharged engine.

New, larger ventilated brake discs at the front ensured better braking performance for the XKR. The front brake disc diameter was increased from 326mm to 355mm and the thickness from 30mm to 32mm, which not only improved braking but also the system's resistance to fade.

Exterior and Interior trim changes

Jaguar made some subtle changes to the XK to create a different look for the New XKR. At the front, there

The stylish XKR Convertible not only looked good but was an excellent performer, too. (Nigel Thorley).

Revised frontal treatment with colour coded auxiliary light units and
mesh grilles differentiated the XKR from the XK.
(Jaguar Cars/Nigel Thorley)

The now obligatory bonnet louvres, not just for aesthetic reasons,
but they also served a purpose in improving air flow and cooling.
(Jaguar Cars/Nigel Thorley)

was a new style front bumper with colour-keyed
finish on the front foglamp housings, along with a
different aluminium finish to the upper and lower front
mesh grilles. The bonnet now featured the obligatory
'supercharged' louvres either side of the power bulge.

Moving to the side, the front wing power vents were
now finished in aluminium instead of body colour.

New XKR Coupé and Convertible, both finished in Slate Grey with 20in Senta wheels. (Jaguar Cars/Nigel Thorley)

Revised lower bumper area and four tailpipes for the XKR, along with the new badging. (Jaguar Cars/Nigel Thorley)

Revised seating with stiffer bolsters, XKR logos in the headrests and weave finished alloy trim. (Jaguar Cars/Nigel Thorley)

As if the driver wouldn't realise he was in an XKR, badging appeared in the main instruments which were recalibrated for the extra performance. (Jaguar Cars/Nigel Thorley)

19in Jupiter design alloy wheels were standard (with 20in Cremona alloys as an option). The brake callipers carried the 'R' logo, visible through the wheels.

At the rear, a new 'R' badge, along with an aluminium finish to the 'signature' panel, and the addition of a quad (four tailpipe) exhaust system with a revised lower bumper to accommodate them, differentiated the XKR from the XK.

Changes to the interior started with a unique sports seat design providing additional lateral support for both the driver and front seat passenger, incorporating the 'R' logo in the headrests. The logo also featured on the rev counter, steering wheel and gear selector. Taking a feature from the original ALC show car, the XKR featured a unique 'weave' pattern to the alloy trim panels.

XKR customers could specify the Luxury Sports interior trim option that featured soft grain leather with 16-way, electrically-adjustable seating. The soft grain leather continued to the instrument panel, door trims and centre console areas.

C h a p t e r   **Fourteen**

New XK ongoing developments

As you will read in this chapter, Jaguar continually upgraded the XK and XKR throughout 2007 and 2008.

XK 3.5s?

It is not commonly known or well publicised that, between the start of production prototyping and 2008, Jaguar produced nearly 1300 examples of both the XK Coupé and Convertible, fitted with the 3.5 litre V8 petrol engine, as used at the time in the X-350 XJ saloons. Little is known about these cars except that they were probably specifically built for engine size/tax-conscious markets, like Northern Europe. None are known to remain in the UK, and nothing is known about what happened to them, or if they still exist.

New XK styling pack

At the start of 2007, Jaguar produced a distinctive Exterior Styling Package for the New XK models, as it had done for the X-type and S-type saloons at the time.

The pack consisted of a new front valance, rear valance, upper and lower mesh grilles in a choice of bright or black finishes, and sill appliqués, as well as new exhaust tailpipe finishers. The components were designed for ease of fitment, using existing fittings on the cars. The pack came in primer. ready to be painted to match a car's finish and would have been fitted by a

The X-150 styling kit fitted offered retrospectively for the early XK models. (Jaguar Cars/Nigel Thorley)

Side sill extensions were part of the X-150 styling kit.
(Nigel Thorley)

The styling kit included deeper rear bumper and square tail pipes.
(Jaguar Cars/Nigel Thorley)

Jaguar dealership to a new car, or fitted to an existing car retrospectively. As Ian Callum, Jaguar's Design Director commented, "The enhancements we have made for the XK Exterior Styling Pack give the car an even more stylish and purposeful look by deliberately lowering the visual stance of the car and creating exciting new elements that work with the elegant profile of the XK."

XKR Portfolio

With the New XK and XKR selling well, a new special limited edition XKR Portfolio added to the range in March 2007. The new model was provided with improved luxury and technology, and was available in all worldwide Jaguar markets.

Externally, the XKR Portfolio was fitted with 20in polished Cremona five-spoke alloy wheels as standard. The front wing power vents were now hewn from polished aluminium (instead of body colour on the XK

The XKR Portfolio special edition dating from 2007.
(Jaguar Cars/Nigel Thorley)

and dull alloy on the XKR), and incorporated indicator side repeaters and the Jaguar 'ingot' signature name. An exclusive colour at the time, Celestial Black, was the

The XKR Portfolio Convertible in the European Liquid Silver colour alternative with polished Cremona alloy wheels.
(Jaguar Cars/Nigel Thorley)

The more usual Celestial Black paint finish to the XKR Portfolio. (Jaguar Cars/Nigel Thorley)

Styling and trim enhancements to the interior of the 2007 XKR Portfolio. (Jaguar Cars/Nigel Thorley)

standard exterior paint colour finish on the Portfolio (with Liquid Silver as a paint option for the UK and Swiss markets).

Jaguar Special Vehicles department teamed up with world-leading brake manufacturer Alcan to create the largest, most powerful brakes ever fitted to a production Jaguar at that time. These included massive 400mm front disc brakes, 45mm larger than the standard XKR model, retarded by powerful 6-piston callipers. At the rear, 4-piston callipers operated on 350mm discs. Race-developed, crescent-shaped grooves were cut into the

New at the time alloy trim treatment for the XKR Portfolio. (Jaguar Cars/Nigel Thorley)

surface of the discs to prevent a build-up of deposits on the brake pads, and improve braking performance under extreme use. By allowing the heat created within the system to dissipate quickly and efficiently, the Portfolio's brakes produced fade-free performance, whilst maintaining refinement and stopping power. The callipers were finished in red, with 'R' branding, visible through the alloy wheels.

Internally, the Portfolio benefited from a unique, engine-spin aluminium veneer, while customers also had the option of Satin American Walnut veneer. A new alloy and leather gearshift selector, soft-grab door handles, contrast stitching throughout the cabin, leather-edged mats with a Jaguar logo, and distinctive Portfolio treadplates on the doorsills, completed the effect. Note, this was a limited edition model, unrelated to later Portfolio models.

The Portfolio was fitted with a new Bowers & Wilkins hi-fi speaker system, tuned specifically for the XKR's cabin. High-output, low-distortion Kevlar mid-range speakers, and specially designed aluminium-dome tweeters delivered superb mid-range and extended high-frequency responses.

XKR-S

At the 2008 Geneva Motor Show, Jaguar announced a rather special limited edition XK, the XKR-S. Only available as a Coupé, this was reportedly the fastest production XK at the time.

The beginnings of this car went back to 2006, when, following the completion of development work on the XKR, a test vehicle was still available. Work commenced, initially unofficially, on an even more driver-focused car, which eventually lead to the formal introduction of the XKR-S.

The original XKR-S with body skirts and lowered suspension.

Using the existing 4.2-litre supercharged engine, the engine management system was recalibrated to provide 420bhp @ 6250rpm (416PS) and 413lb ft of torque @ 4000rpm. This gave a 0 to 60mph time of just 5.2 seconds, with an electronically-limited top speed of 174mph, attained by reducing drag via a specific aerodynamic package.

To match the performance, the XKR-S featured the Alcan braking system, first seen on the XKR Portfolio model mentioned previously.

Work was also carried out for the XKR-S on the suspension, with new springs, anti-roll bars and unique dampers, and all aspects of the suspension system were retuned. A faster ratio steering rack was also used for quicker reaction and optimum feel.

With the revised handling package, the ride height was reduced by 10mm compared to the XKR and the car sat on unique-at-the-time 20in Vortex alloy wheels with specialist tyres.

Finally, the four-tailpipe exhaust system was re-tuned to provide a more 'hard edged' sound, particularly under acceleration.

The XKR-S Coupé was available in Ultimate Black exterior paintwork, and carried suitable badging on the boot. Styling changes included a new front aerodynamic splitter, side sill extensions, and revised rear spoiler and diffuser panel.

Internally, the soft grain leather upholstery was finished in Charcoal with Ivory twin-needle contrast stitching. Leather finishing, and contrast stitching continued to the instrument panel top, centre console, inner door panels and rear side panels. Piano Black veneer was used for the finishing touches, along with a Charcoal Alston luxury headlining. Finally the instrument cluster was recalibrated to take account of the improved performance and XKR-S branding featured on the leather trimmed steering wheel, alloy and leather gear selector, bright aluminium pedals and headrests. The XKR-S also benefited from the Bowers & Wilkins hi-fi system used in the Portfolio model.

Only for sale in European markets, a total of 200 XKR-S models were produced at this time, although the model designation would crop up later in production as you will see in Chapter 16.

XK60 Special Edition

Mid-year 2008 also saw the 60th anniversary of the famous XK120, Jaguar's first postwar sports car and, to commemorate this, Jaguar launched a special series of the New XK for the UK market, aptly named XK60. With the introduction of the XKR Portfolio and XKR-S models, the XK60 provided the opportunity to update the normally-aspirated cars with lots of enhancements, without a price increase! This model at the time therefore replaced the existing XK models.

The upgrades (for both Coupé and Convertible models) included the standard fitment of 20in Senta alloy wheels and some distinctive exterior body enhancements, like a new front spoiler and rear valance panel, chrome-finished power vents and bright upper and lower front grille meshes, special tailpipe finishers and appliqués on both sides of the car, most of which were once offered as the styling package reviewed earlier.

Internally only a more sporty alloy gear selector and surround differentiated the XK60 from previous XKs.

The XK60 model, the normally-aspirated production cars introduced in 2008. (Jaguar Cars/Nigel Thorley)

Chapter Fifteen

Enter the 5.0-litre

Enter the 5.0-litre

On 12th January 2009, Jaguar announced major powertrain changes to its range of cars, including the introduction of the all-new AJ-V8 Gen III engine in the XK range, delivering more power and performance with greater efficiency. The XKs were also to be given a more dramatic look in readiness for the launch in March of that year of three core models in the new XK range: the XK, the highly-equipped XK Portfolio, and the supercharged XKR.

The 5.0-litre XK is launched in 2009, here seen in Coupé form with body colour power vents incorporating the new 'Jaguar' insignia and indicator repeaters. (Jaguar Cars/Nigel Thorley)

The new 5.0-litre AJ-V8 Gen III engines

The new AJ-V8 Gen III engines were the most advanced and efficient Jaguar had ever produced. They bore little resemblance to the out-going 4.2-litre units. The naturally-aspirated 5.0-litre engine delivered 385PS (SAE) – 26% more power than its 4.2-litre predecessor, and 380lb ft (515Nm) of torque – 23% more. The XKR's supercharged 5.0-litre version delivered a mighty 510PS (510bhp SAE) and 461lb ft (625Nm) of torque – improvements of 23% and 12% over the supercharged 4.2-litre engine.

On the road, maximum speed remained electronically controlled at 155mph (250kph). However, these power and torque gains, allied to the lightweight aluminium

body architecture of the XK, dramatically improved acceleration times. For the naturally-aspirated XK, 0-60mph was cut from 5.9 seconds to 5.2 seconds (0-100kph from 6.2 to 5.5 seconds); for the supercharged XKR, 0-60mph was cut from 4.9 seconds to 4.6 seconds (0-100kph to 4.8 seconds from 5.2). The supercharged XKR was also impressively efficient, with combined fuel economy of 23mpg and a CO_2 rating of 292g/km – an improvement over the previous XKR – and 16% and 17% better, respectively, than the equivalent figures for the BMW M6. Crucially, the naturally-aspirated XK also continued to beat its closest rivals on economy and CO_2 ratings, with an average consumption of 25.2mpg and a CO_2 figure of 264g/km – 7% better than the equivalent figures for the Mercedes-Benz SL500 – thanks to its fuel-efficient engine and significantly lower kerb weight: 1660kg compared to the SL500's 1845kg.

The new Gen III engines were built around a stiff, all-new, aluminium block, with cast-in iron liners and cross-bolted main bearing caps to reduce noise, vibration and harshness. The blocks were high pressure die-cast, providing a superior finish and greater dimensional accuracy. The engines used aluminium heads, with four valves per cylinder, and spheroidal-graphite cast iron crankshafts and forged steel connecting rods. For the first time, the cylinder heads were specified with a secondary (recycled) aluminium alloy thus reducing the environmental impact of manufacturing the new engine.

The 5.0-litre direct-injection petrol engines were also more compact than their predecessors. By relocating the oil pump, overall engine length had been reduced by 24mm. This allowed for improved engine bay packaging to support enhanced safety cell performance, while ensuring overall engine weight was virtually unchanged.

A sixth-generation, twin vortex system supercharger was fitted to the XKR's 510PS engine – a compact Roots-type unit, feeding air through twin intercoolers, which in turn were water-cooled by their own discreet cooling circuit. The new air intake had been radically redesigned – with air delivered through twin air boxes, flow loss was reduced and efficiency increased. The high helix rotor design improved the supercharger thermodynamic efficiency by 16% over the 4.2-litre model. It also improved noise quality to the point where the unit was now virtually inaudible (making supercharger whine a thing of the past). The intercoolers reduced the temperature of the pressurised intake-air and so optimised power and efficiency.

Mechanically, the new supercharger and its intercoolers were efficiently packaged in the 'V' of the engine to deliver a lower overall engine height in support of pedestrian safety requirements.

One of the key features of the new petrol engines (an industry first), was the centrally-mounted, multi-hole, spray-guided fuel-injection system, delivering fuel at a pressure of up to 150bar directly to the cylinder. The positioning of the injectors ensured fuel was precisely delivered to the centre of the combustion chamber, maximising air-fuel mixing and improving combustion control. Fuel was delivered via twin, high-pressure fuel pumps that were driven via an auxiliary shaft in the new engine block. This substantially contributed to improved low-speed, dynamic response.

The charge cooling effects of the direct-injection fuel system allowed the compression ratio of the naturally-aspirated engine to be raised to 11.5:1, further optimising the engine economy. The supercharged engine also benefited from a compression ratio increase to 9.5:1 from 9.0:1 in the previous 4.2-litre.

During the engine warm-up phase, the combustion system employed multiple injection mode strategies to deliver 50% more heat for fast catalyst warm-up and emissions reduction.

The launch of the new AJ-V8 Gen III 5.0-litre petrol engine, used in the XK, XKR and the equivalent XF and XJ saloons.
(Jaguar Cars/Nigel Thorley)

A neat installation of the 5.0-litre Gen III engine meant more space around the engine bay, though little could actually be seen! (Nigel Thorley)

Another innovation involved a new type of variable camshaft timing (VCT) system. Instead of being activated by oil pressure, the four VCT units were triggered by the positive and negative torques generated by opening and closing the intake and exhaust valves. This allowed for a smaller engine oil pump, saving energy and improving fuel consumption. VCT units worked independently on all four camshafts with 62° of authority on the inlet cams and 50° of authority on the exhaust cams. Timing was optimised by the engine control unit for torque, power and economy at every point in the engine's speed range. The new VCT units were capable of a response rate up to three times faster than in previous Jaguar engines, with actuation rates in excess of 150 degrees per second.

The naturally-aspirated engine was also equipped with camshaft profile switching (CPS) on the inlet camshaft. Depending on the engine's running conditions and the demands of the driver, the CPS switched between one profile that was ideal for low-speed driving, and another which gave increased valve lift for high-performance. Hydraulically-actuated two-piece tappets switched between profiles on the tri-lobe camshaft and altered both the lift and duration. The cam lobe profile selected for lower engine speeds had a duration of 214° and lifted the valves 5.5mm. This optimised gas velocity improved low-speed torque and reduced valvetrain friction for improved fuel economy.

For high-speed driving, CPS switched to a cam lobe with a duration of 250° and valve-lift of 10.5mm, allowing greater airflow for high power. Switching was activated at 2800rpm at high load, ranging to 4500rpm at light load conditions.

A new variable inlet manifold (VIM) on the naturally-aspirated engine varied the length of its eight inlet tracts to optimise power and torque throughout the rev range. Vacuum-operated actuators opened valves to select a longer, 680mm, inlet tract at low revs, increasing the rate of both the airflow and the engine torque. As the revs climb beyond 4700rpm, the actuators selected a shorter, 350mm path allowing a greater volume of air into the engine to optimise power. The actuator position was monitored by the engine control unit to improve torque throughout the engine speed range.

An innovative reverse-flow cooling system design was employed to deliver thermodynamic and friction improvements. The reverse-flow cooling system pumped coolant through the cylinder heads before it flowed through the block and returned to the radiator. The resulting cooler cylinder heads allowed more optimum, knock-free, ignition timings.

In addition, the 22kW oil-to-water heat exchanger, packaged at the core of the engine, transferred heat from the coolant to the lubricating oil during warm up, bringing the oil up to operating temperature 14% faster than the cooling system used in the 4.2-litre V8. This marginally improved fuel consumption in the crucial engine warm-up period.

Diamond-Like Carbon Coating (DLC) was used to reduce friction on the fuel pump tappets, and a solid film lubricant to coat the piston skirts. New engine oil had a lower viscosity, contributing to an extension in service intervals from 10,000 miles to 15,000 miles (or 12 months), and both V8 engines were now fitted with an electronic oil-level indicator.

The XK's exhaust 'sound track' was enhanced via valves, which opened to to provide a deeper, more "rewarding note" (as Jaguar put it!), to match the increase in torque at low revs. In addition, the XKR had been engineered to provide an intake feedback system, to enhance the V8 sound commonly absent on supercharged engines. Intake manifold pressure pulsations were fed into an acoustic filter at the rear of the engine tuned to provide an 'edgy' sports car note at high revs. The filter was controlled by the engine management system, which allowed the sound to enter the cabin only under the appropriate driving conditions.

Upgraded transmission

Jaguar/ZF's electronically controlled, 6-speed ZF 6HP28 transmission was operated, either from the steering wheel mounted paddles, or in full automatic mode via the JaguarDrive selector (first seen on the New XJ and XF saloon ranges). Automatic transmission functions were selected simply by turning the rotary shift control, which rose into the driver's hand as the car was started – for instance, a simple push and turn action changed from Drive to Drive Sport.

The supercharged V8 engine with 510PS and 625Nm of torque transmitted its power through an uprated version of the ZF 6HP28 gearbox, with additional clutch plates and an uprated torque converter.

The high levels of torque produced by the new engines made it possible for the torque converter lock-up feature to function at low speeds without slip, and contributed to the official combined fuel economy of 23mpg (12.3 l/100km) in the XKR. The advanced design of the transmission also included a torsional damper to absorb firing impulses from the engine, further smoothing the driveline.

Active Differential Control and Dynamic Stability Control

Another first for Jaguar was the new Active Differential Control (ADC), the final stage of the supercharged driveline. Designed to give improved traction and dynamic stability, the electronically controlled differential continuously adapted to both the driver's demands, and the amount of grip available at each individual wheel. Operated by an internal electric motor and 'ball-and-ramp' mechanism, the differential contained a multiplate clutch, which transmitted or 'vectored' torque to the wheel with most grip, and therefore maximised the car's traction. The multi-plate clutch assembly was designed to prevent excessive differential slip, but differed fundamentally from a conventional traction control system, which uses the brakes to counteract differential slip after it has occurred. Working with other systems such as traction

control and the ABS braking function, ADC significantly improved overall vehicle performance, and provided more precise driving feel.

While the less powerful XK models did not adopt the Active Differential Control of the XKR, they did utilise an upgraded mechanical differential, which delivered outstanding levels of grip and stability under power.

The Dynamic Stability Control system for the new XK range utilised bespoke tuning, with four driver-selectable modes, Normal, Winter, Trac DSC and DSC OFF on all models. Normal mode was ideal for everyday driving, and was the default setting activated automatically on starting. The Winter mode was designed to improve drivability and confidence in more slippery conditions. Trac DSC mode was a sportier setting, allowing the experienced driver to exploit the car's performance fully, and enjoy greater involvement in controlling it. DSC OFF allowed the driver (where circumstances were appropriate) to switch the system's

The new JaguarDrive select-shift gear selector system. (Nigel Thorley)

electronic protection off completely – activated by pushing the DSC control button for ten seconds.

Suspension

The latest generation of Jaguar's Adaptive Dynamics replaced the (CATS) on the previous models. Active damper tuning systems removed many of the compromises of a passive damping system – which had to make a single choice, between softer damping for a comfortable ride, and firmer damping for more tautly-controlled handling. CATS overcame that compromise with automatically switchable damping modes, adapting to the road and how the car was driven. But where CATS only offered two settings: 'soft' and 'firm', the new Adaptive Damping System provided a continuously variable damping strategy between wide extremes.

Its three primary functions were to control body vertical movement, roll rate and pitch rate. Adaptive Damping performed three critical functions, 100 times a second. Firstly, it analysed induced body motions, and set each damper to an appropriate level in order to maintain a constant and level body attitude – maximising control without compromising ride. Secondly, it predicted the roll rate due to steering inputs, and selectively increased damping forces

The 5.0-litre XK Portfolio Convertible here seen in Lunar Grey with the new 19in Caravela alloy wheels. (Jaguar Cars/Nigel Thorley)

to reduce roll – improving handling feel and driver confidence. And thirdly, Adaptive Damping analysed fore and aft pitch rate due to throttle and braking inputs, and, again, varied damping forces to reduce pitch – further improving comfort and control.

Additionally, Adaptive Dynamics improved ride quality by monitoring wheel position 500 times a second, and automatically increasing the damping rate as the suspension approached the limits of its travel. Similarly, it controlled wheel 'hop' on uneven roads, by varying damping to move any wheel out of its natural bouncing frequency.

The JaguarDrive control interface allowed the driver to interact with Adaptive Dynamics by selecting modes for different driving conditions and moods. In Dynamic Mode, Adaptive Dynamics increased body control for a sportier feel. Dynamic Mode also interacted with the engine ECU, to give a more responsive accelerator pedal reaction, and quicker gearshift responses. Winter Mode was introduced on the XF and was now fitted to the XK range, adding another element of dynamic subtlety. Where Dynamic Mode offered a more sporty feel, Winter Mode offered a more damped accelerator pedal response, for progressive control in slippery conditions, with bespoke shift settings that delayed and softened gearshifts, again for better control with low grip.

The XKR offered the most sophisticated dynamic control of all, with Active Differential Control and

Adaptive Dynamics. These functions were managed through the JaguarDrive Control, allowing the driver to change the settings of the Adaptive Dynamics system, which then worked in tandem with the Active Differential Control (ADC) – an electronically controlled alternative to the traditional mechanical differential.

Exterior design

Visible changes to these 5.0-litre XKs reflected the significant changes under the skin. The exterior changes for the naturally-aspirated XK models and the supercharged XKR were highlighted by a distinctive, more purposeful new front end design and revised rear panels. This was accompanied by new LED rear light clusters incorporating fog lamps. plus twin reversing lamps (rather than the previous single lamp unit). The LED technology was included in the integrated side repeater and approach lamps in the exterior mirrors. All the 5.0-litre XK models also featured revised body coloured side power vents.

Beyond the shared changes, subtle differences in detail distinguished each of the three models in the range. All displayed the new front bumper features with stylish, chrome-detailed inserts and further chrome detailing to the upper mesh grille. The XKR was set apart by chrome on its lower mesh grille – finished in black on the XK and XK Portfolio models. All models now featured chrome detailing on window surrounds (Coupé) and rear signature blade, and in addition the XKR came with a new lower rear valance that was finished in body colour, and a revised tailpipe design.

Interior design

The Convertible's triple-lined fabric roof was as before, but the XK Portfolio and XKR models featured suedecloth headlinings as standard.

For both Coupé and Convertible models, a revised centre console was designed to accommodate the JaguarDrive Selector and switchgear. All cars also featured bright sill treadplate inserts. The three-spoke steering wheel now incorporated a leather-wrapped lower spoke and a new 'growler' badge. The XKR's instruments had red pointers, while all models adopted a new white illumination to the instrumentation.

Heated and cooled front seats were now standard equipment on the XK Portfolio and on XKR, with the optional R Performance interior (dependent on market), and available as an option on the XK.

The XK featured 10-way seat adjustability for both driver and passenger seats, with heating and memory functions as standard – while the XKR seats had similar functions but with the unique R seat styling. The XK Portfolio and XKR, with the optional R Performance interior, had 16-way adjustable seats with heating and

The more modern approach to the front end styling of the 5.0-litre XK, in this case in Radiance Red with 20in Kalimnos alloy wheels. (Jaguar Cars/Nigel Thorley)

Portfolio interior of a 5.0-litre Convertible: note the new-style steering wheel. (Nigel Thorley)

memory functions, adjustable side bolsters, and the new cooled seats as standard.

The door casings all featured saddle-stitched lines, and a new interlayer to give a softer touch to the top shoulder of the casing. The leather door pulls also introduced twin-needle stitching, and a soft-feel interlayer for all models. In each door, the modified seat switch pack now included single-piece chrome 'highlight' switches.

There was a wide choice of interior colour options, including a new combination for the XK Portfolio and XKR of Ivory seating with Oyster upper cabin trim and Oyster carpets. Bond grain leather was still standard on the XK interior, and an even higher quality soft-grain leather with contrast stitching became standard in the XK Portfolio and the new R Performance XKR.

Improved quality-looking switch pack for the 5.0-litre models. (Nigel Thorley)

Real wood veneers still featured, but were joined by a new Rich Oak veneer option, alongside the classic Burr Walnut for all three models. The XK Portfolio also offered the choice of an Ebony veneer, while the XKR had its own unique alternative in Dark Oak. A Knurled Aluminium veneer was also available on XK and XK Portfolio models, while Dark Mesh Aluminium was available on the XKR.

User-friendly technology and driving aids

The new 5.0-litre cars, in both Coupé and Convertible form, offered a number of extra driver aids. Among the practical features was intelligent front lighting, incorporating bi-xenon automatic headlamps – with power wash, dynamic headlamp levelling, corner lights activated by the direction indicators to improve visibility while cornering; and the option of Active Front Lighting.

Standard equipment across the XK range included air sensors to optimise cabin air quality through the climate control system, keyless start, cruise control, electro-chromatic fold-back exterior mirrors, and front and rear Park Assist.

Jaguar's Emergency Brake Assist became standard on the new XK, and Advanced Emergency Brake Assist was fitted to all models with Adaptive Cruise Control (ACC). Advanced Emergency Brake Assist uses the ACC radar to calculate distance from, and speed of approach to, the vehicle ahead and pre-charges the brake-line pressure to minimise impact speed if a collision is predicted – with an audible warning to the driver.

Every model in the new 5.0-litre XK range included front, side and thorax airbags, incorporating new technology which reduced the load on the occupant's body if the front airbag was deployed.

New LED rear lighting with twin reversing lights. (Nigel Thorley)

Equipment levels

With the 5.0-litre models came five new alloy wheel designs, some of them replacing earlier ones.

The standard wheel specification was dependent on market and model, but for most markets the range began with the 18in seven-spoke Venus for XK models. The new 19in 10-'V'-spoke Caravela wheel became standard on XK Portfolio and optional on the XK. Dependent on market, the new 19in ten-fan-spoke Artura design was available in painted or chromed finish and in conventional or run-flat types, offered as options on XK, XK Portfolio and (in run-flat form) also on the XKR. Another new wheel, the 19in ten-spoke Tamana design, became standard equipment on the XKR for most markets other than the UK (which specified 20in wheels), and was unique to this model.

New designs of 20in wheels included the twin-five-spoke Kalimnos, standard on the XKR in the UK market, and optional for all XK models in other markets. The twin-seven-spoke R Performance Nevis design was a unique option for the XKR, and another addition to the wheel range.

A new 19in mini-spare was introduced as standard equipment for the XKR, while the weight and space-saving Instant Mobility System still took the place of a spare wheel on other models in European markets, and where 18in wheels were fitted as standard.

With the recent addition of new colour options of Claret, Spectrum Blue, and Kyanite Blue, the exterior colour range for the new XK, XK Portfolio and XKR was extended to no fewer than 15, two of which – Salsa and Kyanite Blue – were reserved exclusively for the XKR.

Revised lighting, signature panel and bumper area for the 5.0-litre models. (Nigel Thorely)

The audio system options for the 5.0-litre XK range included the usual single-slot or multi-disc CD changers, and either Jaguar Premium Sound, or the ultimate, a high-end Bowers & Wilkins hi-fi, the 525-watt system with Dolby® ProLogic®II Surround Sound, three-channel stereo with unique amplifier, Kevlar mid-range speakers with high output and low distortion, and specially designed aluminium tweeters.

Depending on market, a number of Digital Radio options became available: HD radio was available for North American market cars, SDARS satellite radio for North America and Canada, and Digital Audio Broadcasting (DAB) was offered in selected European markets.

Comparison of the original 4.2-litre XK on the right, with the 5.0-litre equivalent on the left, clearly showing the 2009 changes. (Nigel Thorley)

More changes, new models, and the return of a name

The XK range continued to develop with a raft of new editions and upgrades.

80 AWARDS IN 2010 FOR JAGUAR AND LAND ROVER

Jaguar and Land Rover picked up no fewer than 80 awards in 2010 for their cars and customer satisfaction surveys. In line with these, sales were dramatically improved, and, despite the XK being the only sports car produced by the company, in 2010 sales were still improving with a total of 1641 XKs sold compared to 1430 in 2009, an overall improvement of 15%.

The Jaguar XKR 75 Goodwood one-off seen here performing at the Goodwood Circuit from which it took its name.

(Jaguar Cars/Nigel Thorley)

XKR 75/175

The original idea for this special edition began with the work on the first XKR, back in 2006. That had led to the early XKR-S covered in Chapter Fourteen. Now, Jaguar revised the steering and software, upgraded the ECU and exhaust system, all to extract ever more power. The end result was the one-off 523bhp Jaguar XKR 75 Goodwood, painted in lime green (and nicknamed "Kermit" internally), with dark Gunmetal alloys and unique XKR graphics on the side. This was showcased at the 2009 Goodwood Festival of Speed event to commemorate the 75th anniversary of the Jaguar name.

The car was well received, and this encouraged Jaguar to produce an equivalent vehicle for retail sale from October 2010, as a limited edition of just 75 cars, to be sold only in the UK and other European countries

(20 were built in right-hand drive). Many features, both cosmetically and mechanically, would be later seen on other models in the XK range.

All the 'production' XKR 75 cars were finished in Stratus Grey paint, with the option of grey signature striping around the top wing areas. A new front splitter, side-sill extensions, rear diffuser and larger rear spoiler featured in body colour with other exterior trim in black. 20in Vortex forged lightweight alloy wheels, diamond-turned with dark grey finish, sizes 9in front and 10.5in rear, were fitted with rear tyre width increased by 10mm to 295mm. Internally the cars were finished in Charcoal leather with Piano Black veneer and 'XKR 75' sill tread plates. As a final touch, there was a commemorative card with each car, signed by Ian Callum and Mike Cross from Jaguar Cars.

Performance followed the one-off Goodwood, offering 530PS and torque increased to 655Nm (483ft-lb) from 625Nm (461ft-lb), giving the car a top speed of 174mph with a 0 to 60mph acceleration time of just 4.4 seconds. The enhancements included a revised ECU, upgraded torque converter and other suspension, brake and exhaust changes which would find their way into a new XKR-S model (see below).

The exhaust changes involved removing the centre silencer boxes and replacing them with a crossover pipe, while retaining the rear boxes and outlets. The Adaptive Damping software was upgraded with 28% stiffer front springs and 32% rears, accompanied by a 10mm lower ride height. New fully-machined aluminium front and

The XKR 75 special edition, with unusual side graphics rarely taken up by owners. (Jaguar Cars/Nigel Thorley)

revised rear suspension uprights (unique to this model) increased camber stiffness by 30%.

There is no doubt that the XKR 75 was precursor to the XKR-S and option packs (see below).

Ultimately, Jaguar produced a special limited edition for the US and Canadian markets too. Named the XKR 175, with 175 built, it carried most of the cosmetic upgrades of the XKR 75, along with performance enhancements that followed the soon-to-be-announced Speed Pack (see below), but were not as

Arden's interpretation of the XKR 75. (Arden/Nigel Thorley)

The German Startech enhanced XK. (Startech/Nigel Thorley)

performance-oriented as the UK/European XKR 75 models.

Arden 75

Coinciding with Jaguar's launch of the XKR 75, the German conversion company Arden announced its own upgraded model, the Arden 75. Arden's modifications, which included realignment and matching of the engine management system, addition of a high-performance sport exhaust system with sport catalysts, and a matching silencer for a fuller-bodied V8 sound, delivered 580bhp and 720Nm of torque. It claimed performance figures of 0 to 60mph in 4.3 seconds, and a top speed of 189mph.

Brandy coloured interior and bamboo veneer for the German Startech model. (Startech/Nigel Thorley)

The tuning package also included a lowered suspension as a result of using firmer springs, a set of massive 21in multi-part Arden Sportline wheels, handmade stainless steel grilles, daytime running lights, and an Arden-type Jaguar bonnet ornament.

Startech XK

A little-known name as far as the XK is concerned was the Startech company in Germany which produced a range of enhancements to production XKs, introduced at the 2009 Frankfurt Motor Show.

Intended to give a sportier look to the XK both externally and internally, upgrades included a carbon fibre bodykit, Monster J Diamond Edition alloy wheels, sports springs lowering the ride height, and brandy-coloured interior with bamboo woodwork.

2011 model changes

Jaguar announced its new model range at the Geneva Motor Show, in 2011, when subtle changes were made to the existing XK, XK Portfolio and XKR models. A new higher-performance variant of the XK range, the XKR-S was also launched – more on this below, but first to address the changes to the existing models.

The latest lighting technology allowed the front headlamps to be made slimmer, and at the same time incorporated LED signal functions and running lights, to meet changing legislation. Combined with a larger grille and new bumper design, these gave the XK even better recognition.

Each model in the range gained unique styling attributes to distinguish it from its siblings. Chrome mesh grilles, for example, on the XK, were replaced with matt black detailing on the XKR, while the flagship XKR-S (see below) received a unique front bumper.

The front wings, by necessity, were re-styled to suit the new lighting arrangement, and while doing so, changes were made to the power vents along the front wing sides. These were changed from a vertical to horizontal design with a mesh insert, emblazoned with the Jaguar name.

The boot lid was revised with a slimmer chrome finisher, allowing room for the famous Jaguar 'leaper' motif, bringing it into line with the rest of the company's products at the time.

The updated 5.0-litre frontal view with wider mouth, revised shaping to front chrome apertures and new light units. (Jaguar Cars/Nigel Thorley)

There were now 17 paint colours, five of which were new, along with another new range of alloy wheels totalling 11 different designs.

Interior changes

The XK cabin was refreshed with a host of new trim

The addition of the Jaguar leaper to the boot lid came with the 2011 models. (Nigel Thorley)

The revised 5.0-litre models from 2011, in this case with the 20in Takoba alloy wheels. (Jaguar Cars/Nigel Thorley)

The 2012 model year XK Coupé finished in Crystal Blue. (Nigel Thorley)

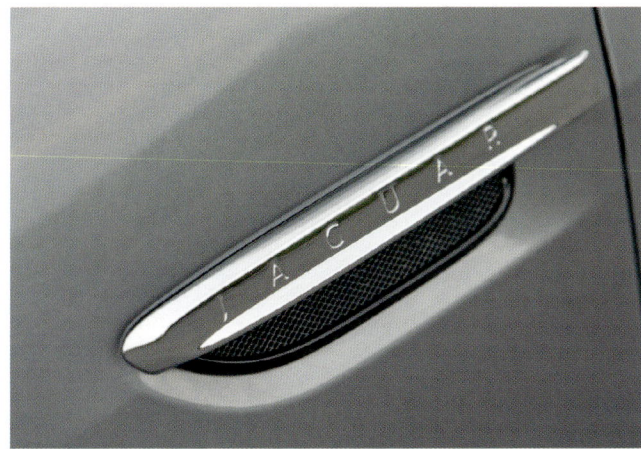

The power vents introduced on the New XK back in 2006 were finally changed to these horizontal vents. (Nigel Thorley)

materials, including Ebony soft-feel paint for the switches, gloss black finish to the centre console, phosphor blue halo illumination, and ambient lighting. New veneers, colour combinations and headlining options allowed owners to create a cabin ambience precisely matching their individual requirements.

Another new leather-wrapped, multi-function steering wheel was added, providing a more tactile feel. 'Jaguar' embossed stainless steel pedals were now an option – standard on the XKR-S.

New Performance front seating became an option for the XK Portfolio and XKR models, featuring integrated head restraints and increased lateral and squab support. The seats were specifically designed to hold the driver and passenger securely and comfortably in place for performance driving. 16-way adjustment of the squab, cushion, lumbar and bolster elements was supplemented by memory and heating functions. Another feature from the XKR-S of Jet Poltrona Frau Italian leather headlining was offered as an option on other models.

Most other features were carried over from the earlier models, but a new reverse parking camera was available with imaging via the central dash-mounted touch-screen.

For the UK and certain European markets only, XKs could be fitted with the tyre repair Instant Mobility System. By adopting IMS, the XK freed up its 30-litre wheel well, which was then carpeted and could hold the specially-designed and tailored XK accessory suitcase.

The enhanced interior of the 2012 model year XK, in this case with the Performance seating. (Nigel Thorley)

The high performance XKR-S Coupé. (Nigel Thorley)

XKR-S returns

At that Geneva Motor Show in 2011, Jaguar unveiled yet another variant to the XK 5.0-litre range, this time under the insignia used earlier in the life of the car – XKR-S, initially in Coupé form only. The most expensive XK yet produced, the XKR-S Coupé would cost £97,000!

With the supercharged AJ-V8 Gen III engine fitted to the XKR, revised fuel mapping, and an active exhaust boosted power and torque to 550PS and 680Nm respectively, the XKR-S was the most powerful Jaguar road car ever, 8% in PS and 9% in torque over the XKR. The car achieved 0-60mph in just 4.2 seconds, and joined the exclusive '300km/h' club, with a limited top speed of 186mph. Jaguar promoted the XKR-S as not only extremely powerful but also efficient, emitting just 292g/km of CO_2.

The 6-speed ZF automatic transmission was revised to

With 550PS performance from the XKR-S version of the V8 engine, it was the most powerful Jaguar road car produced at the time. (Nigel Thorley)

optimise upshifts and allow for the increased top speed. The XKR-S enhanced the XKR's electronic systems, and refined the inherent stiffness of the lightweight aluminium architecture to create what Jaguar termed "the most dynamic and exciting Jaguar yet."

The double wishbone front suspension was comprehensively revised, with a new fully-machined steering knuckle. This significantly increased camber and castor stiffness by 0.13 degrees per kilonewton to transform the accuracy and weighting of the steering for greater levels of connection, feedback and precision. The rear suspension geometry was also revised with rear wheel steer optimised for maximum agility, while spring rates were increased at both ends of the car by 28%.

Comprehensive revised front suspension for the XKR-S. (Nigel Thorley)

A reprogrammed Active Differential was installed for the XKR-S model. (Nigel Thorley)

Unique carbon fibre spoiler for the XKR-S. (Nigel Thorley)

Black Vulcan wheels and trim for the XKR-S. (Nigel Thorley)

The Active Differential was programmed to reduce steering sensitivity at the very high speeds of which the car was capable, increasing stability and driver control. Bespoke software for Jaguar's Adaptive Damping was written for the XKR-S, ensuring both total body control, and maximum traction and grip. Changes to the TracDSC mode altered intervention levels to allow the experienced driver to explore the outer edges of the performance, rewarded by the motorsport-inspired soundtrack from the exhaust, which featured an active pneumatic valve.

The Jaguar High-performance Braking System, fitted as standard, was more than a match for the car's seductive performance. Huge brake discs, 380mm at the front and 376mm for the rear, in combination with aluminium callipers, and pad area increases of 44% front and 31% rear in comparison to the XK, provided outstanding levels of power, stability and feel.

The suspension changes and performance exhaust system from the XKR-S were also available as part of a new Dynamic Pack option for the XKR model (see later).

Extensive Computational Fluid Dynamics, wind tunnel, and track work had resulted in the aerodynamic design changes applied to the XKR-S to enable it to perform and maintain stability at speeds of up to 186mph. These aerodynamic design changes gave the front of the car a dramatic and bold appearance. Vertical feature lines ran down from the edges of the oval air intake into a new bumper design which incorporated a wider, lower air intake, a carbon fibre splitter and twin side nacelles. At the edges of the bumper, vertical panels channelled air down the side of the car along new sills, which served to both smooth the horizontal airflow, and emphasise the 10mm reduction in ride height of this model.

A unique rear wing with a carbon fibre inlay worked in conjunction with a rear apron featuring a carbon fibre diffuser. The result was a reduction in overall lift of 26%, and balanced aerodynamics front and rear to keep the car perfectly pinned to the road.

The exterior changes were highlighted by the application of gloss black to the exterior brightwork, complemented by the dark 'technical' finish of the lightweight forged 20in Vulcan alloy wheels. These reduced the unsprung mass by nearly 5%, and also provided better traction and grip levels, thanks to wider rear tyres (Pirelli P-Zero 255/35 ZR20 front and 295/30 ZR20 at the rear), specifically developed for the car. Through the wheels could be seen the Jaguar High-performance brake callipers, finished in either red or gunmetal.

Internally, the XKR-S had the new Performance front seats, with carbon-leather trim, as standard. With their integrated headrests, racing harness cut-outs and increased side and squab support, these were an ideal match for the XKR-S high performance. Exclusive to the XKR-S was a carbon-patterned and soft-grain leather

Arguably the most luxurious of any ultra high performance GT car was the XKR-S. (Jaguar Cars/Nigel Thorley)

The most aggressive XK front yet for the XKR-S. (Jaguar Cars/Nigel Thorley)

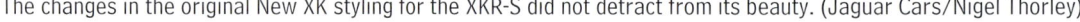

The changes in the original New XK styling for the XKR-S did not detract from its beauty. (Jaguar Cars/Nigel Thorley)

interior with contrasting micro-piping and stitching. As previously mentioned, the Jet Poltrona Frau Italian leather headlining was standard on the XKR-S.

Other XKR-S standard interior features included a soft leather-wrapped steering wheel, and Jaguar embossed bright stainless steel pedals. Soft feel paint was used for switchgear, and there was a gloss black centre console area.

At the launch of the XKR-S at Geneva, Mike Cross, Jaguar's Chief Engineer, Vehicle Integrity, commented: "The XKR-S encompasses everything a performance Jaguar should be; as capable, precise and thrilling on your drive home as it is at the Nürburgring. Every response delay has been minimised in order to give the car a more connected feel in the manner in which it steers, handles, stops and goes."

XKR-S Special Carbon Fibre Pack

Inspired by the launch of the XKR-S, Jaguar added a special Exterior Pack, only available for this model. It featured carbon fibre bonnet louvres with the

Detail of the XKR-S Convertible interior. (Jaguar Cars/Nigel Thorley)

'supercharged' script, carbon fibre finishes to the side power vents, door mirror caps and lower boot lid finisher.

XKR-S Convertible

It wasn't until November of 2011 that Jaguar announced a Convertible XKR-S was joining the Coupé model. The XKR-S Convertible, like the Coupé was available in a range of six colours, including Polaris White and British Racing Green. The only differences between the Coupé and Convertible XKR-S models were that the rear damper top mounts were stiffened. At the time Mike Cross commented: "Because the XK was designed as a Convertible it has great structural integrity. This allowed us to apply the XKR-S Coupé's sporting suspension settings to create a convertible with no compromises. Its blend of great speed, precision and dynamism is given an extra dimension with the roof down and that thrilling exhaust soundtrack."

2011 XK UK PRICING

With the introduction of the XKR-S Coupé prices at the time were:

XK Coupé	£65,000
XKR Coupé	£78,500
XKR-S Coupé	£97,000
XK Convertible	£71,000
XKR Convertible	£84,500

The introduction of the XKR-S Convertible.
(Jaguar Cars/Nigel Thorley)

Fast and Black

Jaguar kept visitors busy at the same 2011 Geneva Motor Show when it also announced a new XKR Special Edition that incorporated two new option packs, Speed and Black – also available separately for other XK models.

The XKR Speed Pack

The Speed Pack allowed customers to extend the car's top speed from 155mph (250km/h) to an electronically-limited 174mph (280km/h), thanks to a unique engine and transmission recalibration.

To ensure the XKR with Speed Pack remained stable at high speeds, the Coupé used a revised front aerodynamic splitter and larger rear spoiler to provide increased balance and a reduction in lift. The XKR's computerised Active Differential Control also adjusted to reduce steering sensitivity at very high speeds, further improving stability and driver control.

Customers who ordered the XKR Coupé with the Speed Pack were offered a paint palette that was part of the Jaguar Designers' Choice Programme – a range of colours specifically chosen to complement the performance potential of the car: Ultimate Black, Polaris White, Salsa Red, Liquid Silver, Lunar Grey, Kyanite Blue and Spectrum Blue.

Fitment of the Speed Pack also included body-coloured side sills and rear diffuser, and a chrome finish to the window surrounds, upper and lower mesh grilles, side power vents and boot lid finisher. Red brake callipers with a Jaguar 'R' logo sat inside 20in Kasuga alloy wheels.

The Speed Pack XKR with special graphics.
(Jaguar Cars/Nigel Thorley)

The XKR Black Pack

The Black Pack was created to provide more visual impact, with glass black alloy wheels and exterior detailing.

Like the Speed Pack, XKRs fitted with the Black Pack had a paint palette that was restricted to colours that Jaguar's design team believed to be ideal for creating a coupé with immediate exclusivity. The Black Pack models were therefore only available in Ultimate Black, Polaris White or Salsa Red initially but boasted 20in gloss black Kalimnos alloy wheels. Further gloss black finishing was applied to the window surrounds, front grilles and side power vents. Optional red-painted brake callipers were also available with the black alloy wheels, while body-coloured front and rear spoilers and boot lid finisher rounded out the package. Customers also had the option to apply a sweeping 'XKR' side body graphic running along the door sills.

In addition to the Black Pack's exterior changes, the Jaguar Designers' Choice Programme also selected a range of interior trims that supported the visual impact of the car. All XKRs with the Black Pack were trimmed with Charcoal leather hides that could be personalised with a range of colour stitching and grain. Three interior finishes and veneers for the fascia and door trims were also available – Dark Oak, Dark Mesh Aluminium and Piano Black.

The Black Pack car. (Jaguar Cars/Nigel Thorley)

XKR Dynamic Pack

There was also an enhanced version of the Speed Pack – the Dynamic Pack. This included all the features of the Speed Pack, along with extensive revisions (like those for the XKR-S) to the suspension, including a stiffer knuckle for improved steering precision, revised spring and damper settings, and Adaptive Dynamics. Ride height was lowered by 10mm and the Dynamic Pack also featured 20in Vortex alloy wheels, forged and lightweight with a gloss black and diamond turned finish, plus distinctive black painted brake callipers.

With Dynamic Pack also available, the options listing for XK owners was extensive. (Jaguar Cars/Nigel Thorley)

Artisan Special Equipment Coupé in Celestial Black.
(Jaguar Cars/Nigel Thorley)

Artisan SE

In 2012, Jaguar kept the programme of new editions rolling, with the introduction of the Artisan Special Edition XK models in both Coupé and Convertible form.

The main thrust of the special features of these models was in the interior. The Performance styled front seats were fitted with the very finest Scraffito grain leather, along with the rear seat backs, door casings and instrument binnacle, in just two colour schemes, Navy or Truffle. These were accompanied by contrast micro-piping and twin-needle contrast stitching. The two choices continued to the carpets, with either London Tan or Ivory edging.

There were also two options of veneer, either a traditional dark Shadow Walnut or Dark Figured Aluminium. For the Coupé, there were two choices of headlining, either Jet (black) or Canvas Poiltrana Frau leather. For the Convertible, there was a choice of Black, Blue, Grey or Brown hood colours. Finally, Special Edition treadplates and stainless steel paddles completed the interior 'make-over'.

Artisan Special Equipment Convertible in Rhodium Silver.
(Jaguar Cars/Nigel Thorley)

As well as the standard fitment of Performance seating with 16-way adjustment and heating, these SE models also featured the top-end Bowers & Wilkins 525W sound system, and a heated steering wheel.

These Special Equipment models were only available in a choice of three exterior paint finishes, Celestial Black, Polaris White or Rhodium Silver. They were fitted with 20in Orona alloy wheels in a polished finish.

Pricing for the UK Artisan Special Equipment models were £77,350 for the Coupé and £82,500 for the Convertible.

Artisan interior for the SE model. (Jaguar Cars/Nigel Thorley)

Indian Special Edition XKR

A further special edition of the Artisan SE model was rolled out by Jaguar Motors India, also in both Coupé and Convertible forms.

In a range of six colours this time, Celestial Black, Ultimate Black, Crystal Blue, Lunar Grey, Polaris White, or Rhodium Silver. Interior trim finishes and colours, alloy wheels, and other equipment followed the same listing as with the Artisan SE models.

The Indian take on the SE model. (Jaguar Cars/Nigel Thorley)

Chapter Seventeen

The grand finale

Jaguar was on a high by the end of 2012 – number one manufacturer in the latest JD Power and Associates/ *What Car?* UK Vehicle Ownership Satisfaction Survey; success somewhat tempered for XK fans in 2013, as the advent of the new two-seater F-TYPE signalled the final run-down of the XK sports car range. However, Jaguar was sending it off in style – bringing out, in 2013, the most exciting and fastest model of all.

The most powerful XK ever, the XKR-S GT, initially produced for the US, with an extra ten made for the UK market. (Jaguar Cars/Nigel Thorley)

XKR-S GT

With the launch of Jaguar's fastest XK, at the Geneva Motor Show in 2013, Adrian Hallmark, Jaguar's Global Brand Director said: "The XKR-S GT is the most extreme iteration of the Jaguar R Brand's performance focus. Utilising race car derived technology, all-aluminium construction and an uncompromised approach to aerodynamic efficiency, the result is a car as capable on the track as it is exhilarating on the road."

The XKR-S GT was developed by Jaguar's Engineered to Order Division (ETO) to be the ultimate track-focused, road-going iteration of the XK Coupé. Extensive aerodynamic

Unique frontal treatment, alloy wheels and yellow callipers make the XKR-S GT instantly recognisable. (Jaguar Cars/Nigel Thorley)

The 'bad boy' of the XK range, the XKR-S GT. (Jaguar Cars/Nigel Thorley)

and suspension changes, and the addition of carbon ceramic brakes all combined to give the XKR-S GT race-car-inspired connected feel and braking performance. Initial production would be limited to just 30 cars, for the North American and Canadian markets only. However, as interest was intense for this new variant, a further ten were built, destined for buyers in the UK, at a price of around £135,000.

The specially finished interior for the XKR-S GT. (Jaguar Cars/Nigel Thorley)

A range of bespoke carbon fibre components, including an extended front splitter, dive-planes and elevated rear wing, all worked to maximise the XKR-S GT's aerodynamic downforce. Technical learning from the development of the then new Jaguar F-TYPE two-seater sports car had also been applied to the XKR-S GT's suspension and steering systems, optimising both agility and sensitivity to driver input.

The stunning performance of the car was provided by Jaguar's proven 5.0-litre supercharged V8 engine, boasting 550PS and 680Nm, driving through the 6-speed transmission and active electronic differential. Combined with the aerodynamic and suspension changes, plus revisions to the traction control system's calibration, the result in straight-line terms was a 0-60mph time of 3.9 seconds. The electronically limited top speed being an incredible 186mph.

The XKR-S GT was only available in Polaris White, with unique graphics and Jaguar R-S GT script on its louvred bonnet, (it has since transpired that at least one owner did receive his car in the exterior colour of his own choice). The Warm Charcoal interior with Red accents featured the Performance seats, finished in soft-grain Warm Charcoal leather and suedecloth, with the Jaguar and R-S GT scripts integrated into the backrests. Jet suedecloth headlining and a Jet suedecloth steering wheel, with aluminium paddle shifters, were also fitted as standard. Script to the treadplates and console highlighted further the exclusiveness of the XKR-S GT.

Pete Simkin, Director ETO Specialist Products at Jaguar commented at the time: "The development of the XKR-S GT demanded an uncompromised approach to enhance aerodynamic downforce, with complementary suspension changes to maximise high-speed cornering ability. In combination with the use of a carbon ceramic braking system, the result is the most focused 'R' model Jaguar has ever built which delivers heightened levels of performance and driver reward."

Ian Callum, Director of Design at Jaguar also commented at the car's launch: "The XKR-S GT has been designed purely by the laws of physics. It has been developed in the wind tunnel and on the racetrack with the sole aim of creating as much high-speed stability and downforce as possible. Nothing has been styled for the sake of it. It's been an exercise in efficiency and the result is a car that's raw, focused and devastatingly quick."

Externally, the XKR-S GT featured a carbon-fibre front splitter of race car wrap-around type – extending forward by 60mm, it started the optimisation of airflow around, over and underneath the car. Aggressive carbon-fibre twin dive-planes and wheelarch extensions furthered the efficiency of airflow around the car, while below the addition of an optimised aluminium front valance served to smooth airflow under the car as well as enhancing engine and brake cooling performance.

A rear carbon-fibre diffuser ensured the smooth exit of air from underneath the car, while the elevated rear wing – also in carbon-fibre – worked in combination with the deck lid mounted spoiler to maximise rear downforce. At its electronically limited top speed of 186mph, the XKR-S GT produced 145kg (320lb) of downforce. Bonnet louvres served as a further engine cooling aid, while also helping aerodynamic performance by improving the airflow through the front end of the car.

There were also significant suspension changes. The front and rear suspension arms, uprights, wheel bearings, bushings and rear subframe were all new, and drew on hardware developed for the F-TYPE. The overall set-up worked to increase lateral suspension stiffness, for greater precision and responsiveness.

Integral to the revised suspension system was its new spring and damper module design. The XKR-S GT has a motorsport-derived twin spring system mated to Jaguar's Adaptive Dynamics damping system – the dampers being ride-height adjustable. Front and rear spring rates were respectively 68% and 25% stiffer than on the XKR-S, while the damper tune was much more track-focused, providing increased levels of body control and grip.

Jaguar's Adaptive Dynamics was specifically tuned for the XKR-S GT so that the suspension parameters changed to deliver a higher level of body control, with maximum traction and grip when the dynamic mode was deployed, offering optimum performance for focused track driving.

The XKR-S GT's front track is 52mm wider than that of the XKR-S, while the rear remains the same. The steering rack was taken from the F-TYPE, with a correspondingly faster ratio and retuned steering valve, giving immediacy of turn-in and response to steering inputs.

The unique 20in forged and lightweight alloy wheels – finished in gloss black – were shod with specially developed Pirelli Corsa performance tyres (255/35 and 305/30 front/rear), giving the XKR-S GT a more muscular stance and greatly increasing its grip and stability.

The XKR-S GT was the first production Jaguar to be fitted with a carbon ceramic braking system. The internally ventilated and cross-drilled lightweight brake discs measure 398mm and 380mm front/rear respectively. Combined with 6-piston monobloc callipers at the front and four piston units at the rear – the yellow callipers being branded with 'Jaguar Carbon Ceramic' script – the XKR-S GT delivered race car levels of fade-free stopping power and brake pedal feel.

Enhanced braking feel came courtesy of the electronic Pre-Fill system. Working in conjunction with the car's DSC system, Pre-Fill pressurised the brakes every time the driver came off the throttle pedal, resulting in a very short and consistent level of travel on the brake pedal. This maximised braking response, reducing the car's stopping distance and delivering increased levels of confidence during high-performance driving. The lightweight nature of the carbon ceramic system meant a reduction in unsprung weight of 21kg – so further enhancing the XKR-S GT's handling. The XKR-S GT's carbon ceramic braking system also had a significantly longer life span than a standard system.

When it came to performance, the XKR-S GT featured a fully active performance exhaust system with valves that opened under load, both enhancing gas-flow, and the car's aural character, while optimising power output.

ETO

Jaguar Land Rover's specialist ETO division is responsible for extending the Jaguar and Land Rover brands with a series of special edition models as well as a range of personalisation options allowing owners to tailor their cars.

The designers and engineers in ETO work alongside the JLR Product Development teams on future products with a focus on offering additional luxury, performance and capability, exploring different facets of the brands' personalities. ETO developed the XKR-S, the XKR-S GT and continue to work on other Jaguar and Land Rover products.

Yet more special editions

More special editions were still to come, in 2014, before the demise of the XK.

XK66

Following the XK60, XK75 and XK175, it was now time for another limited edition, the 2014 XK66 (Coupé and Convertible) – built primarily for the German market – to commemorate 66 years since the introduction of the XK120 sports car in 1948.

Launched in May of that year, and based on the

The limited edition XK66. (Jaguar Cars/Nigel Thorley)

The XK66 interior with special badging. (Jaguar Cars/Nigel Thorley)

existing Portfolio model, XK66 was only available in two colours that referred it back to the XK120 days: British Racing Green or Stratus Grey (or Anthracite, as it was known in XK days). For convertibles, the hood finish was either Black (Stratus paint) or Beige (BRG paint). The cars carried an 'XK66' emblem on the rear and side power vents, with chrome door mirror caps and Union Jack emblems on the wheel valve caps. Alloy wheels were the polished 20in Orona type.

Internally the XK66 was primarily of Portfolio specification, with soft grain leather in a choice of Caramel (light brown) with contrasting Warm Charcoal stitching, or Warm Charcoal with Ivory stitching. Veneer was Burr Walnut with accompanying switchgear in chrome finish. There was also a passenger side

The last special edition the normally-aspirated Signature model. (Jaguar Cars/Nigel Thorley)

plaque reading 'XK66 one of 66' – only 66 XK66 cars were produced, at a price of 99,380 euros (Coupé) and 107,580 euros (Convertible).

XK Signature & Dynamic R

To soften the blow of the forthcoming demise of the XK range, Jaguar introduced two new special editions in 2014: the Signature and Dynamic R, both replacing the existing XK, XK Portfolio and XKR models, but available in both Coupé and Convertible forms. Accompanied by the XKR-S, these were the three models identified for the 2015 model year, with deliveries commencing in March 2014.

The luxury-focused XK Signature with the normally-aspirated 5.0-litre engine was fitted with a host of additional features as standard. These included 20in Kalimnos alloy wheels (or 20in Takoba alloys as an option), and Reverse Park camera. The Signature got luxury-style seating in a choice of Ivory or Charcoal soft grain leather, with Canvas suedecloth headlining, figured Ebony veneer and Bright Metal sport pedals. The colour choice was limited to Polaris White, Ultimate Black, Stratus Grey, Italian Racing Red, Dark Sapphire Blue or British Racing Green.

Replacing the then current XKR, the Dynamic R was packed with equipment, but cost £10,000 less than a similarly specified car would have just months before, and it was £27,500 less to buy than the range-topping XKR-S.

The essence of the Dynamic R was that it took the

XKR's supercharged engine and 6-speed gearbox, and matched them to the Speed, Black, Dynamic and Aerodynamic packs as standard. That provided the better-balanced suspension for performance, exhaust, spoilers, etc, plus a increase in top speed to 174mph.

The XK Dynamic R also showed off new diamond sewn Performance seating in a choice of either Ivory/Charcoal soft grain leather with Ivory contract stitching, or Charcoal/Red soft grain leather with Red contrast stitching. Jet suedecloth headlining was complemented with Piano Black veneers and Bright Metal sport pedals.

Equipped with 20in Vortex diamond turned alloy wheels, there was also the option of 20in Vulcan gloss black lightweight alloys, accompanied by red painted brake callipers. Exterior paint finishes were limited to the same palette as the Signature model.

Prices for Coupé version of these special editions were £54,950 for the XK Signature and £69,950 for the XK Dynamic R.

The Final Fifty

Yet another limited special edition – this time for the US market only – was announced at the 2014 New York Auto Show. Bearing the 'XK Final Fifty Limited Edition' name, and in both Coupé and Convertible styles, all were finished in Ultimate Black paint with Ivory interiors, the Convertibles with Black hoods.

The Final Fifty editions were all XKR models and received various enhancements to standard specification. The bonnets had louvered panel insets, like those of the XKR-S GT. All 50 came with the Dynamic Pack including 20in Vortex wheels, a rear wing, side sill extensions, a rear diffuser and an amplified exhaust system. Internally, Performance seats incorporated diamond-stitched leather, faux suede for the steering wheel, special treadplates and a commemorative plaque signed by Ian Callum.

The Dynamic R special edition. (Jaguar Cars/Nigel Thorley)

End of the line

On 24th July 2014, the very last XK rolled off the Castle Bromwich assembly line at Jaguar Cars Castle Bromwich assembly plant, a not-unexpected announcement, but one that was tempered with

Most of the XK limited editions carried special treadplates. (Jaguar Cars/Nigel Thorley)

Performance seating was part of the standard specification for the Dynamic R model with cross-hatched pleating. (Jaguar Cars/Nigel Thorley)

One of the Final Fifty US XK models. (Jaguar Cars/Nigel Thorley)

sadness from many. To commemorate the occasion, a special event was organised, with the last two XKs lined up alongside the very first X-150 – a 2006 Coupé, a car already in the Jaguar Heritage Trust collection.

The penultimate XK was finished a Polaris White, a naturally aspirated Coupé that was, at the time, handed over by Castle Bromwich Operations Director Nicolas Guibert, to Roger Carroll, Dealer Principal of Rybrook Jaguar in Chester, receiving the car on behalf of its new owner. The actual final car was finished in Italian Racing Red, an XKR Coupé, presented by Nicolas to Mike Beasley, Jaguar's former Managing Director and Vice Chairman of the Jaguar Heritage Trust. In line with tradition, the last car was gifted by JLR to the Trust, and will form part of its collection; aready allocated a special registration number (JH14 XKR).

As well as the end-of-line celebrations. a special display had been mounted in the showroom at the end of R Block in the centre of the factory, to give the wider Castle Bromwich workforce the chance to learn about the long history of the XK, and contribute their own

The final two cars off the Castle Bromwich assembly line in 2014, the red car going to the Jaguar Heritage Trust, the white car, the last customer vehicle, flanked by the very first New XK made in December 2005. (Jaguar Heritage Trust/Nigel Thorley)

personal memories of this model in a special commemorative book. Story boards featuring archive images of the XK from the original launch of the XK120 at Earls Court in 1948, through to the present day, complemented the display of Jaguar Heritage's 1953 XK120, alongside the latest F-TYPE Project 7, symbolising Jaguar's future sports car direction.

The decision to cease production of the XK (Jaguar's sporting GT flagship) was part of Jaguar's wider strategic vision, bringing to an end a production run of 56,798 XKs made since 2006. It is perhaps ironic that as the 1950s XK150 models saw out the use of the XK insignia in 1961 – replaced by the E-type, that the last New XK should again see out the insignia in 2014 – replaced by the F-TYPE.

Russ Varney – one of the key people at Jaguar – project leader of the XKR-S, commented just prior to the shut-down of XK production: "The Jaguar XK could be reborn as a more focused GT car. The heart of Jaguar is in sports cars, and that is why we will now regard the F-TYPE as the halo product for all that we do. However, I don't think that means the XK is dead necessarily. The car straddled the GT and sports car segment, with more of an emphasis on the GT side but probably not enough of an emphasis on the sports car side. There is no reason the XK couldn't exist today as a true contender in that sports car segment.

"We have plans to do lots more with the F-TYPE, and we expect it to cover a lot of bases, but there will still be other areas we want to cover. We need to find the right way to deliver on them, and the XK could be one way of doing that."

At the time of writing, there was no news of an eventual XK replacement, although sources at Jaguar Land Rover have indicated that, when it does eventually arise, it will be bigger, faster and even more luxurious than the previous models. While many look forward to an eventual new model, the existing X-100 and X-150 models will long be held in esteem and eventually, like all other Jaguar sports cars, be considered true classics.

Chapter **Eighteen**

Buying a New XK

If you are considering buying any XK model, reading this book will give you the necessary understanding of the cars and what to look for when buying one. In the first instance, refer back to Chapter Eight, page 97 to the top of page 100, for general advice that applies to all XKs. This chapter will cover specific items relating to the New XK models from 2006 to 2014.

Due to excellent developmental advances, and the integrity of the design of these later cars, there are far fewer issues when buying or maintaining a New XK than with the earlier models. Hence, this chapter is significantly shorter than Chapter 8.

The choice of car

Budget is usually the main constraint for potential buyers, so bear in mind that Coupés will cost less than Convertibles, XKs cost less than XKRs, etc.

The buyer's choice, early X-100 or later X-150 – each have their pros and cons! (Nigel Thorley)

While most would love to buy an XKR or even XKR-S, it is worth noting that the performance of the 5.0-litre normally-aspirated XK is significantly better than the 4.2-litre XKR (particularly the earlier X-100 XKR). For those who are thinking of trading up from an X-100 to an X-150, or for those who are thinking of buying an XK for the first time, why buy an X-150 or why change from an X-100? For a considerable time, the New XKs were so much dearer than their predecessors that they were beyond the price range of many, and that question could be answered by price alone. Now, however, the X-150 models are becoming more affordable. So why choose a New XK over an X-100?

The main areas of superiority are in the bodywork (aluminium – far less susceptible to corrosion), general fit and finish, and technology. Aesthetics and styling are very much a matter of personal choice – many still prefer the more rounded look of the X-100 models. Equipment levels will be superior in the X-150 and marginally more interior accommodation space may also be a benefit. If

Be aware that all XKs are highly complex, so specialist diagnostics equipment may be required to rectify issues. (Nigel Thorley)

you want a car for touring, luggage space is relevant. The original X-100 models' boot space is spacious for a sports car; and the X-150 Coupé has relatively good boot space. However, the X-150 Convertibles are very restrictive, because of the hood and its mechanism.

Maintenance costs and general upkeep will arguably be more economical for the later cars, but you may suffer higher insurance costs, or more expensive British road tax. Cars over ten years of age may be eligible for much cheaper (cherished) insurance and road tax, varying according to the age and emissions of the vehicle.

Finally, you need to take into account availability of replacement parts. The X-100 models now come under the Jaguar Classic Parts supply company umbrella (and not regular dealer supply Jaguar Land Rover). Eventually, there should be a good supply, with parts being remade to meet demand, but, for the foreseeable future, there are likely to be shortages of some parts for these cars. In the case of the X-150, Jaguar, like other manufacturers, will need to ensure supply for some time to come, and some of the technology applies to other Jaguar models.

4.2 or 5.0-litre

If you have made a decision to buy an X-150, then which to

Wheels and tyres are very expensive to replace, so beware damaged wheels, uneven tyre wear, or mismatched tyre types and sizes. (Nigel Thorley)

do you buy, 4.2-litre or 5.0-litre? Mike Horlor, the XK Forum Co-ordinator for the Jaguar Enthusiasts' Club, has owned both– here are his thoughts:

"Both 4.2-litre and 5.0-litre versions of the XK are reliable (thus far). There have been few mega mileage examples of the 5.0-litre engine around to test ultimate reliability and it is still possible to argue that, in the long run, the added complication of the later engines' valve gear could make them more sensitive to poor maintenance (missed oil changes or poor quality oil). Only time and mileage will tell.

"It is the difference in performances of the 4.2 and 5.0-litre equivalent models where the largest differences exist. Not only more powerful courtesy of its direct fuel-injection system, the 5.0-litre also produces its power in more economical fashion. Both 4.2-litre and 5.0-litre naturally aspirated models share similar fuel economy figures, whereas the combined fuel consumption figures for the 4.2 XKR and 5.0 XKR are marginal, failing to do justice to the naturally aspirated 5.0-litre ,which, in the real world, is notably quicker than the 4.2-litre it replaced, yet has a significant mpg advantage over the supercharged cars. This is particularly so at the lower speeds most of us use in daily life. So, if there is any doubt, when considering buying a naturally aspirated XK, that it will prove brisk enough, that doubt should be quickly dispelled by driving a 5.0-litre which has a similar or better mpg performance than the 4.2 model.

"For supercar performance, the 5.0-litre supercharged cars take some beating. All are seriously quick cars and there is little on the road which can match them and certainly not at today's secondhand prices. Good value they may be, but it's hard not to be tempted to flex the right foot to the detriment of fuel consumption and tyre wear, not to mention their licence losing abilities.

"To match the sporty performances of the XKRs in a straight line, as power outputs have risen, the suspension settings have become progressively stiffer, to the detriment of ride quality. None is a bone shaker and all are still excellent long distance tourers. However, the owner of an early XK8 on 17in wheels with its near saloon car ride qualities would be surprised how 'stiffly' a modern 5.0-litre XKR rides.

"Fortunately for secondhand values, only small changes to the exterior looks of these cars have been made since production started in 2006. So small have the changes been that the loss of the external radio aerial in 2007 was a major talking point at the time. The biggest variations have been in wheel patterns, which exist in a bewildering variety to suit all tastes. Jaguar has well and truly moved away from the time when it only offered one or two choices of alloys.

"If a decision is taken to buy a 5.0-litre, then the exterior styling changes come automatically. Internally, there were many changes from the onset of the 5.0-litre cars, which make them a nicer place overall 'to be in'. If a wide range of 'toys' is most important to your choice of car, either select an XKR which has always enjoyed a high specification, or a 5.0-litre Portfolio model."

Body and trim

The X-150 was an entirely new design, and owed little to previous models, and, in view of its aluminium construction, there are few issues to concern an intending buyer over corrosion. The fit and finish of panels was always excellent, as was the paintwork, so the major pointers are to look at the condition of the paintwork, possible body repairs from accident damage, ill-fitting or damaged wheels and trim, and one specific area of possible corrosion.

It is not unknown for the New XK bodywork to suffer from a minor form of aluminium corrosion caused by faulty preparation or interaction between the aluminium and other trim/metalwork. This will normally show itself in the form of bubbles lifting the paint in specific areas around the car, namely the door tops and rear wings, where they meet the chrome trim areas ,and also on the boot rear tonneau panel between the boot lid (Convertibles) and the hood trim. This was a more major concern with the first aluminium bodies built for the X-350 (XJ) saloons, and is certainly not a major problem for XKs, but should be noted, as the cost of repair and repaint can prove expensive.

Paintwork was excellent, so should still be, regardless of the age of the car. Look therefore for dull areas caused by oxidisation of the paint through lack of care, or differing colours of panelwork, where specific areas have been painted before. If so, investigate further on the inside of panels where possible, running your hands across the offending area, feeling for filler or undulations in the finish. Note, however, that the front noses of these cars, and some of the sill appliqués and rear bodywork almost always show a slight difference in colour. These are of different materials and were painted separately to the bodywork when new, so this is normal. Also note that opening the bonnet may reveal apparently

Aluminium corrosion is a minimal issue with New XKs, but be aware of it. (Nigel Thorley)

Although body and paintwork are long lasting, many XKs suffer badly from minor bodywork scuffing and pebble rash. (Nigel Thorley)

There's not a lot visible underneath an XK because of protective and aerodynamic panelling. (Nigel Thorley)

'unfinished' semi-matt' areas of paint on the inner wings and panels. Again, this was normal and nothing to worry about. Normal wear and tear will include pebble rash at the front of the car, around wheelarch areas, the bonnet, and even windscreen, causing minor (or some major) chips, which could cost a lot to repair. Significant damage to the windscreen can result in a failed MoT (or similar road worthiness test).

Look for damage to the front nose section from minor contact, check the lower grille and valance areas for damage, the sills for damage caused by contact with high kerbs, and similarly scuffs at the back bumper area, where there may have been minor contact.

Pay careful attention to the alloy wheels, as they are easily damaged and are expensive to replace. Most obvious will be edge damage from kerbing, much of which can be repaired quite easily these days by specialists. However, all alloy wheels are vulnerable and the larger and more designer led they are, the more likely they are to be severely damaged – in many cases in ways undetectable to the naked eye. Any major contact with a kerb, or running a wheel with a flat or

Interiors wear very well so beware badly stained mats, carpets and scuffed sill areas. (Nigel Thorley)

deflated tyre, will cause the wheel to become 'oval'. This can lead to an imbalance in the handling of the car. It is also not unknown for damaged wheels to be welded up and reused on the assumption this is satisfactory – it is not and is dangerous. So the inside of the wheels should be thoroughly checked.

It will be unusual for these cars to be fitted with unbranded tyres, but do check, not just the condition, but also the size and type of tyre, to ensure they are suitable for such a high-performance vehicle. Most models have larger and wider wheels with low profile tyres – they are inevitably expensive to replace, and should be done so at least in pairs per axle, to ensure good balance and effective handling.

There isn't a lot to investigate on the underside of an X-150. With rubberised panels to create a smooth airflow, it is difficult to see anything. However, do check for obvious fluid leaks – these cars are usually totally free of them. However, it is not unknown for earlier cars to suffer differential leaks; this can only be fixed by the replacement of other components in the drivetrain, as these earlier differentials are no longer available new.

There isn't a lot of separate trim, particularly chrome on these cars, but do check for damage, as some replacements can prove expensive. Look for damaged door mirrors, scratched or chipped glass, cracked light lenses, etc. It isn't unusual for owners to have fitted some aftermarket accessories, like extra chrome surrounds to the lighting, etc. All such matters are down to personal taste, but shouldn't make a difference to the price you pay for a car.

Finally, what about the exterior paint colour? With so many colour options over the years, there is plenty of choice to suit most tastes. It was also not unusual for original owners to choose a customised colour, which may not suit all tastes. It is worth pausing, before accepting a customised scheme, unless the price of the car makes it worthwhile – or unless you particularly like it yourself!

Interior trim

A vast array of finishes and trim colours have been available for the New XK models over the years. It's down to personal choice whether you prefer black to ivory, bond grain leather to fine grain, alloy trim to wood veneer.

Areas to look out for include the driver's seat bolster, which can become scuffed and scratched, due to constantly getting in and out of the car. In most cases, this can be repaired by professional treatment, but if severely worn, new leather may have to be let in, which

LED lighting on the later cars may be an MoT issue in future, necessitating complete light replacement. (Nigel Thorley)

will prove expensive. Apart from this, the leather trim is particularly hard wearing, so beware of any major issues with it, like severe cracking from long exposure to water, or bad discolourisation through contact with the sun or incorrect cleaning methods.

All the cars were equipped with carpet overmats which will protect the main carpeting. Are they still there and, if so, in what condition? – not easy to obtain now in the exact colour you require, and the carpets themselves would be expensive to replace if needed.

The wood and alloy trim wears well and, if necessary, can be replaced, but only in matched sets to ensure a uniform finish. Headlining doesn't usually suffer, although, as with all the trim, regular smokers will have created their own problems, through strong smells and discolouring of the materials. Modern textiles like suedecloth are not that easy to clean, so care should always have been taken with such trim areas.

It is not unknown for early differentials to leak and, if they do so badly, then it isn't just the differential that needs replacing (as they are no longer available), but other aspects of the drivetrain as well. (Nigel Thorley)

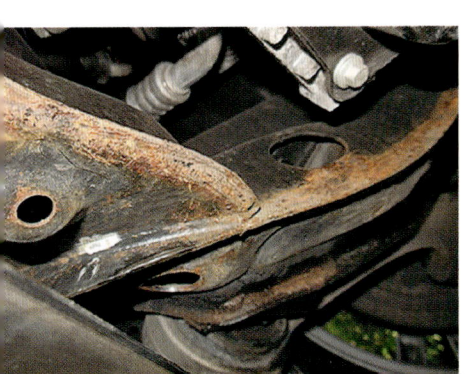
Minor surface rusting like this is not unknown, and is not a problem with underside components of these cars. (Nigel Thorley)

Electrics and lighting

The electrics and electronics in these cars is far superior to earlier Jaguars, so give very few problems. Externally, check the lighting, particularly the digital light units, which, when certain LEDs fail, can lead to an MoT failure. The cost of repair is high, because you have to replace the whole light unit. Similarly, check the xenon lighting at the front – another very expensive area for replacement if there are issues.

When sitting in and road-testing a prospective car, check that everything –and I mean *everything* – works (and correctly). Something quite innocuous could be hiding a major electrical issue, so beware. Check, particularly, that all is well with the touch-screen and all its operations.

Mechanicals

Mechanicals in these cars are very long lived. The engines do not carry forward any of the known issues associated with the X-100 V8s units such as timing chain tensioners, water pumps, etc. The 5.0-litre unit is an entirely different engine in every detail to the 4.2-litre and, so far, has proved incredibly reliable and trouble free.

Refer to Chapter Eight, page 103, for checking engine numbers relating to the V5 document, and that the car has a full service history (either with a franchised Jaguar dealership or a reputable independent Jaguar specialist), backed up with physical evidence of the work done (not just a fully stamped service book).

Road test

It is vital to road test a car before considering a purchase, to ensure it runs well, has no hesitations or harshness in the engines, gearboxes, with no rattles and knocks from the suspension or undue noises from the drivetrain. All in all, however, the longevity of the New XK models, and the very few recalls and service instructions put out over the years, is testament to how good these cars are.

A road test is vital before buying one of these cars. (Jaguar Cars/Nigel Thorley)

Owning, running and caring for your New XK

An overview

Modern technology makes these later XKs a lot more reliable, but also difficult for the DIY enthusiast or traditional hands-on car owner to maintain. Computerised online diagnostic systems are required to determine and rectify many issues that crop up, which limits the investigation and work that can be carried out by the average owner. Therefore, when issues arise, it is usually down to helpful assistance from someone 'in the know,' the internet, or by using a Jaguar franchised dealership or independent Jaguar specialist to discover the remedy. The New XKs are a product of today's world – much better in many respects, built for efficiency, cost-effectiveness and longevity of service. Demands put on manufacturers have ensured better fuel consumption; longer and cheaper service intervals, but these have come at the cost of higher degrees of complexity.

The concept of construction has also changed dramatically since the older X-100 steel-bodied cars. Safety issues relating to impacts, emissions controls, etc, all played their part in directing Jaguar, like all other car manufacturers, down a route to much more sophisticated and complicated systems. Airbags, pedestrian safety systems, complex cruise control and 'fly by wire' technology have changed motoring and maintenance for ever.

General servicing

When it comes to general servicing, there is less to do and less one can do. With 10,000/15,000-mile service intervals, and very low oil consumption, little needs attending to between services, and a DIY enthusiast can carry out basic servicing work, such as checking coolant hoses, brake pipes and so on, using the Jaguar service guide. Please also refer to Chapter Nine of this book. Other more specific matters are covered below.

Some things are hard to check – for instance, the 5.0-litre engines have no conventional dipstick to check oil level, and the oil filter cover located at the top of the engine needs a special adaptor to loosen it, to allow residual oil in the filter housing to drain back into the engine during an oil change.

Outside normal service procedures, main areas of concern are drivebelt renewal (normally at 150,000 miles), supercharger belt replacement (105,000 miles), brake fluid changes (every two years), and coolant changes (at ten-year intervals). These intervals are only recommendations – items such as the belts should be checked regularly, as they can wear much earlier. You may find the air-conditioning system needs purging; or the radiators get clogged with debris and insects, which can affect the cooling efficiency of the core. Attending to these matters separates the car that is regularly – and properly – maintained, from an 'average' one.

The 5.0-litre cars have a Service Interval Indicator, read via the onboard diagnostics. At each service, the dealer is supposed to reset this indicator, something

The oil level of 5.0 litre engines is checked via the car's instrument panel, not by conventional dipstick. (Nigel Thorley)

the average DIY maintainer will not be able to do, so be aware of this.

Other maintenance

Whilst servicing, and some other maintenance work is quite possible to do yourself, other, more involved work is not only very complex but awkward, requiring specialist tools which are too costly to be viable for the average home-maintenance person to buy. The factory equivalent of workshop manuals don't exist for these models, and you can't buy publications like the Haynes manuals or even a Jaguar Heritage CD for them. There is the Jaguar Global Technical Reference website, however, at www.jaguartechinfo.com – a subscription site which is quite comprehensive, with technical information on these cars. Service schedules, instructions and other useful information can be found there.

In this chapter, we can only cover some items relevant to the later cars, beyond normal servicing. Firstly, reiterating an item covered in Chapter Nine, the gearboxes are identified as 'sealed for life' and supposedly not in need of oil or filter changes. In reality, as with the earlier models, they do need an oil and filter change regularly. This is not a DIY job as special equipment and oil is required. It is suggested that the oil and filter are changed at around 80,000 mile intervals.

The differentials are also 'sealed for life' yet later cars do actually have a drain plug! On the very early 4.2-litre cars, the rear differentials were supplied by the Vistean company and, over time, they can leak oil and even become slightly noisy. Cars were later fitted with differentials from the Dana company. The earlier differentials are no longer available, so if one needs changing, the replacement will include other expensive items such as a new propshaft, and even driveshafts.

Wheel bearings and bushes can be a common problem, due to the weight of the car and the large wheels and tyres. The usual way to check for wheel bearing wear is by jacking up the car and rocking each wheel side to side, and back and forth providing a 'feel' for the amount of wear in the components. When on the road, listen for unusual rumbling noises that might be associated with wheel bearings becoming worn. It is vital these are changed before they deteriorate badly.

There are numerous bushes on the suspension system, all of which wear over time and mileage. They can cause knocking noises, and affect the handling and tyre wear. Most are easy to replace, but the rear wishbone bushes are an integrated component in the lower alloy wishbone arms. Jaguar recommend that when these need replacing, the whole arm is changed, not just the bush. This is because of possible damage to the lightweight alloy arms. However, some reputable independent specialists are now offering refurbished arms fitted with new bushes on an exchange basis, making the work cheaper. It is also quite common for the front lower wishbone bushes to settle slightly in service, and this may cause a very small additional amount of toe-out from the initial factory setting, although still possibly within maximum Jaguar tolerances. If spotted in time, resetting the tracking towards the centre of the acceptable range can help extract maximum life from the tyres.

Sometimes issued are raised from apparent problems with the Jaguar electronic handbrake. These are normally down to the rear discs and pads being well worn and nearing the time they should be replaced. This causes an erroneous message to be sent to the dashboard: 'Electronic Park Brake Fault'. Usually, once new discs and pads are installed, the problem goes away.

Some drivers use 'left foot braking,' a procedure particularly common with automatic transmission cars, whereby the left foot is used to press the brake pedal, while the right foot stays on the accelerator pedal. It's a practice used by many competitive drivers, and enables a fast throttle response before and immediately after braking. However, with modern technology cars, like the New XK, this is a major problem. The very action of applying the brake pedal at the same time as lifting off the accelerator pedal causes the car's electronics to receive conflicting signals, one calling for brakes and the other calling for power. This triggers fault messages and, at worst, trips the car into 'limp home mode,' restricting performance. If you want to continue with left foot braking, then the answer is to ensure your foot is completely OFF one pedal before applying the other.

Many of these cars are equipped with the larger 19in and 20in wheels, and it is worth checking the tyre pressures regularly. Although tyre wear is relatively good for a car of this size, any slight fluctuation in pressures will adversely affect wear and can affect the handling of the car, just as worn wheel bearings and bushes can. Correct tracking and keeping the wheels in balance can not only affect tyre wear but also the balance and handling of the car.

In order to keep the car running correctly, the battery needs to be kept in tip-top condition. Even the slightest reduction in battery voltage can cause problems – for instance, erroneous warning messages may appear on the dashboard; or elements of the car's system stop functioning properly, or, worse, the car won't even start. It is therefore strongly advised that, if a car is not in regular use, a trickle charger is fitted to the battery to maintain its condition. Surprisingly, these cars can actively maintain electronic systems for hours after a car has been parked up and locked. A simple matter of pressing a button on the remote control key fob later can reactivate electronic systems in the car for some time afterwards.

A particular issue for these cars is that if the car's battery was replaced, the car would not start. Jaguar supplied a software update and connection lead change that rectified the problem. Dealers should have made contact with owners to carry out the change during routine servicing.

Occasionally, a 'low battery' warning relating to the key fobs may be caused by a faulty casing. Early fobs had an issue with the back of the casing which allowed the battery to move on its contacts. A new backing can be fitted which puts more pressure on the circuit board, providing a better battery contact.

The ground studs (one in each wheelarch by the damper area) tend to corrode from road dirt ingress, and can even fall off. The studs are the main ground point for the headlight units, so if one fails, the whole light will stop working. Jaguar supply new studs which are easily fitted to the body without any major work.

The New XKs have LED rear and high level brakelight units fitted. A certain number of the LEDs must be illuminated to pass the MoT. It is likely that similar regulations apply to road worthiness tests in other countries. The individual LED bulbs cannot be replaced, so a complete unit has to be substituted.

There are small rubber panels that form airflow ducts which look like mini-mud flaps, and are situated under the edges of the front wings/sill area. They are often removed when other work is being carried out, or can be broken off over raised kerbs and the like. Keep an eye on their fixings, and replace them if they are not there or get damaged. They are an important part of the aerodynamics of the car, and can even affect fuel consumption!

The 5.0-litre cars have the rotary JaguarDrive control – actually just an electrical switch. Electrical failure can leave a car with its gearbox locked in park position, unable even to be moved on to a recovery vehicle. Fortunately, Jaguar anticipated this problem, and there is an emergency procedure to deal with it. There is an access hatch below the centre console, which hides a lever to release the transmission lock mechanically and place the gearbox in neutral.

It is not unknown for the dashboard touchscreen to become slightly loose when work has been carried out in that area. If that happens, it can result in the screen either not working at all, or not working in certain modes.

These small rubberised panels are actually a vitally important part of the car's aerodynamics package. (Nigel Thorley)

Additional maintenance and care issues

Since the first edition of this book, other matters have come to light concerning the later (X-150) models. As previously mentioned, although these New XK models were much improved both in technological and build matters compared to the earlier X-100 cars, problems still occur as the cars get older with higher mileages.

The engines (both 4.2-litre and 5.0-litre) fitted to these later cars had a head-start in all areas, with much improved components that largely eliminated basic hardware weaknesses. However, a rare issue relates to occasional variable valve timing (VVT) unit wear, revealed by excessive noise following cold starts.

A minor issue for 5.0-litre cars can be engine noise, especially when compared with 4.0-litre and 4.2-litre versions. 5.0-litre engines have direct fuel injection working at very high pressures, produced by noisy pumps. Careless under-bonnet maintenance can all too easily dislodge and loosen the acoustic pump covers, fitted to reduce what is quite a din.

Other than the points already noted, XK reliability has always been good, and it improved still further with the introduction of these aluminium-bodied cars.

Owners of modern cars, including Jaguars, have come to appreciate that battery voltage is key to reliable electronic operations. Storing a car without using it for a few weeks at a time is a death sentence for batteries facing multiple battery draining electronic modules, and it opens the way to displays of spurious dashboard warning lamps and wasted garage visits for diagnostics sessions. The use of a battery conditioner is essential for vehicles kept this way.

Fitting a new battery to a New XK (particularly a convertible) is not a simple task, and it must be the correct size, shape and voltage to match the car. Later XKs (2006 MY onwards) have an on-board battery management system (BMS module) to add more control to charging and discharging. When replacing a battery on these cars, it is necessary to reset the BMS using an appropriate diagnostics system, forcing it to recognise that it now has a new battery with different requirements from those of the old failing battery.

After eliminating the battery as a possible culprit for electrical glitches, the next common issue affecting the electrics of some aluminium cars has been corrosion of the earthing studs. Fortunately, these can easily be cleaned or replaced to restore their function.

Time has still yet to reveal common failure patterns

The two types of space-saver wheels for XKs. The red one can only be used with cars fitted with a standard braking system.

The position of the battery in a New XK can make it difficult to change for a DIY owner, and, back then, most cars required reprogramming to accept the new battery!

within these later cars' electronics systems. Faults to date have been examples of one-off failures in a largely reliable system. Touch screens slightly loose within their frames, causing apparently multiple inputs as they move and touch, were one of the few issues creating a failure pattern of blank or unreactive screens.

Among mechanical components on later cars, settling of front wishbone bushes resulting in excessive toe-out should be monitored to avoid high front tyre wear. All the XK range of cars are relatively heavy grand tourers, and, driven enthusiastically, they will wear out suspension bushes and wheel bearings.

Rare accounts have come through of issues with the Pedestrian Safety System (see page 147) that controls the bonnet area upon pedestrian impact. Upon deployment, the system lifts the rear edge of the bonnet to deflect any impact with a pedestrian, avoiding greater injury to them. It has not been unknown for the system to deploy accidentally, possibly through some impact with a large pot-hole in the road. Jaguar has not issued any service bulletins about this to date, and there is no way of preempting the situation. However, if the system does deploy, it is a very costly exercise to replace the parts involved.

Naturally, aluminium cars do not rust like their steel forebears. Nevertheless, they do incorporate various mild steel stiffeners in the suspension/under-body area. After a few years of being pounded by salt and road debris, these stiffeners should be checked for rust, and preferably be protected by repainting or adding a protective wax coating to maintain their integrity.

As most of these later XKs have larger alloy wheels, some, like all XKRs with performance braking systems, have space-saver wheels fitted in the boot areas. For normally aspirated models with standard braking systems, the usual *red* 18in space-saver is okay. However, for all cars fitted with the enhanced braking systems, a *black* 19in space-saver with the lower profile tyre must be used. Some of the very late XK models will have neither, and instead have a Tyre Repair Kit.

None of these cars is DIY-friendly. From 1996 to 2014, the cars became ever more packed with electronics, with the need for sophisticated diagnostics and special tools to work on them. The good news is that reliability increased steadily with time, and the final 4.2-litre and 5.0-litre cars have shown themselves to be capable of high mileages with minimal unscheduled maintenance costs.

Chapter Twenty

Modifications and miscellanea

A significant number of accessories, enhancements and upgrades have become available for all the XK models over time. From the very beginning, Jaguar itself offered a range of interesting (and sometimes useful) accessories for the car. Also, from about 1999, outside companies started to take a keen interest in the car, initially just offering accessories or aesthetic add-ons, the range has now expanded to include major styling changes and mechanical/performance enhancements.

Factory accessories

Apart from the R-Performance options brochures and lists, Jaguar has produced a considerable range of 'accessory' publications for the XK. The first, published in July 1996 and updated in a larger format at launch in October, offered a diverse range of useful items from a small 14-piece attaché case Tool Kit, to an Inclination Sensor to detect unauthorised jacking/towing of the vehicle. One of the more useful safety products was Alpha Dotting, the microscopic particle implant of the vehicles identification number at various locations around the car.

Useful items to avoid damage to trim included a hard pre-formed ABS protective liner for the boot, a soft tailored boot mat and, for the interior front seat, fitted covers in washable nylon. A very practical accessory was plastic headlamp covers to protect the glass from stone chips and cracking, a similar item available for

If you're looking for period factory-supplied accessories for your XK, there is plenty of choice in this incredible range of brochures. (Nigel Thorley)

the early fog lamps as well.

From the beginning, Jaguar offered a range of luggage fitments for the XK, from a boot lid mounted rack (with or without an aerodynamic matching suitcase) to ski-holders and even bike holders. Jaguar even offered various sets of fitted suitcases for the boot, none of which proved very popular because of cost – these included a set of five traditional vulcanised black cases with straps, a six-piece set in soft fabric and leather, and even a set of seven rigid suitcases, not all of which fitted in the boot!

The 1998 catalogue followed the same format as the car brochures, with virtually the same range. A new lockable Security Box that fitted in the boot was now available, for valuables like passports and jewellery, and luggage retainers for the boot floor could be added. There was also an aftermarket add-on Satelite Navigational system (CD based), with the remote screen sited to the right of the driver in front of the fresh air vent.

Yet another brochure, in 1999, heralded a revised range: now the accessory Tool Kit was in the form of a zip case (and came with a pair of gloves), and the range included a Front Bonnet Protector – a vinyl cover to guard against stone chips. Jaguar also offered the Star TAC 130 mobile phone system, with a phone unit fitted in the centre console storage area. By this time, Reverse Park Sensing had become an aftermarket fit as well.

The Millenium brochure offered a reduced range of accessories for the XK. For colder climes, an Engine Block Heater was now listed. From 2001, an Auxiliary Power Socket could be fitted in the glovebox or boot, ideal for charging mobile phones, for example.

By 2004, the range of items had been dramatically reduced and, indeed, brochures covered most Jaguar models instead of just the XK cars. Entirely new accessories for the XK were an all-wood rim steering wheel, and an improved range of storage and sports holding equipment.

With the introduction of the X-150 models, in 2006, Jaguar introduced new accessories and add-ons. Early on, the range was quite small, but later expanded to include personalised badging, illuminated boot tread strip, luggage space extenders, and enhancements packs mentioned in Chapter 16 (Aerodynamic, Speed, Black).

Alloy wheels

The choice of factory-supplied alloy wheels has been extensive, and sometimes confusing. Most popular from the initial range available for buyers of the X-100 models, were the 18in Flute or chromed plate 17in Revolver, fitted during build or aftermarket. Alternatively, and rarely seen, was the option of the XJR 17in five-spoke, exposed nuts, wheel. Another rarity, offered most of the time, were winter quality tyres fitted to conventional steel wheels (with plastic hub caps à la X-300).

For the X-150 models, the initial choice of wheels was between the 18in Venus, 19in Carella, or 20in Senta, with a 19in Sabre run-flat type available a few months later. For the slightly later XKR model, 18in wheels are not available, and, at the time, especially for the XKR, 19in Jupiter and 20in Cremona were supplied extra. [Do you mean exclusively for the XKR or particularly in the case of the XKR?]

As the extensive deletions and additions to the alloy wheels range can be confusing, all the wheel types can be found, detailed by year and with accompanying pictures, in Appendix 9 on page. Suffice at this point to say that the wheels listed are not interchangeable between X-100/X-150 models, and that wheel-type can also depend on the fitment of uprated brakes and other issues.

Incredible to think, but yes, all these suitcases were made to – and do – fit in the boot of an XK8, providing you have a space saver! (Nigel Thorley)

Fitted luggage is now available for the X-150 Coupe and Convertible models. (Nigel Thorley)

A typical Paramount Performance 'Grand Prix' XKR with many of their improvements included, providing over 400lb ft of torque. (Nigel Thorley)

An example of the extremes that can be gone to in creating a unique version of your New XK. (Ultimate Auto)

R-Performance (X-100) models

The introduction of R-Performance options from 1999 for the X-100 models provided even more variances in specification.

Essentially, the products available covered improved brakes, and handling packages, with a new range of alloy wheels. However, various items were an only-fit with selected other products from the range. For example, the uprated Brembo brakes could only be fitted with one of the larger alloy wheel sets.

Initially the alloy wheel range was made up of:

    18in BBS Milan
    20in BBS Paris
    20in BBS Detroit

(and at this stage, a new Winter Tyre was offered fitted to an open ten-spoke alloy wheel).

By 2001, a new 20in Montreal wheel was offered, and, in 2002, Recaro sports seats with soft grain leather, matching steering wheel and gear knob; and even an Aluminium Pack, with instrument surrounds, foot pedals and gearlever surround was available. By 2004, a more expansive approach was given to R-Performance, with a comprehensive brochure covering all Jaguar models. For the XKs specifically another 20in split-rim alloy wheels was added to the range, the Sepang.

Outsiders

During 1999, outside companies started to take an interest in the Jaguar X-100. Paramount Performance, for example, was already promising a wide range of options, many of which came from the German Arden Company. Arden itself introduced a 460bhp version of the XKR, which also took some styling cues from the XK180.

Called the A-type, it was produced with a carbon fibre body, remapped electronics, race tuned exhaust

system and lowered suspension, along with further weight savings – suggesting a top speed in the region of 190mph with 0 to 60mph in 4.5 seconds Six-pot callipers on the front wheels and four-pot at the rear improved the braking system. Externally, the reformed body panels gave the car a more aggressive look, as did the wider mouth at the front, and new lighting treatment all round.

Since then, Paramount Performance has produced a whole range of options to bring the cars up to particularly high-performance standards, with enhanced trim and styling. Many other companies have joined the fray, with the likes of Adamesh, Racing Green and XKZ Zarhan, all offering a wide range of updates and enhancements for these models.

Similarly for X-150 models, many more companies like Paragon, Design XKR, and the ones mentioned above, to name but a few, are offering a wide range of accessories and upgrades for these cars. There is an amazing choice of cosmetic enhancements with trim, improved lighting, body kits, alloy wheels, plus more

Wire wheel conversions are more common with X-100 cars but Dayton now offers similar for the X-150 models. (Dayton)

involved performance, suspension and brake upgrades – the lists can seem endless.

How to improve the looks of your XK

If you have or expect to purchase an XK, there is so much you can do without going to the extremes of some of the Paramount and Racing Green projects. It is all down to how much money you want to spend and what type of car you want to end up with.

For example, let's take wheels again. If you don't like the wheels that Jaguar offered there is still plenty of choice, providing you take care to ensure the wheels you buy will actually fit. Lots of businesses, even local companies, can offer a wide range of wheels to suit your requirements. Motor Wheel Services, well known for its supply of classic wire wheels, now offers a range of specially developed wire wheel conversions for the XK models. Supplied as a bolt-on fit, no special temporary or permanent adaptations are required on the existing XK hubs. The wheels are built to a high quality to take the stress to which a modern and relatively heavy car like the XK can subject them. They are chrome plated, and any existing tyres can be fitted to them. All you have to remember is that they are more difficult to clean than conventional wheels!

For the ultimate improvement to a Convertible, this torpedo effect aluminium tonneau cover can be finished in any body colour and fits neatly behind the rear seat when the hood is erect. (Racing Green Ltd)

Fancy a nose job? Any colour, most shapes, take your pick from the many after-market alternatives available. (Nigel Thorley)

Wrapping a car is a new process which can result in a complete change of exterior colour scheme or something more 'dramatic' like a chrome effect! (Superior Auto Design)

Could something like this be a 'warp' too far for some XK owners? It's all down to personal taste! (Paramount Performance)

If you are looking for a bit more veneer and something different to leather, then how about this door trim? (Paramount Performance)

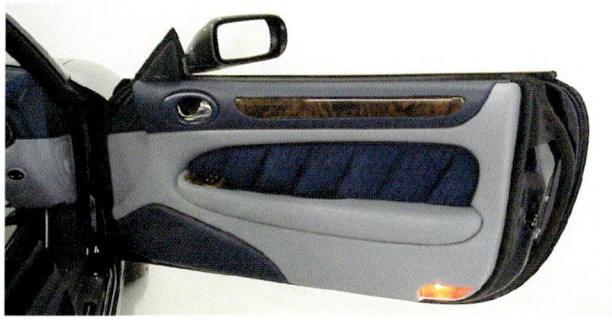

Adamesh and similar companies offer enhancements to existing X-100 and X-150 trim like chromed surrounds to light units. (Nigel Thorley)

A relatively modern feature is vehicle 'wrapping', a form of plastic wrap that is shrunk around the car to change the exterior colour or even add logos, designs, etc. This was introduced for commercial and public service vehicle businesses as it was a much more cost-effective way of personalising transport, and of course, when such vehicles are sold, the wrap can be removed leaving the original finished. Now that trend is appearing on cars. If you find the right car for you at the right price, but want to change the colour, this may be the way to do it. The plus point is that it protects the original surface underneath, and is surprisingly economical to remove without damaging the factory paint.

If you want to substantially change the look of your XK's interior, then think about contacting companies like Racing Green, Adamesh, or Northelle in Germany. All offer a range of options, from individually chosen wood veneer with unique grains to Piano Black finishes and even high contrast upholstery/trim options. Seats can even be re-trimmed to suit, and you can accommodate upgraded sound systems and alarms, etc.

How to improve safety and comfort

Reverse park aids can be fitted to cars that predate the availability of such systems from Jaguar or its dealerships. Widely available from many outlets, aftermarket kits like the 'Third Eye' can be fitted easily and safely to the X-100s. The general principle is that sensors fitted to the rear bumper face are activated when reverse gear is selected. A signal beam senses obstacles at a preset distance and emits an intermittent 'bleep', the bleeps getting more frequent the closer the car gets to the obstacle(s).

Prices will vary for these kits, which are in the main cheaper than buying direct from a Jaguar dealership. It is important, in view of the width of the XK, to

Or go all the way and have the seats re-upholstered as well. (Paramount Performance)

select a kit with *four* sensors, not two or three – four will provide a good spread of beam. Each kit comes complete with detailed instructions.

After measuring up to ensure the sensors are correctly positioned as shown in the kit instructions, the bumper can be drilled. Take care not to damage surrounding paintwork. The sensors and their housings will be clearly different from one another and marked as such: it is vital that they are fitted as instructed so that the beams can function correctly.

Feed the wires through into the boot area (which may involve removing some of the boot trim), where the system's control box/pick-up unit must be mounted. This has to be connected to one of the car's reversing light circuits, as it will pick up the signal when reverse is selected and the reversing lights come on. The other wire from the pick-up unit goes to the audible warning bleeper, which has to be accommodated somewhere inside the car.

Various companies offer headlight bulb upgrades for non-xenon equipped X-100s and they claim the bulbs dramatically improve light output with up to 50 per cent more light on the road.

Safety Devices produced specially made roll-over cages for the X-100s, so perhaps we will see XKs on the tracks alongside the XJSs, XJ Saloons and XK/E-type sports cars which participate in the Jaguar Enthusiasts Club Series one day.

Jaguar never produced a hard top for the X-100 Convertible models so this was left to outside contractors. Both Arden and LS Design produced examples, the latter made from a double-skinned shell

The Arden hardtop for XK Convertibles isn't cheap and can be difficult to store when not on the car. (Paramount Performance)

of glass fibre fitted with Velour or leather trim. Cost when new was around £5500, dependent on trim finish.

Classic Additions and Adamesh offer a range of aftermarket items for all XK models. From fitted indoor or outdoor car covers in various colours, they progressed to producing stainless steel mesh grilles and wind deflectors for the Convertibles, which turned out a lot cheaper than the Jaguar-supplied items.

If you don't have an X-100 already equipped with a satnav system, you might consider SmartNav from Traffic-master. It is a specialist fit (and it was recommended by Jaguar themselves), with nothing on show inside the car except for a small screen (if you want it). Otherwise you just have a button that connects you directly to their control centre and you simply voice request your requirements, which are downloaded to your car and then voice directions are given. As a 'real time' system it even keeps track of traffic conditions and informs you accordingly, changing your route when necessary, and actually in some uses is still a better system to the integrated system in the X-150s!

How to improve performance

Various companies have produced, and still continue to produce, a range of enhanced exhaust systems for XK models. Many claim improved performance and sounds, and there are now so many, it isn't possible to list them all here – a search on the internet will reveal a vast array.

Engine management upgrades is another area now well catered for, with a wide range including modified induction systems for the X-100 engines, supercharger pulley changes to increase rotational speed, and ECU re-mapping. Steering, suspension and brakes are also very well covered, with systems to provide switchable steering response, stiffened suspension, larger brakes, and even a paddle shift gear change system for the X-100 models. Again, many companies offer these services. However, one should bear in mind that Jaguar fine-tuned these cars' drivetrains for the best performance/drivability/efficiency, so any such changes should be reviewed carefully before purchase, to weigh up the cost, affects on the car's performance/handling, and even on-going maintenance and care.

For budding home-mechanics, with the finance and expertise, and specialist Jaguar independent garages working on XKs these days, the Autologic diagnostics system is a notebook-sized casing with its own integrated 12in colour touch screen that utilises solid-state technology and connects to the car's own interior

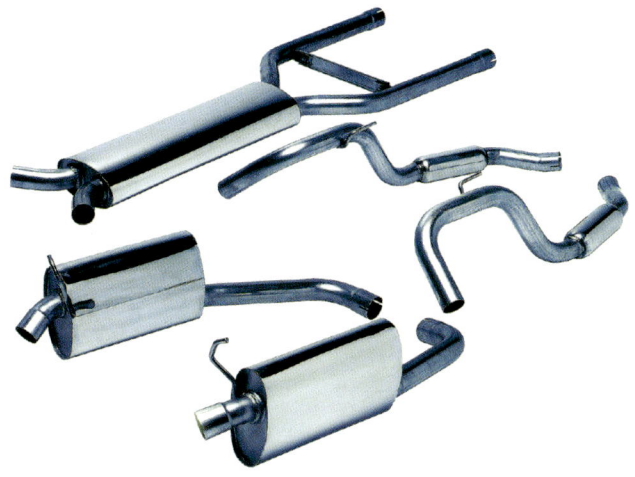

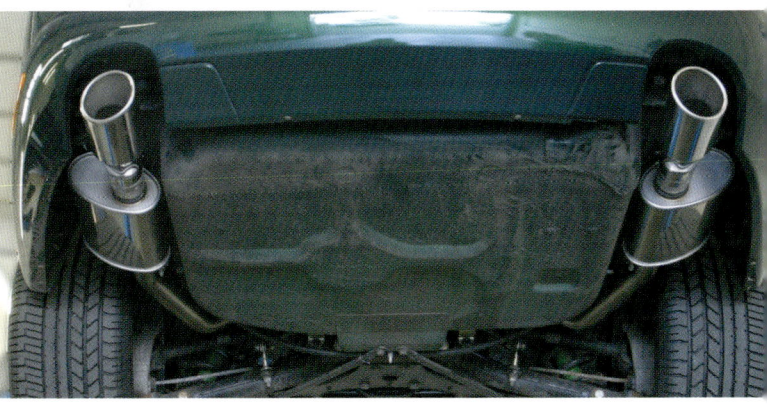

One of the many after-market exhaust systems available for the XK, this one a Tiger system from Double S. (Double S Exhausts)

The XK lends itself to a whole range of options for exhaust systems, many of which follow the original lines so don't hang lower, with a choice of pipe diameter to create more or less sound as the owner requires. This conversion was carried out by Elite & Performance of Derby (Nigel Thorley)

multi-pin socket, from where the Autologic unit also gets its power. It has the ability to download and upload information from the Diagnos.co.uk website, providing quick and easy access to expertise when a problem needs attention. This also means any changes in the software can be made quickly and efficiently. The equipment can provide valuable services such as modifying the engine management systems, programming other electronics, and even reprogramming key-fobs – just like a Jaguar dealership diagnostic system.

Lastly, if you don't want to improve the momentum performance of your XK, you can certainly dramatically improve the fuel consumption with an LPG alternative fuelling system. These are getting more sophisticated all the time, the price of LPG is still significantly below that of petrol/gasoline, and with modern techniques it is easy to fit a system without losing too much space in the boot, although you will have to resort to a can of tyre sealant instead of a spare. There are more difficulties to consider with the installation in an X-150, and the most important thing is whether such an installation is worth it financially. If you don't intend to cover a lot of miles in your XK, it could take years to recoup the cost of installation.

As you can tell, there is so much to go at for the XK models and more is being offered as time goes on. You can choose to keep your XK as original as it left the factory, or can make it truly individual – the choice is yours.

Classic Additions provide this wind deflector, ideal for keeping the lady's hair in place when the top is down. (Nigel Thorley)

It is feasible to fit an LPG conversion to an XK. (Nigel Thorley)

No, it's not an F-TYPE, but an aluminium XK converted to a style reminiscent of the former, but with unique touches, created by Grantley Engineering in Yorkshire to special order.

Examples of the last two face-lift versions of the New XK: on the right the post-2009 5.0-litre, and on the left the last of the line Dynamic R 5.0-litre.

Appendices

1: XK8/XKR (X-100) 4.0 litre and 4.2 litre maintenance schedule

Work	10,000 miles	20,000 miles	30,000 miles	40,000 miles	50,000 miles	60,000 miles	100,000 miles	Other notes
Replace engine oil, filter & sump washer	X	X	X	X	X	X	X	
Visual check for fluid leaks	X	X	X	X	X	X	X	
Inspect brake pads (brake rotor conditon on pad change)	X	X	X	X	X	X	X	
Replace air cleaner element (normally aspirated engine)				X			X	
Replace air cleaner element (supercharged engine)				X			X	
Replace fuel filter						X		
Replace sparkplugs						X		
Replace pollen filter		X		X		X		
Check drive belt tension wear indicator	X	X	X	X	X	X	X	
Renew drive belt (normally aspirated engine)								150,000 miles
Renew supercharger drive belt							X	
Check brake fluid level	X	X	X	X	X	X	X	
Check coolant level and specific gravity	X	X	X	X	X	X	X	
Check windscreen washer reservoir level	X	X	X	X	X	X	X	
Check battery electrolyte level	X	X	X	X	X	X	X	
Check power assisted steering fluid level	X	X	X	X	X	X	X	
Check condition of wiper blades	X	X	X	X	X	X	X	
Check condition of all tyres, pressures, etc.	X	X	X	X	X	X	X	
Oil door locks, hinges, wax protect brake/fuel lines, etc.	X	X	X	X	X	X	X	
Check lights, horn and other electrics	X	X	X	X	X	X	X	
Replace gearbox oil and filter							X	
Replace brake fluid								2 years
Renew coolant, flush radiator and check hoses								10 years or 150,000 miles
Road Test	X	X	X	X	X	X	X	

2: New XK/XKR (X-150) 4.2 litre maintenance schedule

Work	10,000 miles	20,000 miles	30,000 miles	40,000 miles	50,000 miles	60,000 miles	100,000 miles	Other notes
Replace engine oil, filter & sump washer	X	X	X	X	X	X		
Visual check for fluid leaks	X	X	X	X	X	X		
Inspect brake pads (brake rotor conditon on pad change)	X	X	X	X	X	X		
Replace air cleaner element (normally aspirated engine)			X			X		
Replace air cleaner element (supercharged engine)		X			X	X		
Replace fuel filter						X		
Replace sparkplugs			X			X		
Check drive belt tension wear indicator	X	X	X	X	X	X		
Renew drive belt (normally aspirated engine)							X	
Renew supercharger drive belt				X				
Grease drive shaft universal joints	X	X	X	X	X	X		
Check brake fluid level	X	X	X	X	X	X		
Check coolant level and specific gravity	X	X	X	X	X	X		
Check windscreen washer reservoir level	X	X	X	X	X	X		
Check battery electrolyte level	X	X	X	X	X	X		
Check power assisted steering fluid level	X	X	X	X	X	X		
Replace windscreen wiper blade rubbers	X	X	X		X	X		
Renew windscreen wiper blades				X				
Check condition of all tyres, pressures, etc.	X	X	X	X	X	X		
Oil door locks, hinges, wax protect brake/fuel lines, etc.	X	X	X	X	X	X		
Check lights, horn and other electrics	X	X	X	X	X	X		
Replace gearbox oil and filter					X			
Replace brake fluid								2 or
Renew coolant, flush radiator and check hoses						X		4 years
Road Test	X	X	X	X	X	X		

3: New XK/XKR (X-150) 5.0 litre maintenance schedule

Work	15,000 miles	30,000 miles	45,000 miles	60,000 miles	75,000 miles	90,000 miles	Other notes
Replace engine oil, filter & sump washer	X	X	X	X	X	X	
Visual check for fluid leaks	X	X	X	X	X	X	
Inspect brake pads (brake rotor conditon on pad change)	X	X	X	X	X	X	
Replace air cleaner element (normally aspirated engine)			X			X	
Replace air cleaner element (supercharged engine)			X			X	
Replace fuel filter							
Replace sparkplugs							105,000 miles
Replace pollen filter	X	X	X	X	X	X	
Check drive belt tension wear indicator							
Renew front accessory drive belt (N/A models)							150,000 miles
Renew front accessory drive belt (supercharged models)							105,000 miles
Check brake fluid level	X	X	X	X	X	X	
Check coolant level and specific gravity	X	X	X	X	X	X	
Check windscreen washer reservoir level	X	X	X	X	X	X	
Check battery electrolyte level	X	X	X	X	X	X	
Check power assisted steering fluid level	X	X	X	X	X	X	
Check condition of wiper blades	X	X	X	X	X	X	
Check condition of all tyres, pressures, etc.	X	X	X	X	X	X	
Oil door locks, hinges, wax protect brake/fuel lines, etc.	X	X	X	X	X	X	
Check lights, horn and other electrics	X	X	X	X	X	X	
Replace gearbox oil and filter							
Replace brake fluid							2 years
Renew coolant, flush radiator and check hoses							10 ys or 150,000 miles
Road Test	X	X	X	X	X	X	
Reset service indicator announcement indicator	X	X	X	X	X	X	
Reset engine oil level indiactor	X	X	X	X	X	X	

4: XK8/XKR (X-100) exterior colour availability by year

Colour	1996	1997	1998	1999	2000	2001	2002	2003	2004	2005
Spindrift (white)	X	X	X	X*	X					
White Onyx						X	X	X	X	X
British Racing Green	X	X	X	X	X	X	X	X	X	X
British Racing Green (Metallic)							X	X	X	X
Emerald (Dark Green)					X	X				
Aquamarine	X	X	X							
Sherwood (Mid Green)	X	X	X							
Alpine (Pastel Green)				X*	X					
Seafrost (Pastel Green)					X	X	X	X	X	X
Sapphire (Dark Blue)	X	X	X	X	X	X				
Westminster (Dark Blue)					X	X				
Antiqua (Mid Blue)	X	X	X	X						
Pacific (Mid Blue)					X	X	X	X	X	X
Adriatic (Mid Blue)							X	X		
Amaranth (Purple)			X	X						
Ultraviolet (Purple)									X	X
Ice Blue (Pastel)	X	X								
Zircon (Pastel Blue)							X	X	X	X
Mistral (Blue/Grey)					X	X				
Titanium (Grey)	X	X			X	X	X			
Meteorite (Silver)			X	X						
Platinum (Silver)					X	X	X	X	X	X
Quartz (Dark Grey)							X	X	X	X
Slate (Dark Grey)							X	X	X	X
Anthracite (Black)	X	X	X	X	X	X				
Ebony (Black)							X	X	X	X
Midnight (Black Met)							X	X	X	X
Topaz (Gold)	X	X	X	X	X	X	X	X	X	X
Roman Bronze						X				
Carnival (Dark Red)	X	X	X	X	X	X	X	X		
Pheonix (Red)				X**	X	X	X	X		
Salsa (Red)									X	X
Radiance (Darker Red)									X	X

Specials

Colour	1996	1997	1998	1999	2000	2001	2002	2003	2004	2005
Copper Black (S/Victory Models)										X
Frost Blue (S/Victory Models)										X
Bay Blue (S/Victory Models)										X
Satin Silver (S/Victory Models)										X
Jupiter Red (Portfolio Models)								X		
Coronado Blue (Portfolio Models)								X		

Note:
* indicates not available on XKR models in that year.
** indicates only available on the XKR model for that year.

5: XK/XKR (X-150) exterior colour availability by year

Colour	2006	2007	2008	2009	2010	2011	2012	2013	2014
White Onyx	X								
Porcelain White	X	X	X	X					
Polaris White					X	X	X	X	X
British Racing Green	X	X							
Jaguar Racing Green	X	X*							
Botanical Green			X	X	X	X	X		
Emerald Fire Green		X	X	X					
Seafront Green	X	X							
Liquid Silver	X	X	X	X	X				
Rhodium Silver							X	X	
Lunar Grey	X	X	X	X	X	X	X	X	X
Quartz Grey	X								
Slate Grey	X	X							
Zircon Blue	X								
Vapour Grey			X	X	X				
Pearl Grey			X	X	X				
Stratus Grey					X	X	X		
Frost Blue		X	X	X	X				
Crystal Blue					X	X	X	X	
Azure Blue			X	X					
Spectrum Blue					X	X	X	X	
Blue Prism		X							
Ultraviolet Blue	X								
Indigo Blue	X	X	X	X	X	X	X	X	X
Kyanite Blue				X**	X**	X**	X**		
Midnight Black	X	X							
Ultimate Black			X	X	X	X	X		
Black Amethyst							X	X	X
Ebony Black	X	X	X	X	X	X	X	X	X
Salsa Red	X	X	X	X**		X**			
Carnelian Red								X	X
Radiance Red	X	X	X	X		X			
Claret Red				X	X	X	X		
Winter Gold	X	X	X	X					
Cashmere Gold					X*	X*	X*	X*	X*
Caviar Brown					X*	X*	X*	X*	X*

Notes:

* XK model only

** XKR model only

Specials

Name	Colour	2006	2007	2008	2009	2010	2011	2012	2013	2014
XKR Portfolio	Celestial Black		X	X						
	Liquid Silver		X	X						
XKR-S Coupe	Ultimate Black				X					
XKR 75/175	Stratus Grey					X				
	Arisan SE									
	Polaris White							X	X	
	Celestial Black							X	X	
	Rhodium Silver							X	X	
	Indian Special Edition									
	Celestial Black								X	
	Ultimate Black								X	
	Crystal Blue								X	
	Lunar Grey								X	
	Rhodium Silver								X	
XKR-S	Polaris White						X	X	X	X
	British Racing Green								X	X
	Ultimate Black						X	X	X	X
	Stratus Grey						X	X	X	X
	Italian Racing Red						X	X	X	X
	French Racing Blue						X	X	X	X
XKR-S GT	Polaris White/Graphics									X
XK66	British Racing Green									X
	Stratus Grey									X
SignatureXK DynamicXKR	Polaris White									X
	Ultimate Black									X
	Stratus Grey									X
	Sapphire Blue									X
	British Racing Green									X
	Italian Racing Red									X

Name	Colour	2006	2007	2008	2009	2010	2011	2012	2013	2014
Final Fifty	Ultimate Black									X
Speed & Dynamic Packs	Polaris White						X	X	X	X
	British Racing Green								X	X
	Ultimate Black						X	X	X	X
	Liquid Silver						X	X		
	Stratus Grey						X	X	X	X
	Satelite Grey								X	X
	Rhodium Silver								X	X
	Spectrum Blue						X	X		
	Kyanite Blue						X	X	X	X
	Salsa Red						X	X		
	Italian Racing Red								X	X
Black & Black Dynamic Pack	Polaris White						X	X	X	X
	Ultimate Black						X	X	X	X
	Stratus Grey							X	X	X
	Satelite Grey								X	X
	Rhodium Silver							X	X	X
	Salsa Red						X	X		
	Italian Racing Red								X	X

6: XK8/XKR UK brochures

Year	Models	Cover	Description	Pages	Identity Code
1996	XK8	Black/Red car nose	"The Car is Back" – Abridged teaser with reply form	6	JLD/10/22/21/96
1996/7	XK8	Black/Blue half hose	"The Cat is Back" – Full launch brochure with development pics, specs, etc.	50	JLD/10/01/21/96
1996/7	AJ-V8 engine	Green	"Refined Power", Launch information		
1997	XK8	Blue portrait with sea	Range brochure including X-300 saloons	28	JLD/10/02/00.96.1
1998	XK8	Cream Landscape	Combined brochure with V8 saloons. Last section only on XK8	32	JLD/10/02/00/98
1998	XK8	Green Square	Completely new brochure on XK models with new pics, etc.	36	JLD/10/01/21/98
1998	XKR	Red nose close-up	Launch brochure for the XKR in square format	14	JLD/10/01/36/98
1999	XK8/XKR	Cream Red Car	Square format revision of launch XKR and 1998 green XK8 brochure	44	JLM/10/02/03/99
2000	XK8/XKR	Blue/Black Bonnet	Square format, major revisoin of previous XK brochures.	44	JLM/10/02/03/00
2000	Silverstone	Mesh Grille	Portfolio style with loose leaf pages to celebrate special edition XKR		
2001	XK8/XKR	Green Car at speed	Square format, Complete revision based on model changes	50	JLM/10/02/03/01
2001	XKR 100	Green R-Per	Large portrait format, fold out card on commemorative model (includes XJR)		JLM?10/02/14/02
2001	XK8/XKR	Green "Art of Performance"	Square format, fold out colour feature on XKs and XJs with large poster on rear		JLM/10/01/00/01
2002	XK8/XKR	4 car line up	Small (A5) landscape range brochure covering X-type, S-type & XJ saloons	32	JLM/10/15/00/02
2002	XK8/XKR	4 car line up	Supplementary, updated version of above A5 landscape range brochure	32	JLM/10/15/00/02.5
2003	XK8/XKR	Silver XKR Nose	Large portrait format, entirely new brochure with separate colour chart	62	JLM/10/02/03/03
2003	XK8/XKR	Silver XKR Nose	Abridged version of above in same format	24	JLM/10/20/03/03
2003	XK8/XKR	Silver, inset pictures	Smal (A5) landscape range brochure covering X-type, S-type & XJ saloons	24	JLM/10/15/00/03
2004	XK8/XKR	Black XKR at speed	Landscape format, another completely new style of brochure	50	JLM/10/02/03/04
2004	XKR 400	Black box sleeve	Prestige landscape format for limited edition model with silver sleeve plus box	34	J4849
2005	XK8/XKR	Black XKR in Sleeve	Landscape format, another new brochure style with good colour detail	40	JLM?10/02/03/04.5
2005	Carbon Fibre	Black Sleeve (holes)	Limited edition quality landscape format for Carbon Fibre model	42	J5213
2005	4.2 S	Oil Skin Sleeve	White luxury hard-backed landscape format for last models	40	JLM/10/02/24/06
2005	XK8/XKR	Black "Born to Perform"	Small square format full range brochure with all Jaguar models	52	JLM/10/15/00/05
2006	New XK	Blue tint Power Vent	Large format 28 page launch information with specs, colours, etc.	28	JLM/10/24/03/07
2007	New XK	White XK centre section	Large format detailed brochure of orignal New XK with full details and specs	50	JLM/10/02/03/07
2007	New XK	White blue XK front	A4 sized 'Vehicle Personalisation' accessory brochure to accompany above	34	JLM/10/29/03/07
2007	New XK/XKR	Half Front view sunset	Large format detailed brochure of XK plus XKR	40	JLM/10/02/03/07.25
2007	New XK/XKR	Half Front view sunset	A4-sized three-fold price list with options and interior pictures	6	JLM/10/03/03/07.25
2007	XKR Portfolio	Headlight/wheel detail	Unique landscape brochure for the new XKR Portfolio model	16	JLM/10/02/29/08
2008	All New XKs	Black car front at speed	12 ½ x 7 ½ landscape quality brochure on all models, specs and equipment	60	JLM/10/02/03/08.1
2008	All New XKs	Black car front at speed	Accompanying price listing for above	12	JLM/10/03/03/09
2008	XK60	Black boxed XK60 script	Small limited deal brochure just on this model within a black cardbox casing	120	None given
2008	XKR-S	Black XKR-S at speed	Hardback special publication for the original low volume model		
2009	All New XKs	Black car rear view lights	12 ½ x 7 ½ landscape quality brochure on all models, updated	68	JLM/10/02/03/0`09
2009	All New XKs	Black car quarter windows	Accompanying price listing for above	12	JLM/10/03/03/0109
2009	XKR/XFR	Black box with red brochure	Landscape quality brochure covering the facelift XKR along with XFR model	20	JLM/10/15/0/8/0310
2010	All New XKs	Black car front at speed	12 ½ x 7 ½ landscape quality brochure on all models with facelifted front	72	JLM/10/02/03/0310
2011	All New XKs	Red XK at speed	12 ½ x 7 ½ landscape quality brochure on all models, specs and equipment	44	JLM/10/25/03/0411
2011	XKR-S	Blue car front side view	First unique brochure on the new XKR-S model in small format	36	None given
2011	XKR-S	Carbon fibre style slip-case	Blue car at speed on cover of quality landscape brochure on this model	32	JLM/10/02/35/1211
2011	XKR-S/R/SFR	Red slip-case	Quality landscape brochure covering the sports and saloon -R models plus XKR	32	JLM/24/03/08/0611
2012	All New XKs	Silver XK at speed/sunset	12 ½ x 7 ½ landscape quality brochure on all models, specs and equipment	44	JLM/10/02/03/0812
2012	SE	White cover with XK insignia	Brochure cover, the Artisan Special Equipment models in detail	24	JLM/10/85/03/-412
2014	All New XKs	Collage of racing images	Large format square Celebration brochure, including last of special editions	32	JLM/10/02/03/0214

Specials

Year	Models	Cover	Description	Pages	Identity Code
2006	New XK/XKR	White with silver XK insignia	Rare large portrait format hardbound pictorial book on the cars	56	None given
2006	New XK	White box	Boxed set of individually-printed styling images of the original New XK		None given
			Various Press Packs and Accessories listings and price lists were available		

7: Specifications XK & XKR

	XK8 4.0 Coupé	XK8 4.0 Convertible	XKR 4.0 Coupé	XKR 4.0 Convertible
cc	3996	3996	3996	3996
Bore (mm)	86	86	86	86
Stroke (mm)	86	86	86	86
Compression ratio (to 1)	10.75	10.75	9	9
bhp (@ rpm)	290 @ 6100	290 @ 6100	370 @ 6150	370 @ 6150
Max torque (lb ft @ rpm)	290 @ 4250	290 @ 4250	387 @ 3600	387 @ 3600
Automatic transmission	ZF 5-speed	ZF 5-speed	Mercedes 5-speed	Mercedes 5-speed
Wheel size (std) front	8in x 17in	8in x 17in	8in x 18in	8in x 18in
Wheel size (std) rear	8in x 17in	8in x 17in	8in x 18in	8in x 18in
Braking system	Ventilated discs, ABS, split circuits, park brake on rear			
Steering	Rack & pinion variable ratio			
Steering turns lock to lock	2.8	2.8	2.8	2.8
Turning circle	36ft 2in	36ft 2in	36ft 2in	36ft 2in
Suspension (front)	Independent unequal length wishbones, steel coil springs, telescopic dampers, anti-roll bar		Independent unequal length wishbones, steel coil springs, telescopic dampers, anti-roll bar Adaptive Technology	
Suspension (rear)	Independent double wishbone driveshafts acting as double links, concentric steel springs, dampers, anti-roll bar		Independent double wishbone driveshafts acting as double links, concentric steel springs, dampers, anti-roll bar, Adaptive Technology	
Top speed	155mph	154mph	155mph	155mph
0–60mph acceleration	6.4 seconds	6.7 seconds	5.2 seconds	5.3 seconds
Average fuel economy	22.9mpg	23.3mpg	22.5mpg	22.2mpg
Overall length (mm)	4760	4760	4760	4760
Overall width (mm)	1829	1829	1829	1829
Overall height (mm)	1296	1306	1296	1306
Wheelbase (mm)	2588	2588	2588	2588
Unladen weight (kg)	1615	1705	1640	1750
Front track width (mm)	1504	1504	1504	1504
Rear track width (mm)	1498	1498	1498	1498
Boot volume (litres)	327	307	327	307
Fuel tank capacity (litres)	75	75	75	75

	XK8 4.2 Coupé	XK8 4.2 Convertible	XKR 4.2 Coupé	XKR 4.2 Convertible
cc	4196	4196	4196	4196
Bore (mm)	86	86	86	86
Stroke (mm)	90.3	90.3	90.3	90.3
Compression ratio (to 1)	11	11	9.1	9.1
bhp (@ rpm)	300 @ 6000	300 @ 6000	400 @ 6100	400 @ 6100
Max torque (lb ft @ rpm)	310 @ 4100	310 @ 4100	408 @ 3500	408 @ 3500
Automatic transmission	ZF 6-speed	ZF 6-speed	ZF 6-speed	ZF 6-speed
Wheel size (std) front	8in x 19in	8in x 19in	9in x 20in	9in x 20in
Wheel size (std) rear	9in x 19in	9in x 19in	9in x 20in	9in x 20in
Braking system	Ventilated discs, ABS, split circuits, park brake on rear			
Steering	Rack & pinion variable ratio			
Steering turns lock to lock	2.8	2.8	2.8	2.8
Turning circle	36ft 2in	36ft 2in	36ft 2in	36ft 2in
Suspension (front)	Independent unequal length wishbones, steel coil springs, telescopic dampers, anti-roll bar		Independent unequal length wishbones, steel coil springs, telescopic dampers, anti-roll bar Adaptive Technology	
Suspension (rear)	Independent double wishbone driveshafts acting as double links, concentric steel springs, dampers, anti-roll bar		Independent double wishbone driveshafts acting as double links, concentric steel springs, dampers, anti-roll bar, Adaptive Technology	
Top speed	155mph	155mph	155mph	155mph
0–60mph acceleration	6.1 seconds	6.3 seconds	5.2 seconds	5.3 seconds
Average fuel economy	24.9mpg	24.7mpg	22.9mpg	22.6mpg
Overall length (mm)	4776	4776	4776	4776
Overall width (mm)	2015	2015	2015	2015
Overall height (mm)	1296	1306	1296	1306
Wheelbase (mm)	2588	2588	2588	2588
Unladen weight (kg)	1685	1775	1735	1815
Front track width (mm)	1504	1504	1504	1504
Rear track width (mm)	1498	1498	1498	1498
Boot volume (litres)	327	307	327	307
Fuel tank capacity (litres)	75	75	75	75

8: Specifications New XK

	New XK 4.2 Coupé	New XK 4.2 Convertible	New XKR 4.2 Coupé	New XKR 4.2 Convertible	New XK 5.0 Coupé
c.c	4,196	4,196	4,196	4,196	5,000
Bore (mm)	86	86	86	86	92.5
Stroke (mm)	90.3	90.3	90.3	90.3	93
Compression ratio (to 1)	11	11	9.1	9.1	11.5
Bhp (@ rpm)	300 @ 6000	300 @ 6000	420 @ 6250	420 @ 6250	385 @ 6500
Max torque (Lbs.Ft @ rpm)	310 @ 4100	310 @ 4100	413 @ 4000	413 @ 4000	380 @ 3500
Automatic transmission	ZF 6 Speed	ZR 6 Speed	ZF 6 Speed	ZF 6 Speed	ZF 6 Speed
Wheel size (std) front	18in, 19in or 20in	18in, 19in or 20in	18in, 19in or 20in	18in, 19in or 20in	18in, 19in or 20in
Wheel size (std) rear	18in, 19in or 20in	18in, 19in or 20in	18in, 19in or 20in	18in, 19in or 20in	18in, 19in or 20in
Braking system	Ventilated Discs, ABS, split circuits, Park Brake on rear				
Steering	Rack & Pinion variable ratio				
Steering turns lock to lock	2.8	2.8	2.8	2.8	2.8
Turning circle	36in	36in	36in	36in	36in
Suspension (front)	Ind. unequal length wishbones, steel coil springs, telescopic dampers, anti-roll bar		Ind. unequal length wishbones, steel coil springs, telescopic dampers, anti-roll bar, adaptive technology		
Suspension (rear)	Ind. double wishbone, driveshafts acting as double links, concentric steel springs, dampers and anti-roll bar		Ind. double wishbone, driveshafts acting as double links, concentric steel springs, dampers and anti-roll bar, adaptive technology		
Top speed	155mph	155mph	155mph	155mph	155mph
0 to 60mph acceleration	5.9 seconds	6 seconds	4.9 seconds	5 seconds	5.2 seconds
Average fuel economy	25 mpg	25 mpg	22.9 mpg	22.9 mpg	25.2 mpg
Overall length (mm)	4791	4791	4791	4791	4794
Overall width (mm)	2070	2070	2070	2070	2028
Overall height (mm)	1322	1329	1322	1329	1322
Wheelbase (mm)	2752	2752	2752	2752	2752
Unladen weight (kg)	1595	1635	1665	1715	1660
Front track width (mm)	1560	1560	1560	1560	1560
Rear track width (mm)	1608	1608	1608	1608	1608
Boot volume (litres)	330	313	330	313	330
Fuel tank capacity (litres)	70.6	70.6	7.06	70.6	70.6

	New XK 5.0 Convertible	New XKR 5.0 Coupé	New XKR 5.0 Convertible	XKR-S Coupé	XKR-S Convertible	XKR-S GT Coupé
c.c	5,000	5,000	5,000	5,000	5,000	5,000
Bore (mm)	92.5	92.5	92.5	92.5	92.5	92.5
Stroke (mm)	93	93	93	93	93	93
Compression ratio (to 1)	11.5	9.5	9.5	9.5	9.5	9.5
Bhp (@ rpm)	385 @ 6500	510 @ 6000	510 @ 6000	542 @ 6000	542 @ 6000	550 @ 6500
Max Torque (Lbs.Ft @ rpm)	380 @ 3500	461 @ 2500	461 @ 2500	502 @ 2500	502 @ 2500	502 @ 2500
Automatic transmission	ZF 6 Speed	ZF 6 Speed	ZF 6 Speed	ZF 6 Speed	ZF 6 Speed	ZF 6 Speed
Wheel size (std) front	18in, 19in or 20in	18in, 19in or 20in	18in, 19in or 20in	20in	20in	20in
Wheel size (std) rear	18in, 19in or 20in	18in, 19in or 20in	18in, 19in or 20in	20in	20in	20in
Braking system	Ventilated Discs, ABS, split circuits, Park Brake on rear					
Steering	Rack & Pinion variable ratio					
Steering turns lock to lock	2.8	2.8	2.8	2.8	2.8	2.8
Turning circle	36in	36in	36in	36in	36in	36in
Suspension (front)	Ind. unequal length wishbones, steel coil springs, telescopic dampers, anti-roll bar, adaptive technology			Extensive changes – see text within chapters		
Suspension (rear)	Ind. double wishbone, driveshafts acting as double links, concentric steel springs, dampers and anti-roll bar, adaptive technology					
Top speed	155mph	155mph	155mph	186mph	186mph	186mph
0 to 60mph acceleration	5.3 seconds	4.6 seconds	4.6 seconds	4.2 seconds	4.2 seconds	3.9 seconds
Average fuel economy	25.2 mpg	23 mpg	23 mpg	23 mpg	23 mpg	23 mpg
Overall length (mm)	4794	4794	4794	4794	4794	4794
Overall width (mm)	2028	2028	2028	2028	2028	2028
Overall height (mm)	1329	1322	1329	1312	1319	1319
Wheelbase (mm)	2752	2752	2752	2752	2752	2752
Unladen weight (kg)	1669	1753	1800	1795	1840	1840
Front track width (mm)	1560	1560	1560	1560	1560	1560
Rear track width (mm)	1608	1608	1608	1608	1608	1608
Boot volume (litres)	313	330	313	330	313	313
Fuel tank capacity (litres)	70.6	70.6	70.6	70.6	70.6	70.6

For specific special edition models, refer to text within the chapters.

9: Alloy wheel range XK & XKR 1996 to 2005

Design	1996	1997	1998	1999	2000	2001	2002	2003	2004	2005
17in Revolver	X Std XK8	X	X	X	X	DCL	–	–	–	–
17in Revolver Chrome	X	DCL	–	–	–	–	–	–	–	–
18in Flute	X	X	X	X	X	DCL	–	–	–	–
17in Sport (XJR)	X	X	X	X	DCL	–	–	–	–	–
18in Double Five	–	–	–	X Std XKR	X	X	X	X	X	DCL
17in Lamina	–	–	–	–	–	X Std XK8	X	DCL	–	–
18in Impeller	–	–	–	–	–	X	X	DCL	–	–
17in Gemini	–	–	–	–	–	–	–	X Std XK8	X	X
18in Hydra	–	–	–	–	–	–	–	X Std XKR	X	X
18in Centaur	–	–	–	–	–	–	–	X	X	DCL
19in Apollo	–	–	–	–	–	–	–	X	X	X Std Prem XK
18in Aris	–	–	–	–	–	–	–	–	–	X Std R Prem/S
17in Winter Steel	X	X	X	X	X	X	X	X	DCL	–
18in Winter Alloy	–	–	–	X	X	X	X	X	X	X
18in Milan (R-Per)	–	–	–	X	X	X	X	DCL	–	–
20in Paris (R-Per)	–	–	–	X	X	X	X	X	DCL	–
20in Detroit (R-Per)	–	–	–	X	X	X	X	X	X	X
20in Montreal (R-Per)	–	–	–	–	–	–	–	X	X	X
20in Sepang (R-Per)	–	–	–	–	–	–	–	–	X	X

DCL = discontinued line

17in Gemini   17in Lamina   17in Revolver   17in Revolver (Chrome)   17in Sport

17in Winter Steel   18in Aris   18in Centaur   18in Double Five   18in Flute

18in Hydra   18in Impeller   18in Milan   18in Winter Alloy   19in Apollo

20in Detroit   20in Montreal   20in Paris   20in Sepang

10: Alloy wheel range New XK 2005 to 2014

Design	2006	2007	2008	2009	2010	2011	2012	2013	2014
18in Venus	X	X	X	X	X	X	X	X	
19in Carelia	X	X	X						
19in Sabre (runflat)	X	X	X						
19in Jubiter		X	X						
19in Caravella				X	X	X	X	X	X
19in Artura				X	X	X	X	X	X
19in Tamana					X	X	X	X	X
20in Senta	X	X	X						
20in Cremona		X	X						
20in Pegasus			X						
20in Vortex			X	X	X				
20in Kalimnos				X	X	X	X	X	X
20in Nevis				X	X	X	X	X	X
20in Selena						X	X	X	X
20in Takoba						X	X	X	X
20in Venom						X	X	X	X
20in Kasuga						X	X	X	X
20in Vulcan						X	X	X	X
20in Orona						X	X	X	X

18in Venus   19in Artura   19in Caravela   19in Carelia   19in Jupiter

19in Sabre Runflat   19in Tamana   20in Cremona   20in Kalimnos   20in Kasuga

20in Nevis   20in Orona   20in Pegasus   20in Selena   20in Senta

20in Takoba   20in Venom   20in Vortex   20in Vulcan

11: Trim colourways

XK/XKR 1996 to 2005

Model		1996	1997	1998	1999	2000	2001	2002	2003	2004	2005
Sports models	Oatmeal Leather/Charcoal Facia	X	X	X	X	X	X	X	–	–	–
	Charcoal Leather/Charcoal Facia	X	X	X	X	X	X	X	X	X	X
	Cream Leather/Charcoal Facia	X	X	–	–	–	–	–	–	–	–
	Oatmeal Cloth/Charcoal Facia	X	X	X	X	X	–	–	–	–	–
	Charcoal Cloth/Charcoal Facia	X	X	X	X	X	–	–	–	–	–
	Ivory Leather/Charcoal Facia	–	–	X	X	X	X	X	X	X	X
	Nimbus Leather/Charcoal Facia	–	–	–	–	X	X	X	–	–	–
	Dove Leather/Charcoal Facia	–	–	–	–	–	–	–	X	X	X
	Heritage Tan Leather/Charcoal Facia	–	–	–	–	–	–	–	X	X	–
	Cranberry Leather/Charcoal Facia	–	–	–	–	–	–	–	X	X	–
	Heritage Tan/Charcoal Leather/Charcoal Facia	–	–	–	–	–	–	–	X	X	–
	Cashmere Leather/Sable Facia	–	–	–	–	–	–	–	–	–	X
	Ivory Leather/Sable Facia	–	–	–	–	–	–	–	–	–	X
Classic models	Oatmeal Leather/Antelope Facia	X	X	X	X	X	X	X	–	–	–
	Cream Leather/Sable Facia	X	X	–	–	–	–	–	–	–	–
	Charcoal Leather/Charcoal Facia	X	X	X	X	X	X	X	X	X	X
	Teal Leather/Dark Teal Facia	X	X	X	X	–	–	–	–	–	–
	Cashmere Leather/Sable Facia	–	–	X	X	X	X	X	X	X	X
	Ivory Leather/Sable Facia	–	–	X	X	X	X	X	X	X	X
	Nimbus Leather/Slate Facia	–	–	–	–	X	X	X	–	–	–
	Dove Leather/Charcoal Facia	–	–	–	–	–	–	–	X	X	X
	Heritage Tan Leather	–	–	–	–	–	–	–	X	X	–
	Cranberry Leather	–	–	–	–	–	–	–	X	X	–
	Heritage Tan/Charcoal Leather/Charcoal Facia	–	–	–	–	–	–	–	X	X	–
	Cranberry/Charcoal Leather/Charcoal Facia	–	–	–	–	–	–	–	X	X	–
	Ivory Leather/Charcoal Facia	–	–	–	–	–	–	–	–	–	X
Dash trims											
	Stained Maple/Birds Eye Maple	X	X	X	X	X	X	X	X	X	X
	Burr Walnut Veneer	X	X	X	X	X	X	X	X	X	X
	Elm	–	–	–	–	–	–	–	–	X	–
	Piano Black	–	–	–	–	–	–	–	–	–	X
Hood colours											
	Black	X	X	X	X	X	X	X	X	X	X
	Stone	X	X	X	–	–	–	–	–	–	–
	Blue	X	X	X	X	X	X	X	X	X	X
	Green	X	X	X	X	X	X	X	X	X	X
	Dark Beige	–	–	X	X	X	X	X	X	X	X
	Light Beige	–	–	–	X	X	X	X	X	X	X

New XK 2005 to 2014

Year and model	Seats	Stitching	Facia	Soft trim	Hard trim	Veneer	Steering wheel	Hood
2006-07 XK	Caramel/Ivory/ Warm Charcoal	Matching	Matching	Caramel/Slat Blue/ Warm Charcoal	Aluminium	Knurled Aluminium/Poplar/Burr Walnut	Leather/Wood & Leather	Beige/Dark Beige/Blue/ Black
2007 XKR	"	"	"	"	"	Aluminium Weave	R	"
2008 XK	"	Ivory/Warm Charcoal/ Slate Blue	Matching/Slat Blue	"	Aluminium/ Piano Black	Knurled Aluminium/Satin American Walnut/Burr Walnut	Leather/Wood & Leather	Beige/Blue/Dark Grey/ Black
2008 Portfolio	"	"	"	"	"	"	"	Dark Brown/Burgandy/ Dark Green
2008 XKR	"	"	"	"	"	Aluminium Weave	R	As XK
2009 XK	"	"	"	"	Aluminium	Knurled AluminiumRich Oak/Burr Walnut	Leather	Beige/Blue/Dark Grey/ Black
2009 Portfolio	"	Ivory/Warm Charcoal	Warm Charcoal/ Slat Blue/Oyster/ Caramel	Warm Charcoal/ Slate Blue/Oyster/ Caramel	Piano Black/ Aluminium	Knurled Aluminium/Rich Oak/Burr Walnut/ Figured Ebony	"	Beige/Blue/Dark Grey/ Black/Burgandy/Dark Green/Brown
2009 XKR	"	Ivory/Warm Charcoal/ Cranberry	"	"	"	Dark Mesh Aluminium/Burr Walnut/Rich Oak/Dark Oak	R	
2010 XK	"	Matching	Warm Charcoal/ Caramel	Warm Charcoal/ Caramel	Aluminium	Knurled Aluminium/Burr Walnut/Satin American Walnut	Leather	Black/Blue/Beige/ DarkGrey
2010 Portfolio	"	Warm Charcoal/Ivory	Warm Charcoal/ Ivory/Slate Blue/ Oyster	Warm Charcoal/ Slate Blue/Oyster	Aluminium/ Piano Black	Knurled Aluminium/Burr Walnut/Satin American Walnut/Figured Ebony/Piano Black	Leather/Wood & Leather	Black/Blue/Beige/Dark Grey/Burgandy/Dark Green/Dark Brown
2010 XKR	"	WarmCharcoal/Ivory/ Cranberry	Warm Charcoal/ Caramel/Oyster	Warm Charcoal/ Caramel/Oyster	Aluminium/ Piano Black	Dark Mesh Aluminium/Burr Walnut/Rich Oak/Dark Oak/Piano Black	Leather	"
2010 XKR 75/175	Warm Charcoal	Warm Charcoal	Warm Charcoal	Warm Charcoal	Aluminium/ Piano Black	Piano Black	Leather	
2011 XK	Caramel/Ivory/ Warm Charcoal	Matching	Matching	Matching	"	Knurled Aluminium/Burr Walnut/Satin American Walnut/Satin Rosewood/Satin Elm/Rich Oak	Leather	Black/Blue/Beige/Dark Grey/Burgandy/Dark Green/Dark Brown
2011 Portfolio	"	London Tan/Ivory/ Caramel	Warm Charcoal/ Oyster/Slate Blue	Warm Charcoal/ Oyster/Slate Blue	"	Bright Knurled Aluminium/Figured Ebony/ burr Walnut/Satin Elm/Satin Rosewood/ Rich Oak/Piano Black	"	"
2011 XKR	Warm Charcoal/ Ivoy/London Tan/ Red	Warm Charcoa/Ivory/ London Tan/Redl	Warm Charcoal	Warm Charcoal/ Ivory/London Tan/red	"	Dark Mesh Aluminium/Dark Oak/Burr Walnut/Satin Elm/Satin Rosewood/Rich Oak/Piano Black	"	"
2011 XKR-S	Warm Charcoal	Reims Blue/Ivory/Red	"	Warm Charcoal	"	Dark Linear Aluminium/Piano Black	"	Black
2012 XK	Caramel/Ivory/ Warm Charcoal	Matching	Caramel/Warm Charcoal	Warm Charcoal/ Ivory	Aluminium/ Piano Black	Piano Black/Bright Knurled Aluminium/ Gloss Rich Oak/Satin Rosewood/Burr Walnut/Satin Elm/Satin American Walnut	Leather	Dark Brown/Blue/Dark Grey/Dark Green/Beige/ Black/"/Burgandy
2012 Portfolio	Caramel/Ivory/ Warm Charcoal/ Oyster/London Tan	Caramel/London Tan/ Ivory	Caramel/Warm Charcoal/Ivory/ Oyster	Warm Charcoal/ Ivory/Oyster	"	Knurled Aluminium/Gloss Rich Oak/Satin Rosewood/Burr Walnut/Satin American Walnut/Gloss Figured Ebony	"	"
2012 XKR	Warm Charcoal/ Ivory/Warm Charcoal with Red/ Warm Charcoal with London Tan	Warm Charcoal/London Tan/Red/Ivory	Warm Charcoal	Warm Charcoal/ Ivory/Red/London Tan	"	Piano Black/Dark Mesh Aluminium/Gloss Dark Oak/Gloss Rich Oak/Satin Rosewood/ Burr Walnut/Satin Elm	"	"

Year and model	Seats	Stitching	Facia	Soft trim	Hard trim	Veneer	Steering wheel	Hood
2012 XKR-S	Warm Charcoal	Reims Blue/Red/Carbon with Ivory/Ivory	Warm Charcoal	Warm Charcoal	"	Dark Linear Aluminium/Piano Black	"	"
2012 Artisan SE/Indian	Truffle/Navy	London Tan/Ivory	Truffle/Navy	Truffle/Navy	"	Shadow Walnut/Dark Figured Aluminium	"	Black/Blue/Brown
2013-14 XK/Portfolio/XKR	As 2012	As 2012	As 2012	As 2012	As 2012	As 2012	As 2012	As 2012
2013-14 XKR-S GT	Warm Charcoal	Red	Warm Charcoal	Warm Charcoal	Piano Black	Piano Black	Leather	Black
2013-14 XK66	Warm Charcoal/Caramel	Warm Charcoal/Ivory	Warm Charcoal/Caramel	Warm Charcoal	Aluminium/Piano Black	Burr Walnut	"	As Portfolio
2013-14 Signature/Dynamic R	Warm Charcoal/Ivory	"	Warm Charcoal/Ivory	Warm Charcoal/Ivory	"	Figured Ebony	"	"
2013-14 Final Fifty	Ivory	Warm Charcoal	"	"	"	Piano Black	"	Black

12: XK production figures

Model X-100	1995	1996	1997	1998	1999	2000	2001	2002	2003	2004	2005	Totals
XK8 Coupe	8	2925	5141	3319	1701	1514	1723	1203	985	627	602	19748
XK8 Convertible	12	4187	9765	7662	6196	5907	4404	2910	2280	2003	1434	46760
XKR Coupe			11	1402	1530	1778	1659	1053	936	708	584	9661
XKR Convertible			12	838	1994	3042	2949	1695	1455	1075	835	13895
Totals	20	7112	14929	13221	11421	12241	10735	6861	5656	4413	3455	90064

Model X-150 *	2005	2006	2007	2008	2009	2010	2011	2012	2013	2014		Totals
XK 4.2 Coupe	197	5385	2394	1458								9434
XK 4.2 Convertible	204	6565	2212	1425								10406
XKR 4.2 Coupe		1075	3419	1816								6310
XKR 4.2 Convertible		1025	2879	1361								5265
XK 5.0 Coupe				50	1171	1250	1113					3584
XK 5.0 Convertible				70	1166	1220	1113	1762	1461			6792
XKR 5.0 Coupe				101	1144	1763	1404					4412
XKR 5.0 Convertible				60	1049	1368	974	2222	1399			7072
XK 3.5 Coupe	5		261	364								630
XKR 3.5 Convertible	7		93	544								644
Totals	413	14050	11258	7249	4530	5601	4604	3984	2860	0		54549

* The total figures are correct for X-150 models BUT there is no present breakdown from Jaguar Land Rover for the actual production figures per model for 2013 and 2014.

13: XK specialists

This list is purely a guide and should not be considered as definitive or, indeed, a recommendation of the work carried out. It is merely a list of known specialists of the models covered in this publication. Obviously, it does not include the many Jaguar franchised dealerships, nor does it cover the many specialists outside of the UK.

Anybody contemplating placing work should first ensure the company or individual has the expertise and equipment necessary to carry it out, get a reasonable estimate of the cost and time involved, and, ideally, get references from other XK enthusiasts who may have used them.

International clubs

There are numerous small organisations around the world catering for the Jaguar marque, many of which are one-country or area based. For example, in the USA and Australia a single organisation oversees and co-ordinates the work of many small regional Jaguar clubs.
• Jaguar Clubs of North America (JCNA). An organisation formed to bring together the 50 or more small clubs and organisations in the States looking after 6000 Jaguar enthusiasts. Website: www.jcna.com.
• Australian Council of Jaguar Clubs. There are several Jaguar clubs in Australia, all of which can be contacted through the Australian Council of Jaguar Clubs – www.jaguar-acjc.org.au.
• Jaguar Enthusiasts' Club. The world's largest Jaguar marque club, based in the UK. With over 20,000 members worldwide (with local regional get-togethers), it caters for all Jaguar models but with a particularly strong XK membership. As well as an award winning full colour, 140 page glossy monthly magazine (free to members), the Club also boasts its own classified advertisements website for the sale and purchase of cars and parts, many national and international events, shows and tours, plus a regular XK Seminar, an XK Forum, and even the hire and sale of all the specialist tools required to work on these cars. It also carries the largest available range of Jaguar merchandise, including clothing and books, and has a special Club-specific car insurance scheme – www.jec.org.uk, email: jechq@btopenworld.com or tel: 0117 969 8186.
• Jaguar Drivers' Club. The oldest UK Jaguar club, offering external and social events for all Jaguar owners including XKs. A monthly glossy magazine is supplied free to members, and a range of merchandise is available. Jaguar Drivers Club, 18 Stuart Street, Luton, Bedfordshire, LU1 2SL – www.jaguardriver.co.uk.

- The XK8 Enthusiasts Club. A business set up as a club to look after the interests of XK owners, with a digital magazine, helpful advice, events and an annual special XK get-together – www.xkec.co.uk.

Monthly magazines with regular XK content

- Jaguar Driver. Organ of the Jaguar Drivers' Club (see above), and free on subscription to the club, 86 pages.
- Jaguar Enthusiast. Organ of the Jaguar Enthusiasts' Club (see above), and free on subscription to the club. 140 pages, full colour with regular articles, including technical, on the XK range, extensive classified advertisements, parts for sale, etc.
- Jaguar World Monthly. The only regular Jaguar monthly magazine available on the UK High Street. Comprehensive coverage of all things Jaguar.

Brochures, handbooks, press releases and other paperwork

- The Jaguar Heritage Trust. Maintaining all factory records and information on behalf of Jaguar Cars Limited, it can supply (for a fee) a wide range of information, photos, etc, relating to the XK models. From time to time it also has various press releases, brochures, etc, for sale, and now produces a range of CDs covering paperwork, maintenance information, etc, for some of the XKs. Website: www.jdht.co.uk.
- Andrew Swift. Well-known enthusiast and collector of written matter relating to the Jaguar marque. He can supply all manner of specialist paperwork on the majority of XK models and other Jaguars. To contact him, telephone +00 44 114 2685158.

Sales, servicing, other maintenance and enhancements

- Arun Limited – West Sussex. Sale of pre-owned Jaguar XKs. www.arunltd.com.
- Autologic – Suppliers of specialist Autologic soft and hardware suitable for the XK models. www.autologic-diagnostics.co.uk.
- Berkshire Jag Components – Parts for X-100 models. www.berkshirejagcomponents.com.
- Chiltern of Bovingdon – Hertfordshire. Sales of pre-owned Jaguar XKs. www.chilternjag.co.uk.
- Classic Additions – Devises. Range of after-market accessories like mesh grilles, car covers and wind deflectors. www.classicadditions.com.
- David Manners Limited – West Midlands. Major supplier of new parts for all Jaguars, including some XK items. www.jagspares.co.uk.
- David Marks Garages – Nottingham. Specialist independent Jaguar service and other maintenance. Any work carried out from 10,000 service to engine changes. Technical Expert Advice supplied to the Jaguar Enthusiasts Club. www.davidmarksgarages.co.uk
- Dorset Sports Cars – Sales of pre-owned Jaguar XKs www.dorsetsportscars.co.uk
- E & E Services – Milton Keynes. Independent Jaguar specialists service for modern Jaguars. www.eandeservices.co.uk

- Elite & Performance Limited – Derby. Modern Jaguar service plus brake, suspension and engine upgrades, uprated exhaust systems and body kits. www.eapj.com
- Eurojag – Co. Durham. Jaguar dismantlers including accident damage XK8s. www.eurojag.com
- Furniture Clinic – Leather care and repair specialists. www.furnitureclinic.co.uk
- Jaguar at Beechdown – Devon. Pre-owned Jaguar XKs for sale. www.beechdownjaguar.co.uk
- Jaguar Classic Parts – Suppliers of parts for models that have been out of production for a minimum of ten years. www.jaguar.co.uk/about-jaguar/jaguar-classic/jaguar-classic-parts or email jhparts@jaguar.com
- Jagutek – Cambridge. Modern Jaguar servicing plus new and used parts. www.jagutek.co.uk.
- Kent Jaguar Centre – Sevenoaks. Modern Jaguar servicing and diagnosis and parts supply. Tel: 01959 533305.
- Kings Road Garage – Hertfordshire. Pre-owned Jaguar XK car sales. www.kingsroadgarage.co.uk
- Les Pauls Jaguar Specialists – Essex. Pre-owned Jaguar car sales, service and maintenance including air conditioning. www.lespaulsmotors.co.uk.
- Lodsworth Garage – Sussex. Modern Jaguar service, air conditioning service and repair. www.lodsworthgarage.co.uk.
- Myrtle Productions. Range of upgraded interior woodwork, steering wheels and gear knobs for the XK range. www.myrtleltd.com.
- Nene Specialist Cars – Peterborough. Modern Jaguar service, maintenance and diagnosis including air conditioning, wheel alignment, etc. www.nenejags.co.uk.
- North Wales Jag Centre – Repair specialists and spare parts for XKs. Tel: +00 44 1492 870150.
- Paragon Design – Norfolk. Range of body kits for XK range. www.paragondesignuk.com.
- RG Bate (Engineering) Ltd. Birkenhead. Independent Jaguar specialist for service and other maintenance. www.rbateuk@aol.com.
- Racing Green Limited – Hampshire. Extensive range of upgrades and enhancements for the XK models, from new interior woodwork, body kits, exhausts, to major performance changes. www.racinggreen.co.uk.
- Sheffield Prestige – South Yorkshire based modern Jaguar servicing, plus parts and other maintenance and car sales. www.sheffieldprestige.co.uk
- SNG Barratt Group – Shropshire. Major suppliers of new parts, including some XK items. www.sngbarratt.com.
- Simon March & Co – York. Modern Jaguar service and maintenance. www.simonmarch.co.uk.
- Surrey Jag Centre – Modern Jaguar service and diagnosis. www.surreyjag.co.uk.
- The Jaguar Specialists Ltd – Devon. Modern Jaguar service and maintenance. www.thejaguarspecialists.co.uk.
- XKZ Exhaust Systems – Specialist after-market exhaust systems for XKs. Email: chris@ebrueton.co.uk.

Also from Veloce Publishing ...

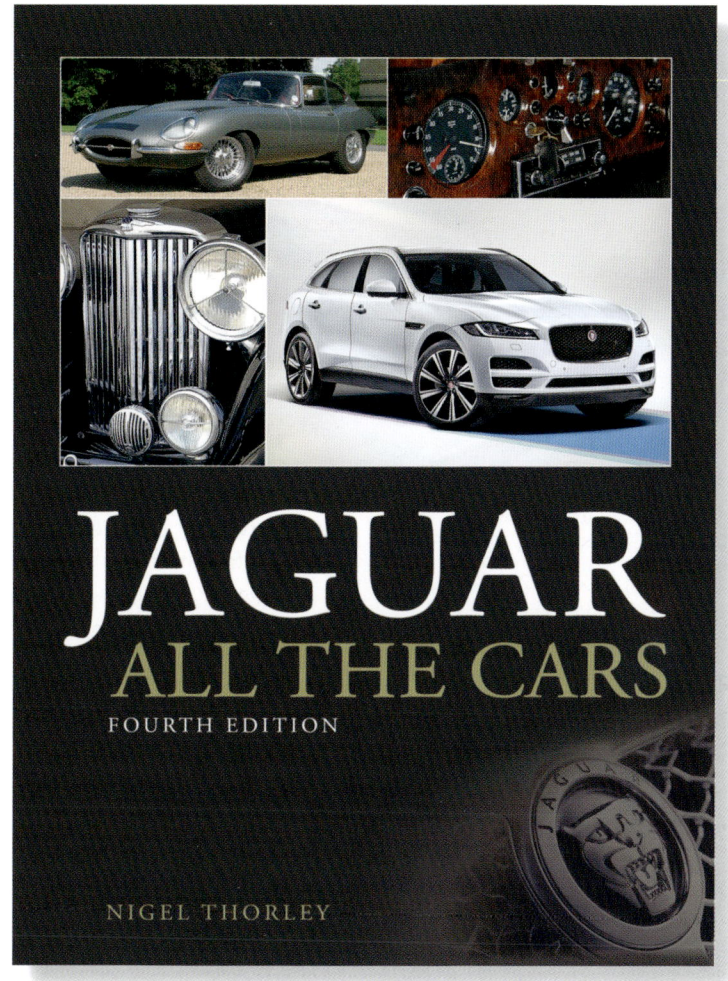

This significantly enhanced Fourth Edition of *Jaguar – All the cars*, brings the Jaguar model story right up-to-date. The only publication available covering the entire range in precise detail, with a revised engine chapter, updated chapters on existing models, and new chapters on the very latest Jaguar models.

ISBN: 978-1-845848-10-1
Hardback • 23.5x17cm • 360 pages • 700 pictures

For more information and price details, visit our website at www.veloce.co.uk
• email: info@veloce.co.uk • Tel: +44(0)1305 260068
* prices subject to change, p&p extra

Also from Veloce Publishing ...

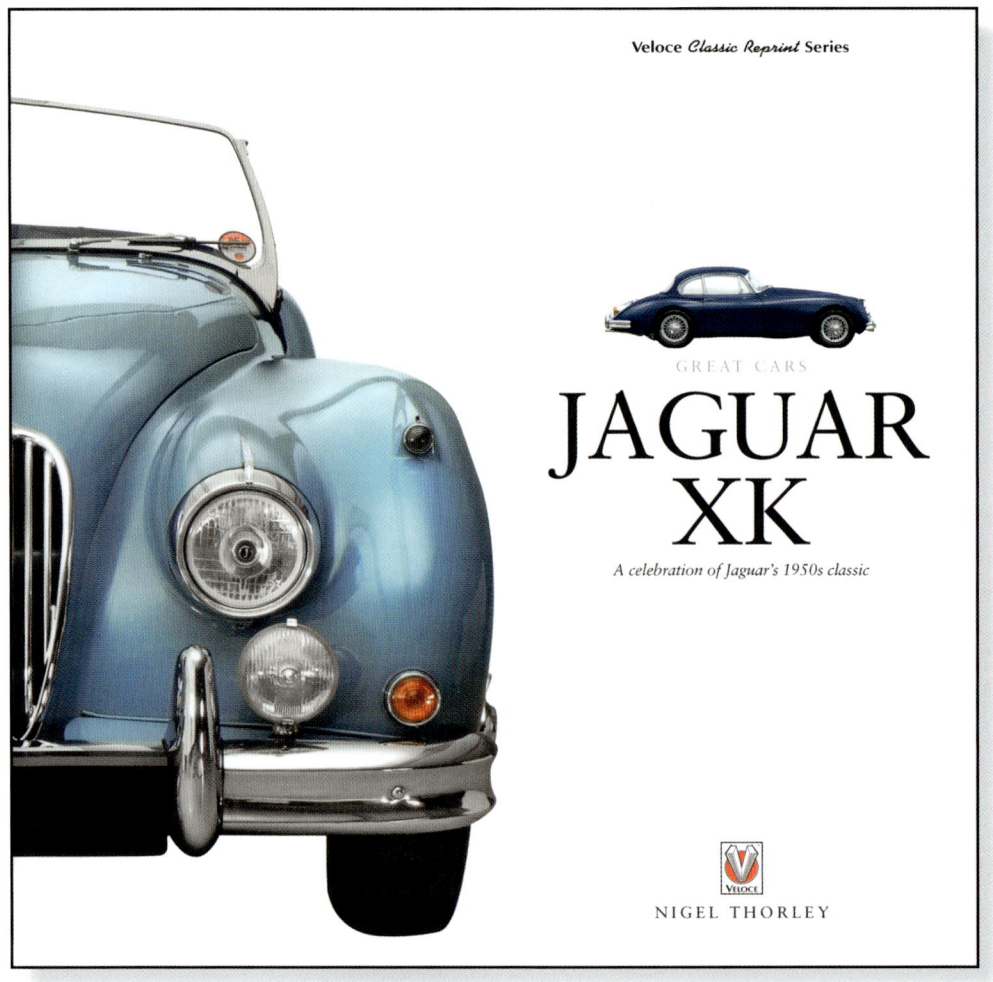

Focusing on the Jaguar XK 120, 140 and 150 model ranges, respected Jaguar historian Nigel Thorley tells the story of this important range of cars. Includes studio photography.

ISBN: 978-1-787113-02-2
Hardback • 25x25cm • 152 pages • pictures

For more information and price details, visit our website at www.veloce.co.uk
• email: info@veloce.co.uk • Tel: +44(0)1305 260068
* prices subject to change, p&p extra

Also from Veloce Publishing ...

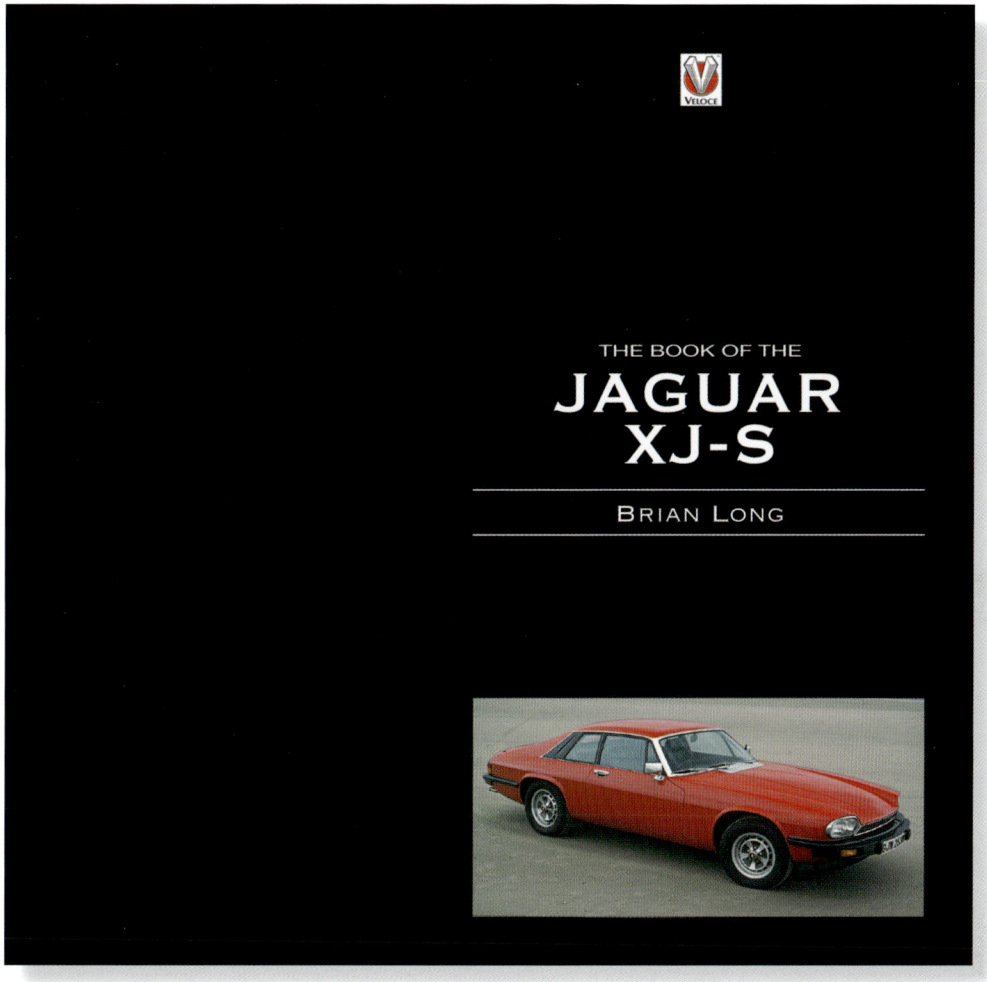

The definitive history of Jaguar's E-Type replacement, the XJ-S. This Jaguar offered a combination of supercar performance and grand tourer luxury, and is now eminently collectable. Includes rare photos of the prototypes that didn't make production.

ISBN: 978-1-845844-01-1
Hardback • 25x25cm • 160 pages • 290 colour pictures

For more information and price details, visit our website at www.veloce.co.uk
• email: info@veloce.co.uk • Tel: +44(0)1305 260068
* prices subject to change, p&p extra

The Essential Buyer's Guide™ series …

… don't buy a Jaguar until you've read one of these!

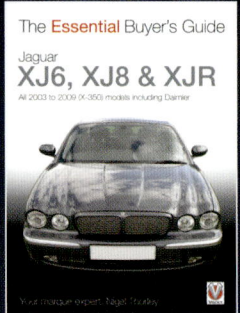

978-1-845844-34-9

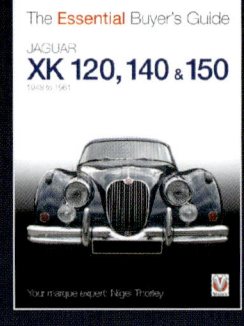

978-1-845843-77-9

978-1-845841-19-5

978-1-845840-77-8

978-1-845844-45-5

978-1-845844-62-2

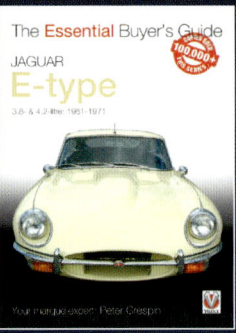

978-1-904788-85-0

978-1-845841-92-8

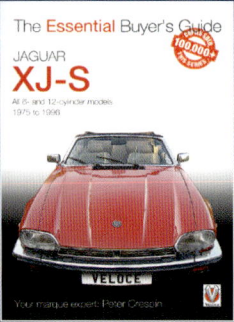

978-1-845841-61-4

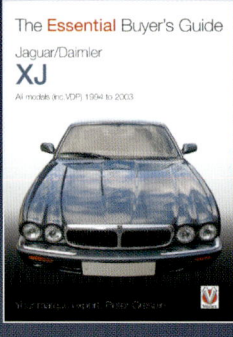

978-1-845842-00-0

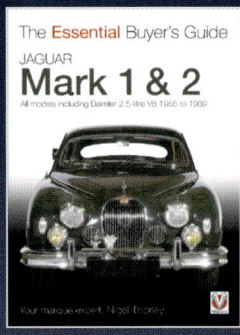

978-1-845843-60-1

978-1-845848-06-4

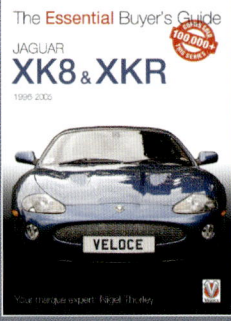

978-1-845843-59-5

For more details and the full range of
Essential Buyers Guides visit
www.veloce.co.uk or email info@veloce.co.uk

Index

Active Differential Control 169, 184
Adamesh 209, 210
Adaptive Cruise Control 71, 77, 86
Adaptive Dynamics 170, 185, 190
Adaptive Restraint 77, 84
Advanced Brake Assist 172
Advanced Lightweight Coupé 91, 131-133, 138, 146
Aerodynamic Pack 193
Air conditioning, 124-126
Airbags 37
AJ-V8 4.2/5.0 litre comparison 196, 197
AJ-V8 Gen III Engine 166-169, 180, 181, 190
AJ6/AJ16 Engine 23, 25, 32
AJV8 Engine 12, 23-25, 29, 30, 32-34, 56, 63, 72, 83, 84, 100, 103, 104, 106-111
Alcan brakes 164
Alloy wheels 36, 39, 55, 68-70, 85-88, 91, 92, 100, 160, 165, 173, 175
Arden 175, 176, 207, 210
Artisan Special Equipment (SE) 186, 187
Aston Martin 10, 19, 25, 27, 28, 42, 44, 46, 47, 58, 81
Audio systems 72, 75
Austin Powers 78
Autocar magazine 22, 28, 44, 45-47, 58-60, 68, 70, 72
Autosport magazine 60
Awards 39, 88, 154, 174

Battery 116
Beasley, Mike 194
BEN charity 43
Bibiana Boerio 131, 142
Birmingham Int Motor Show, 43
Black Pack 184-185, 193
Blackpool 7
Bloxham factory 28
Bluebooth 148
BMW 41, 44, 47, 60, 78
Boole, David 50
Bowers & Wilkins HiFi 165, 173, 187
Brakes 114, 118
British Car Auctions 51
British Car magazine 26
British Leyland 8, 10
Brochures 204
Browns Lane Plant 26, 43, 61, 140, 141
Budget Rent a Car 53
Bumper bar mountings 127, 130

Callum, Ian 14, 134, 141, 190, 193
Callum, Moray 14
Car magazine 46, 60
Car Trends magazine 60
Carbon Fibre Special Edition 91, 92
CATS Suspension 36, 57, 69, 75, 144
Chrysler 86
Classic Additions 210
Classic Trim 36, 37-39
Continental tyres 101
Cooling system 109-111
Corrosion 98-100, 105, 197-199
Crash testing 48
Cross, Mike 183

Daimler 25
David Marks Garages 6
Dayton 207
Diagnostics 211
Digital Radio 173
Dover, Bob 11, 12, 25
Dyble, Stuart 77
Dynamic Pack/Dynamic R 181, 185, 192, 193
Dynamic Stability Control, 85, 169

E-type 8, 12, 14, 16, 18, 23, 30, 32, 39, 42, 44
Egan, John 10
Engineer magazine 39
Exhausts 211

F-type 8, 9, 22, 29, 72-74, 188, 190, 194
Ferrari 44
Final Fifty Special Edition 193, 194
First hand report (X-100) 50, 51
Ford 11, 19, 22, 24, 25, 27-29
Fuel system 110

Gaydon 42
Geneva Motor show 29, 42, 54, 164, 183, 184
Government support 26
Greenwell, Joe 50, 68

Haden, Bill 14
Hallmark, Adrian 188
Hancock, Sheila 54
Harman Kardon 38
Helfet, Keith 15
Hoods 126, 127, 153, 171

Indian Special Edition 187

J D Power Survey 67, 78, 79, 188
Jaguar Accessories 203, 204
Jaguar Designers Choice 185
Jaguar Engineered to Order (ETO) 188, 190, 191
Jaguar Enthusiasts' Club 6, 43
Jaguar Heritage Trust 6, 81, 194
Jaguar Land Rover 6
Jaguar World magazine 78, 95
JaguarDrive 169, 204

Karmann 27

Lamborghini 44
Lawson, Geoff 12, 14, 15, 31, 40, 44
Lexus 24, 44, 72, 86
Lotus 44, 58
LPG 211
LS Design 210

Market sector 134
Maserati 44, 67, 70
Mercedes Benz 27, 41, 44, 47, 56, 60, 62, 86, 87
MG Rover 41
Motor Wheel Services 208
Motorsport magazine 47, 59

Nikasil 53, 72, 103, 106-109
Northelle 209

Ogihara company 27

Paintwork issues 101
Paragon Design 207
Paramount Performance 207, 208
Park brake 201
Performance Car magazine 44
Performance Seating 181, 186, 187, 190, 193
Pininfarina 8
Pirelli tyres 36, 55, 63, 69, 75, 101, 131, 181, 190
Police XK 53
Pollock, Fergus 31
Porsche 41, 44, 58, 60, 67, 70
Portfolio US Special Edition 87
Portugal 26
Premium pack 91
Prices 44, 57, 58, 69, 75, 86, 91, 95, 96, 154, 183, 187, 190

R-Performance 68-70, 78, 80, 85, 87, 89, 171, 207
Racing Green 208, 209
Radford factory 25
Rain sensing wipers 72
Recaro seats 85, 87, 91
Reverse park sensors 210
Road & Track magazine 45, 79
Royal College of Art 42

S Special Edition 91-96
S-type 64, 67, 81
Sabre Ruedas magazine 91
Safety 105, 139-141, 149, 152, 153, 204, 210
Sales figures 51, 52
Satellite navigation 71, 86, 210
Scheele, Nick 14, 43, 50, 68
Security 37
Service information 115-127, 200-204
Service recalls 52
Signature Special Edition 192, 193
Silverstone Special edition 74, 75
Simkin, Pete 190
Speed limiter 90
Speed Pack 184
Sport Trim 38
SS models 8
Starlech 176
Stewart, Jackie 18
Suspension/rolling chassis 112-115
Suspension/rolling chassis 5.0 litre 170
SVO Dept 62, 70, 81
Swallow Sidecar Company 7

Technology Pack 91
Telephone systems 77, 78
Teves braking system, 28, 36, 72
Thaw, John 54
Timing chains 104, 108, 109
Toys & models 52, 53
TVR 44, 47, 70, 86
Tyre Pressure Monitoring, 150

Ultimate Auto, 207
Unipart Balloon 50

V12 Engine 23, 24, 31
Varney, Russ 194
Veloce Publishing 6
Victory Special Edition 91-95

Walter Thompson Marketing, 40, 72
Warranty changes 83
What Car magazine 60, 188
Whitley Engineering Centre 14, 16, 28, 31
William Lyons 7, 15, 18
William Walmsley 7

X-100 general 8, 9, 14-49, 61, 65-68, 70-72, 75-78, 82-86, 88, 89, 99-112, 113-117
X-150 5.0 litre 166-171, 177, 178
X-150 design 134-139, 145-147, 151
X-150 general, 98, 134, 135, 138-154, 161, 195, 8
X-150 Styling Pack 161, 162
X-150 Suspension/Rolling Chassis 144
X-300 11, 23, 25, 26, 28, 36, 62

X-308 19
XJ220 12, 14, 18, 25, 27, 39, 62, 64
XJ40 10, 23, 25, 27
XJ41/42 8-10, 28, 29
XJ6 9
XJK Independent specialist 6
XJR 55-57
XJS 8, 9, 11-16, 22, 23, 25-28, 30, 32, 36, 41, 42, 44, 62
XK 3.5 161
XK Engine 23, 32
XK Goodwood 174, 175
XK Portfolio 172, 178, 179
XK120 8, 9, 16, 32, 54, 138
XK140 8
XK180 61-65, 67, 68, 72, 81
XK6 67, 68, 72
XK60 165
XK66 191, 192
XKR (X-100) general 54-60, 62-64, 66, 67, 69-72, 75, 77, 80, 81, 83-86, 88-96, 98-118
XKR (X152) general 155-160
XKR 100 Special Edition 78
XKR 75/175 Special Edition 174, 175
XKR Portfolio 163, 164
XKR-R prototype 80, 81
XKR-S 164, 165, 177, 179-184
XKR-S Carbon Fibre Pack 183
XKR-S GT 188-191

ZF transmissions/steering 25, 29, 34, 35, 56, 57, 82-84, 111, 112, 138, 143, 169, 180, 190